Mysterious Apocalypse

MYSTERIOUS APOCALYPSE

Interpreting the Book of Revelation

ARTHUR W. WAINWRIGHT

Abingdon Press

Nashville

MYSTERIOUS APOCALYPSE
INTERPRETING THE BOOK OF REVELATION

This book is printed on recycled, acid-free paper.

Library of Congress Cataloging-in-Publication Data

Wainwright, Arthur William.
    Mysterious apocalypse : interpreting the book of Revelation / Arthur W. Wainwright.
        p.   cm.
    Includes bibliographical references and index.
    ISBN 0-687-27641-1 (pbk. : alk. paper)
    1. Bible. N.T. Revelation—Criticism, interpretation, etc.—History. I. Title.
BS2825.2.W27   1993
228'.06'09—dc20   93-9094
                                                                           CIP

Scripture quotations, unless otherwise noted, are from the New Revised Standard Version Bible, Copyright 1989 by the Division of Christian Education of the National Council of the Churches of Christ in the USA. Used by Permission.

Those noted AV are from the King James, or Authorized, Version.

Front cover art: *The Son of Man Among the Seven Candlesticks* (Rev. 1:10-17). Woodcut from Luther's *Das newe Testament Deutzsch* (Wittenberg: Melchior Lotter the Younger for Christian Doring and Lucas Cranach the Elder, September 1522), in the Richard C. Kessler Reformation Collection, Pitts Theology Library, Emory University. Used with permission.

93 94 95 96 97 98 99 00 01 02 — 10 9 8 7 6 5 4 3 2 1

MANUFACTURED IN THE UNITED STATES OF AMERICA

To the memory of my mother and father,
Doris and Alfred Wainwright

CONTENTS

ACKNOWLEDGMENTS

In writing this book, I have received help from many people, to whom I am very grateful. The research has been supported in part by the National Endowment for the Humanities and the University Research Committee of Emory University. John Hayes, Patrick Graham, and Steven Darsey have been very helpful in making suggestions and providing information, and many others have drawn my attention to relevant literature. Brenda Stevenson has loyally provided me with secretarial assistance, and my wife has given me constant support in preparing this work. And Channing Jeschke, librarian of the Pitts Theology Library, Emory University, has always been ready to facilitate my research.

A. W. W.

ABBREVIATIONS

AV	Authorized (King James) Version
BJRL	*Bulletin of the John Rylands Library*
CCL	Corpus Christianorum, Series Latina
CCM	Corpus Christianorum, Continuatio Mediaevalis
CSCO	Corpus scriptorum Christianorum Orientalium
CSEL	Corpus scriptorum ecclesiasticorum Latinorum
ET	English Translation
ExpT	*Expository Times*
GCS	Die griechischen christlichen Schriftsteller der ersten drei Jahrhunderte
HDR	Harvard Dissertations in Religion
HE	Eusebius, *Historia Ecclesiastica*
HTR	*Harvard Theological Review*
JTS	*Journal of Theological Studies*
NTS	*New Testament Studies*
PG	Patrologiae cursus completus, series Graeca
PL	Patrologiae cursus completus, series Latina
RB	*Revue Biblique*
RÉAug	*Revue des Études Augustiniennes*
RelSRev	*Religious Studies Review*
SC	Sources Chrétiennes
TLZ	*Theologische Literaturzeitung*
TU	Texte und Untersuchungen
TZ	*Theologische Zeitschrift*

CHAPTER ONE

A BOOK OF HIDDEN MEANINGS

The book is known as Revelation, but much of it remains a mystery. It records the visions received by a man named John on the desolate island of Patmos, some twenty miles from the mainland of the Roman province of Asia. According to tradition, John, the son of Zebedee, was one of the twelve apostles, an exile on that lonely island in the Aegean Sea because he had borne witness to his Christian faith. For centuries the visions that he recorded have challenged and baffled the ingenuity of interpreters. Scholars, theologians, poets, painters, politicians, and revolutionaries have found a host of meanings in John's book. In Greek its title is *apokalypsis,* which means "revelation," and in English it is known as "the book of Revelation" or "the Apocalypse." Its name implies an unveiling of hidden truths, but it often seems to conceal them.

It is a book that both fascinates and repels. Its vivid poetical images have captured the imagination of its admirers and awakened hostility in its detractors. No part of the Bible has aroused greater controversy. From early times, Christians have disagreed about its status as scripture. While some of its readers regard it as the most wonderful book in the Bible, others question its right to be there at all. Debate about its worthiness to be included in the scriptures began as early as the second century and, especially in the East, took a long time to resolve. In later times the reformers Luther and Zwingli held it in low esteem, and it continues to produce both negative and positive reactions.

Opinions are divided about its date and authorship. Many scholars think that it was written about 95 or 96, at the end of the reign of the Roman emperor Domitian. Others date it between 64 and 70, either during Nero's reign or under the emperors who succeeded him; and a few interpreters have placed it as early as the time of Claudius (41–54) or as late as the reign of Trajan (98–117). Its authorship has long been a topic of disagreement. The most popular theory is that its author was John, the son of Zebedee, but many scholars suggest that it was written by another person called John or even by somebody who was pretending to be the apostle. These challenges to the traditional viewpoint began in the second and third centuries, but Luther, Zwingli, and Erasmus renewed them in the sixteenth century, and present-day scholars are thoroughly divided on the issue.

Controversy has not been confined to date and authorship, but has extended to the book's possible sources and the situation for which it was written. Above all, there has been contention about its meaning. Commentators have disputed whether its visions and prophecies refer to the author's own days or to later ages. They have debated whether it describes events that have already happened or predicts those that are still to come. Theories have been put forward with uncompromising zeal. Advocates of opposing viewpoints have heaped scorn and invoked damnation on each other, and the debate has been conducted with vigor and animosity.

One way in which accounts of the Apocalypse differ from one another is in their attitudes toward the millennium, the period of a thousand years that is the theme of one of the book's most controversial passages:

> Then I saw thrones, and those seated on them were given authority to judge. I also saw the souls of those who had been beheaded for their testimony to Jesus and for the word of God. They had not worshiped the beast or its image and had not received its mark on their foreheads or their hands. They came to life and reigned with Christ a thousand years. (Rev. 20:4)

Many interpreters treat these words as a prophecy about the future. They argue that the author expected Christ to overthrow Satan and inaugurate a thousand-year reign in company with saints and martyrs. Such an interpretation is known by various names: millenarian, millennial, or chiliastic (from the Greek *chilioi*, meaning "thousand"). Its upholders disagree about a variety of matters. They debate whether the millennium will be on earth or in heaven, whether Christ will reign visibly or invisibly, and whether the resurrection that precedes the thousand years will be a physical resuscitation of bodies or a spiritual renewal of the church. Often the word *premillenarian* designates interpreters who believe that Christ will visibly inaugurate this period of a thousand years, and *postmillennial* describes those who think that his visible appearance will be delayed until the end of the millennium.

Not all scholars think that the millennium is in the future. Many of them, of whom Augustine is the most famous, argue that it refers to the present. They do not insist that it is a literal thousand years, but argue that it extends from the first advent of Christ until the resurrection of the dead and the last judgment. They believe that it began either at his birth or at the time of his crucifixion and resurrection, although some of them think that it was inaugurated in the time of Constantine when the Roman Empire became Christian. These writers do not explain the millennium as a visible reign of Christ on earth; rather, they believe that he reigns in heaven and is spiritually present in the church. Their viewpoint is often known as *amillennial,* although that is a misleading description, since it suggests a rejection of the idea of a millennium; and in fact these interpreters clearly believe that there is one.

Other interpreters treat the millennium as a past event. Usually they date it from the earthly life of Christ until about the year 1000 or from the acceptance of Christianity by the Roman Empire in the early 300s until about 1300. This interpretation was popular among many early Protestants, who argued that the millennium ended at a time of papal corruption and the rise of the Turks. Some scholars regard the millennium not as a reference to a period of time at all, but as a purely symbolic allusion to the perfection or completion of God's action either in the final events or even in the present. If the term *amillennial* is to be used, it is most appropriately applied to them.

Another area of disagreement is the relationship between the prophecies and historical events. Futurists think that most of the visions are concerned with the last days. Church-historical interpreters claim that the book provides a map of history from the time of Christ until his second advent. Preterists think that the prophecies deal for the most part with events in the early years of the church. Modern historical critics are close in their outlook to Preterists, since they examine the Apocalypse in the light of the situation in which it was written. But Augustine and many subsequent interpreters have argued that the book does not focus specifically on the state of affairs in the first century but speaks in general terms of the continuing struggle between good and evil.

Interpreters differ in their accounts of the details in the Apocalypse. They vary in their explanations of the four horsemen, the 144,000 whose names are sealed in heaven, the countless multitude that stands before God's throne, and the army, two hundred million strong, that was to move westward from the Euphrates. They disagree about the identity of the numerous angels whom the book mentions and of the two witnesses who are put to death and rise again. They give conflicting accounts of the book's ferocious beasts: the beast from the bottomless pit, the beast from the sea, the beast from the land, and the scarlet beast, on which the whore of Babylon rides. They dispute about the fall of Babylon and the battle of Armageddon. They discuss whether the New Jerusalem is physical or spiritual, earthly or heavenly, and whether it coincides with the millennium or follows it. For more than 1,800 years, readers of the Apocalypse have raised these questions, and they still disagree as much as ever about the answers.

In recent times, scholars have concentrated on what are often described as critical approaches to the Apocalypse. Some of them attempt to unfold its meaning for the first century and to show how it was related to the events and concerns of those times. Others seek to understand it in the light of the myths of the ancient world. Yet others concentrate on its qualities as literature or discuss it in the light of the social sciences of psychology, anthropology, and sociology. Of those who adopt these critical approaches, some are skeptical about the book's relevance for the present day, but others are convinced that it has insights of permanent value. Critical interpreters have shown great learning and insight, but, like more traditional commentators on the Apocalypse, they have failed to reach agreement about its meaning.

The visionary and symbolic character of the Apocalypse has given rise to a great variety of interpretations. When commentators disagree about the meaning of writings like the Sermon on the Mount, which appear to be clear and easily intelligible, it is only to be expected that they will have difficulty with a book like the Apocalypse, which deliberately cloaks its message in symbols. Ambiguity of meaning is an ingrained characteristic of the book.

In spite of the difficulties it presents to the interpreter, or perhaps because of them, the book's influence extends beyond the world of commentaries and theological treatises. Writers who use it to give expression to their feelings and thoughts do not always seek to explain its meaning. But their use of its language and imagery is evidence of its impact on them. Its visions have etched themselves on their consciousness.

The Apocalypse is the most poetic of New Testament books and recalls some of the most colorful visions in the Jewish scriptures. Its picture of the exalted Christ (Rev. 1:12-16) blends aspects of the vision of Daniel 7. Its four horses (Rev. 6:1-8) are reminiscent of the horses of Zechariah 6:1-3. Its four living creatures (Rev. 4:6-8) resemble both the creatures of Ezekiel 1 and the seraphim of Isaiah 6:2-3. The beast from the sea (Rev. 13:1-2) mingles features of the beasts of Daniel 7. The lament over the fall of Babylon (Rev. 18) has parallels in the oracles about great cities by Hebrew prophets (Isaiah 23; 47; Jeremiah 50–51; Ezekiel 26–27). The description of the New Jerusalem and the new heaven and earth (Rev. 21:1–22:5) reproduces themes from Isaiah 65 and 66. But although the Apocalypse contains numerous echoes of the Jewish scriptures, it rarely gives an exact repetition of its visions. It is different from its antecedents, and the differences are striking.

The book has a fascination of its own. Scholars have long been aware of the deficiencies of its Greek. Its style lacks elegance, and it frequently breaks the rules of grammar. But its beauty and power shine through these imperfections and are among the chief reasons for its appeal. Poets and artists have succumbed to its spell. Visionaries have found it a source of inspiration. Revolutionary leaders have used it to stir the passions of their followers. It has captivated men and women who have been baffled by the abstractions of academic theology.

The subject matter of the Apocalypse as well as its poetry is a reason for its appeal. It deals with cruelty and disloyalty, with courage and faithfulness. It speaks of the last days, the promise of rewards and punishments, and the hope of a new heaven and a new earth. Even when its meaning is obscure, it commands attention, and its very mysteriousness is a source of attraction.

Other books in the Judeo-Christian tradition contain predictions of the last days, of spectacular signs in the heavens, of devastating wars, and of a new heaven and earth. These passages are often described as apocalyptic, although debate continues about the precise meaning of that term. There is apocalyptic material in the Old Testament books of Daniel, Isaiah, Ezekiel, Joel, and Zechariah. The New Testament contains apocalyptic passages, especially in the first three Gospels, the Epistles of Paul, the Epistle of Jude, and the Second Epistle of Peter.

During the two centuries before Jesus' birth and for many centuries afterward, apocalyptic writings were produced in Judaism that never found a place in the Bible. Among them were the Similitudes of Enoch, the Apocalypse of Ezra, Jubilees, and the Testaments of the Twelve Patriarchs. Christian writings in this style that failed to receive acceptance as scripture include the Apocalypse of Peter, the Apocalypse of Paul, and some of the Sibylline Oracles. But of all these works, the biblical books of Daniel and the Apocalypse have won the greatest popularity.

Interpreters of the Apocalypse often relate its message to that of similar works. They seek to understand its relationship to the seventy weeks, the little horn, and the five kingdoms of Daniel. The references in Daniel to 2,300 evenings and mornings, three and a half times, 1,290 days, and 1,335 days have produced an endless supply of conjectures about God's plan in history (Dan. 7:1-28; 8:14; 9:24-27; 12:7, 11-12). Interpreters ask if the return of the Jews to their homeland and the salvation of Israel fit into the picture.

They want to know if any of the beasts of the Apocalypse are identical with the "lawless one" or the "man of sin" in 2 Thessalonians 2:1-12. They connect the Apocalypse with Jesus' prophecies about the abomination of desolation, the darkening of the sun and moon, and the coming of the Son of Man (Matt. 24; Mark 13; Luke 21). In their speculations about the future, they have ranged beyond the scriptures. A favorite hunting ground has been the Sibylline Oracles and the Apocalypse of Ezra. Writers have even turned to literature outside the Jewish and Christian traditions and appealed to predictions made by Latin poets.

The following account of interpretations of the Apocalypse from the second century to the present day deals with leading interpretations of the book but also includes some of the lesser-known viewpoints. The first part, chapters 2–6, examines the attitudes of interpreters to the millennium and considers their changing views about the ways in which the prophecies are fulfilled in the course of history. In the early church the dominant interpretation was chiliastic or millenarian and taught that the thousand years would begin in the future. From the beginning of the fifth until the end of the twelfth century Augustine's theory that the millennium had already begun was the most widely accepted. From the twelfth century until the nineteenth, under the influence of Joachim of Fiore, a large number of Western interpreters treated the Apocalypse as a detailed prophecy of the course of history. Although Joachim sowed the seeds of a revival of millenarian views, it was in Protestant circles after the Reformation that millenarian teaching began to flourish. And at a popular level it thrives in the late twentieth century.

The first part of this book also traces the changing theories about the relationship of the Apocalypse's prophecies to historical events. The earliest interpreters explained the book in relation to persecution by the Roman Empire. But after Constantine became a Christian, accounts of the book related its contents to history only in general terms. From the end of the twelfth century, however, many commentaries treated the book as a prophecy of the details of church and world history; and this style of interpretation prevailed until the nineteenth century.

The second part of this book, chapters 7–9, deals with critical interpretations. Scholars often give the impression that this approach did not begin until the eighteenth century. In fact, critical questions have been asked about the Apocalypse since the second century. At an early date critics challenged the book's authorship and authority, and these challenges were revived at the time of the Reformation. Later generations of scholars have developed theories about the book's sources, its literary genre, its relation to ancient myth, its qualities as literature, its importance in the light of the social sciences, and the extent to which it can be understood in terms of its own age.

The third part, chapters 10–13, deals with the ways in which interpreters have related the Apocalypse to different aspects of life. It shows how they have applied the book to the problems of church, state, and society. It describes its impact on the inner life and on worship and examines its function as part of the common cultural heritage.

This survey does not attempt to cover everything that has been written on the Apocalypse but gives a representative selection of interpretations that illustrates the amazing scope of the book's impact. Until the time of Constantine, the discussion looks with equal emphasis at the treatment of the book in both the eastern and western parts of the Roman Empire. From then onward it focuses chiefly on work done in Western Europe and North Africa, and, in more recent times, in North America and elsewhere.

The history of the Apocalypse is almost as long as the history of Christianity. The book has played a part in most of the church's conflicts. It has been enlisted in support of a variety of causes and has helped to determine people's thought and behavior in many crises. It has made its impact on the rich and the poor, the privileged and the dispossessed, dreamers and persons of action, the church's official leaders and their opponents. Its history is the story of its power of survival and of its ability to give expression to human hopes and fears. But while the strength of its impact is beyond doubt, it remains a tantalizing book with a host of possible meanings and large areas of uncertainty.

Part One

The Millennium and History

CHAPTER TWO

MILLENARIANISM
IN THE EARLY CHURCH

The history of the interpretation of the Apocalypse began in the second century. It was an age of spectacular success for the Christian church, which was spreading across the Roman Empire, but it was also a time of fear and suffering, when members of the church were liable to persecution. In the two hundred years between the composition of the Apocalypse and the conversion of the emperor Constantine, the Christian Bible was taking shape. By the end of the second century most of the writings in the New Testament were accepted as scripture, but serious doubts were raised about the authority and authorship of some of them, including the Apocalypse. The book also gave rise to a sharp conflict of interpretations, and at the heart of the conflict was the teaching about a millennium.

CHILIASM

The belief that Christ will return to earth and inaugurate a thousand-year era of blessedness on the planet has many supporters in modern times. But it is not a new belief. It was held by the earliest interpreters of the Apocalypse, who are generally known as Chiliasts, but can equally well be described as millennialists or millenarians. In their opinion the Apocalypse predicted that Christ would set up a kingdom on earth for a thousand years (Rev. 20:4-5). But the name Chiliast is specially used of Christians who held this view in the early church.

The word *millennium* (from the Latin *mille*, "a thousand," and *annus*, "year") is used to describe this period. The expectation has its parallels in other literature. The notion of a blessed time that precedes the last judgment is found in Jewish writings of the New Testament period. The Ethiopic Enoch affirmed that it would last for three weeks, and the Apocalypse of Ezra prophesied a messianic kingdom of 400 years (Enoch 91:12-17; 4 Ezra 7:28-29). It is also possible that the Apostle Paul expected a millennium when he said that Christ's reign would begin with the resurrection of those who "belong to Christ" and continue until "the end" (1 Cor. 15:20-28). But Paul never indicated the length of that reign. It is the Apocalypse that specifically says that the period will be a thousand years[1]; and it is the Apocalypse that has influenced the Chiliasts in their discussion of the millennium.

The Chiliasts lived in an age of persecution. It was for such an age that they believed the Apocalypse was written. Its author wrote of visions that he received on the isle of Patmos, where he was in exile "because of the word of God and the testimony of Jesus" (Rev. 1:9). He exhorted the members of the churches to resist any attempt to make them give up their faith. His description of the compulsory worship of the beast (Rev. 13:1-18) seems to be an allusion to the Roman practice of enforcing emperor worship. At a time when Christians were tempted to compromise their faith in order to avoid suffering, the Apocalypse called for endurance and obedience, and offered the promise of future happiness.

During this period Chiliasm provided an antidote to the fear of persecution. When people are oppressed, they find consolation in dreams of a better life and focus their anger on the institutions and leaders that threaten them. The Apocalypse satisfies these needs. It provides graphic pictures of the overthrow of evil powers and the establishment of a better world. These pictures were highly attractive to members of the early church. Outbreaks of persecution were spasmodic and sometimes short-lived, but when they occurred, they were ferocious. Christians lived in fear of imprisonment, torture, and death. The Apocalypse brought them a promise of deliverance and of ultimate security.

In the second and third centuries, most of the book's interpreters were Chiliasts. They believed that, when Christ returned to
earth, Christians who had died would rise from the grave and
inherit an earthly paradise together with believers who were alive.
They expected Christ to reign on earth for a thousand years in an
era of material prosperity, in company with martyrs and other loyal
believers. Amid the uncertainty and injustice of the present they
welcomed the prospect of life in that kingdom.

Papias (60–c.130), bishop of Hierapolis in Asia Minor, is the first
Christian writer known to hold these views. His works are lost, but
he was probably indebted to the Apocalypse. According to the historian Eusebius, Papias based his belief on a misunderstanding of
the "apostolic accounts," and other early Chiliasts derived their
views from him.[2] No statements by Papias about the millennium
survive, but Justin Martyr (c.100–c.165), the first writer whose
remarks about the Apocalypse have survived, was a Chiliast. Other
writers in the same tradition were Irenaeus (c.130–c.200), Tertullian (160–c.225), Hippolytus (c.170–c.230),[3] Victorinus (d. 304),
Lactantius (c.240–c.320), Methodius (d. 311), and Commodianus
(probably 3rd cent.).[4]

These writers experienced persecution. Justin, Victorinus, and
probably Methodius were put to death for their faith. Hippolytus
became an exile, and Lactantius suffered the milder punishment
of losing his position as a teacher of rhetoric. Irenaeus was not a
martyr, but his mentor Polycarp was burned to death, and Pothinus,
his predecessor as bishop of Lyons, died as a result of brutal
treatment.[5]

Amid these ordeals the Apocalypse reinforced the faith of early
Christians. It promised them a future in which their fortunes would
be reversed and they would be the wielders of authority instead of
the victims of oppression. They expected a millennium of material
bliss in contrast with the agonies of persecution. The redeemed,
said Justin, will live for a thousand years in Jerusalem.[6] Irenaeus
depicted the joys of the millennium in terms of Isaiah 65. Men and
women, he predicted, will build houses, plant vineyards, and enjoy
the fruits of the harvest.[7] Lactantius's account, also indebted to
Isaiah 65, was even more graphic. People, he said, will continue to

have children, darkness will disappear from the earth, the moon will shine with the brightness of the sun, and the sun will be seven times brighter than before. Honey will run down from the mountains with streams of wine, rivers will flow with milk, beasts and birds will no longer feed on other creatures, and lions and calves will live together.[8]

Chiliasts were divided in their opinion about the place of the New Jerusalem (Rev. 21:1–22:5) in the sequence of events. Irenaeus expected it to descend from heaven after the last judgment. Tertullian and Victorinus thought that it would come down at the start of the millennium. Commodianus made a distinction between the arrival of the New Jerusalem and the coming of the new heaven and earth. Although the New Jerusalem would descend to earth at the beginning of the millennium, the new heaven and earth would not appear until after the judgment.[9] In spite of their disagreements, these writers all agreed that there would be a period of unparalleled bliss on earth.

Montanism, the prophetic movement that arose in Phrygia in the latter part of the second century, predicted the return of Christ to establish a kingdom on earth. The Montanists expected Christ to inaugurate the kingdom in Pepuza, a small town in Asia Minor, rather than in Jerusalem. It is not clear to what extent they used the Apocalypse. The claim of their leader, Montanus, to be the "Parakletos," the Holy Spirit (John 14:16, 26; 15:26; 16:7), suggests that he was aware of writings ascribed to John; and Tertullian, who was fully conversant with the Apocalypse, eventually embraced the teachings of Montanism. At any rate, Montanists expected a material kingdom of Christ on earth and in that respect were in accord with the Chiliasts.[10]

Although they expected a future millennium, Chiliasts had differing views about its proximity. Justin thought that it would begin soon.[11] Tertullian announced that the signs of the event were already in evidence. During a Roman expedition to the East, even pagan soldiers, he reported, saw the heavenly Jerusalem suspended in the sky. The vision came early each morning for forty days. Sometimes it faded gradually; sometimes it vanished instantly; but day after day it reappeared.[12] Hippolytus and Lactantius, however, thought that the millennium was more distant, expecting it to begin about 500, some 6,000 years after what they believed to be the date of the creation.[13]

Fear of persecution had an influence on the Chiliasts' understanding of the Apocalypse's portraits of evil. The book contains several references to beasts, and Chiliasts concentrated their discussion on the three that are described in Revelation 13 and 17. The first of them (Rev. 13:1-10) comes from the sea and is fearsome in appearance. It is like a leopard, with a bear's feet and a lion's mouth, and it has seven heads and ten horns. The second beast (Rev. 13:11) comes from the earth. It has two horns like a lamb but speaks like a dragon, and it makes people worship the beast from the sea. The third of them (Rev. 17:1-18) is scarlet in color. It has seven heads and ten horns, like the beast from the sea. Its heads stand for seven hills and seven kings. Its horns represent ten kings who have not yet received their kingdom. And on it sits a prostitute whose forehead bears the name of Babylon, the wicked city whose destruction is described in Revelation 18. Chiliasts associated these pictures of evil powers with the Roman Empire. Rome had many characteristics of the Apocalypse's Babylon. It was materialistic and oppressive, and its seven hills were reminiscent of the seven heads of the apocalyptic beasts. Irenaeus contemplated the possibility that 666, the number of the beast (Rev. 13:18), might signify *Lateinos,* a name that suggested a Latin ruler. But he decided that it was more likely to mean *Teitan,* a less specific term that conveyed the idea of a tyrant without referring to any particular person or government.[14]

Attitudes toward Rome were not entirely negative. Hippolytus and Tertullian identified the empire with the power that was to restrain the advent of Antichrist (2 Thess. 2:6). But they combined this viewpoint with the recognition that Rome was a source of evil. Tertullian described Rome as the Babylon of Revelation 17–18 and blamed it for the death of martyrs. Hippolytus identified it with the beast from the sea and claimed that Antichrist, a Jew from the tribe of Dan, would be the beast from the land, who would revive the Roman Empire. He contrasted the Roman Empire with the kingdom of Christ. The apostles gather the nations together in the

25

name of Christ, but the empire gathers them together in the name of Satan.[15]

Of all the early Roman emperors, Nero was the most notorious in the eyes of Christians. He was responsible for the savage persecution in the year 64, when he blamed the Christians for a fire that devastated part of Rome. Moreover, he had an execrable reputation among non-Christians as well as among Christians. When he died in a civil war, his disappearance from the scene seemed too good to be true, and the legend arose that he would come back again. The legend took two forms. According to one, he had not really died but was in hiding in the East, and according to the other, he would be raised from death. The Apocalypse supports the second form of the expectation. It describes how one of the heads of the beast from the sea received a mortal wound from which it recovered (Rev. 13:3). The beast "was and is not and is to come" (Rev. 17:8). These statements fit perfectly the expectation that Nero will return from the dead. Victorinus was the first commentator to make the connection. The seven heads of the beast, explains the Apocalypse, refer to seven kings (Rev. 17:9-11). According to Victorinus, the first five of them were the emperors Galba, Otho, Vitellius, Vespasian, and Titus; the sixth was Domitian, the emperor in power when the book was written (Rev. 17:10); the seventh was Nerva, who would reign for only a short time; and the eighth and most wicked of them would be Nero, risen from the dead.[16]

Christians lived not only in fear of persecution but were also exposed to other perils that menaced all the inhabitants of the Roman Empire. Civil wars disrupted the life of the Mediterranean world, and as one emperor ousted another, the empire was in danger of collapsing from within. At the same time armies of foreign nations surged across its borders. Goths invaded the province of Dacia, crossed the Danube, advanced into Thrace, harried the Roman provinces on the southern shores of the Black Sea, and sacked the city of Athens. In their predictions, Lactantius and Commodianus, who lived at the end of the third century, reflected these calamities. They used the phraseology of Daniel to talk of invasions by kings from the north and the east. Commodianus, in language reminiscent of the fifth trumpet vision (Rev. 9:7-11), predicted the capture of Rome by an army of many thousands, some of whom would be Goths. These dangers were at least as threatening as the possibility of martyrdom, and Christians had a greater chance of being killed in such conflicts than in the sporadic outbursts of persecution.[17]

Divisions within the church were among the chief concerns of early Christendom. They too are mirrored in interpretations of the Apocalypse. Gnosticism, which was branded as heresy, was a powerful religious force in the second and third centuries, and Chiliasts attacked its teaching. Gnostics looked forward with anticipation to the separation of the soul from the body. The notion of a physical resurrection was repugnant to them. In their opinion, life after death was a spiritual existence, free from the temptation and inconvenience of the flesh. Justin warned his readers against them. "Do not suppose them to be Christians!" he said. "Right-minded" Christians believe in a resurrection of the flesh and a millennium.[18]

Chiliasts also differed from Gnostics about the scriptures. In using the Apocalypse to assert their reverence for the Old Testament, the Chiliasts may well have been aiming at Gnostics like Marcion, who rejected the authority of the Old Testament. Victorinus, for example, likened the twenty-four elders standing before God's throne (Rev. 4:4) to the books of the prophets and the law, and explained the scroll with the seven seals (Rev. 5:1) as the Old Testament.[19] Such statements affirm the validity and authority of the books of the Jewish Bible.

Gnostics and Chiliasts also disagreed with each other about the number of authentic gospels. Many of these writings were in circulation in the second century, and some of them had a Gnostic emphasis. Irenaeus used the Apocalypse to argue that only four of them, Matthew, Mark, Luke, and John, were genuine. They are represented, he explained, by the four living creatures on each side of the heavenly throne (Rev. 4:6-8). The lion stands for John's Gospel, the calf for Luke's, the human being for Matthew's, and the eagle for Mark's. By making a connection between the living creatures and the Gospels, Irenaeus was the pioneer of a long tradition of interpretation,[20] and the tradition originated with a concern to exclude unwanted writings from the Bible.

An emphasis on the church's unity accompanied the desire to defend the faith against heresy. The Apocalypse contains seven letters (Rev. 2–3), said Victorinus, because the number seven stands for unity, and John wrote them for the whole church, not just for seven congregations.[21] Moreover, the woman clothed with the sun (Rev. 12:1-6) is a symbol of the church, and the sun that clothes her is the hope of resurrection and the promise of glory.[22]

These chiliastic interpreters took account of events that aroused tension and fear in second- and third-century Christians. Their writings reflect the danger of persecution, the threat to the empire from civil war and foreign invasion, and the theological divisions within the church. Chiliasts discerned in the Apocalypse a message that spoke directly to their concerns. It promised an end to the imperfections and injustices of life. It gave them the assurance that God would change their fortunes by a supernatural intervention. Early Christians had neither the desire nor the power to stage a successful rebellion against the might of the Roman Empire. The Apocalypse brought them the promise they needed to hear: Christ would return to earth; he was the rider on the white horse with a sword coming out of his mouth and an iron rod in his hand. He would destroy his enemies, throw the beast and the false prophet into the lake of fire, and establish his glorious kingdom on earth for a thousand years (Rev. 19:11–20:6). It was not the responsibility of Christians to initiate these events; their function was to wait patiently and endure persecution. If they were true to their faith, God would take care of them.

Chiliasts differed from each other in their treatment of several passages in the Apocalypse. Hippolytus and Tertullian regarded the two witnesses of Revelation 11:3-12 as Elijah and Enoch, both of whom were said to have gone to heaven without the experience of physical death. Victorinus, however, identified them with Elijah and Jeremiah, arguing that Jeremiah had not died, since his death was not recorded in the Bible.[23] Writers gave differing explanations of the 144,000 "virgins" who "have not defiled themselves with women" (Rev. 14:4). Tertullian and Methodius claimed that they were literally virgins, while Victorinus believed that they stood for the totality of Jewish Christians in the church.[24] A third interpretation was given by Origen, who was not a Chiliast. He claimed that they stood for both Jewish and Gentile Christians.[25]

These early writers usually gave a general explanation of the Apocalypse's prophecies. Victorinus treated the first four seal visions as allusions to the church's preaching and to wars, famine, and pestilence.[26] His writing bears little trace of the kind of interpretation practiced many centuries afterward by writers who treated the book as a chart of the course of history.

Chiliasts have not left any detailed discussion of their methods of interpretation. But Victorinus made use of the principle of recapitulation, according to which later sections of the book predict the same events as early chapters have done. The bowl visions, for example, which refer to the last days, recapitulate the trumpet visions, and the vision of New Jerusalem recapitulates the vision of the millennium.[27] Although Victorinus did not actually state the principle of recapitulation, he implied it in his observation, "Order is not to be looked for in the Apocalypse. Understanding is to be looked for."[28] This idea was to dominate interpretation for many centuries and was prominent in the work of Tyconius and Augustine.

Other principles were implied, though not stated, by the Chiliasts. They assumed that the Apocalypse was to be explained in the light of Old Testament prophecy. They found a place for the four beasts, the little horn, the king from the north, and other apocalyptic images of Daniel in their schemes of expectation. They used the pictures of a renewal of Jerusalem in Isaiah and Ezekiel to explain the meaning of the millennium and the New Jerusalem. Lactantius went further and cited prophecies that were not in the Bible, such as the Sibylline Oracles and the utopian dreams of the Latin poet Virgil.[29] Another underlying assumption of the Chiliasts was that the Apocalypse spoke of events of their own times. They looked for signs of the last day around them. They believed that the apocalyptic drama had reached its final act, although some of them conceded that several centuries might elapse before that act concluded. Yet, apart from Victorinus, they did not mention the principles by which they explained the book. The Apocalypse seemed relevant to them because it appeared to be designed for their situation, and they responded instinctively to that conviction.

OPPOSITION TO CHILIASM

Until the reign of Constantine, the chiliastic interpretation was in fashion, but it was not uniformly popular. Its opponents looked critically at the Apocalypse and challenged the belief that John the Apostle was its author and that it was inspired by God. In the second century the Alogoi rejected it together with John's Gospel and Epistles and claimed that their author was the heretic Cerinthus. The Roman presbyter Gaius protested against the Apocalypse's claim that natural disasters would be a sign of the end (e.g., Rev. 8:8). He rejected the Chiliasts' claim that the binding of Satan (Rev. 20:1) would take place in the future. Satan, he said, was already bound in chains during Jesus' ministry (Matt. 12:29).[30]

Not all opponents of Chiliasm were negative about the Apocalypse. Dionysius, bishop of Alexandria (3rd cent.) and a pupil of Origen, accused the Chiliasts of misinterpreting the Apocalypse, but he was not hostile to the book itself. He did not understand it, however, according to its obvious, literal meaning but looked for a "hidden and more wonderful" interpretation.[31] Dionysius disputed the tradition that John the Apostle was its author. He thought that the apostle wrote John's Gospel and Epistles, but because of its literary style and the nature of its ideas he concluded that another John, perhaps John the Elder, wrote the Apocalypse. Moreover, although he regarded the Apocalypse as valuable, Dionysius did not say that he accepted it as scripture.[32]

Behind Dionysius's desire to find a hidden meaning was the influence of his teacher Origen (c.185–254), a strong advocate of the spiritual explanation of the Bible. Origen, who was influenced by Platonist thought, rejected a literal interpretation of the prophecy about the New Jerusalem. He regarded it as a heavenly, spiritual city and opposed the idea that it would be a place where the redeemed would eat, drink, marry, have children, and exercise dominion over other people.[33] Origen expressed his intention to write a commentary on the Apocalypse,[34] but if he carried out that intention, the commentary has disappeared. The absence of detailed information about his views of the book creates a serious gap in our knowledge, but it is clear that he was a pioneer of the spiritual interpretation.[35]

In spite of dissenting voices, Chiliasm was the most popular approach to the Apocalypse until the reign of Constantine. It was a mode of thought that met the needs of Christians who lived under the threat of persecution and amid the dangers of war. Chiliasm was not an inevitable reaction to this situation. Origen died after imprisonment and torture, and his father was a martyr. Neither persecution nor the precariousness of the political situation made Origen a Chiliast. The temperaments and thoughts of individuals as well as their circumstances helped to mold their attitudes to the Apocalypse. Many of them sought refuge in Chiliasm, but others reacted differently. Yet until Constantine became emperor and Christianity received official approval, Chiliasm prevailed. It had a more popular appeal than either Gnosticism or the spiritual interpretation characteristic of Origen and Dionysius. Its promise of an earthly millennium and its emphasis on the connection between Antichrist and the Roman Empire were vivid and easy to understand. It had the stamp of popular religion, expressing itself in bright and memorable images, not in abstruse concepts. In times of danger and suffering it nourished the spirits of Christians, strengthened their wills, and emboldened them to persist in their faith.

CHAPTER THREE

THE MILLENNIUM AS THE PERIOD
OF THE CHURCH

THE DECLINE OF CHILIASM

During the fourth century, Chiliasm ceased to be fashionable. With the acceptance of Christianity by Emperor Constantine, Christians were less inclined than before to regard Rome as a force of evil. Moreover, the Chiliasts expected Christ to return to earth after the period of persecution was ended, but their expectation did not harmonize with the course of events. After Constantine became emperor, persecution of mainstream Christians ceased, but Christ did not return. The time was, therefore, ripe for new interpretations of the Apocalypse that gave a different account of the beasts and the millennium.

The Apocalypse still had difficulty in being accepted as scripture, presumably because its opponents believed it to be chiliastic. At the beginning of the fourth century, according to Eusebius, some Christians regarded it as scripture and others did not.[1] The book was slow to win recognition in the Syrian and Armenian churches. It did not appear in Syriac versions of the New Testament until after the fifth century,[2] and the Armenian church did not give it recognition until the twelfth century. It fared better with Greek-speaking Christians. In the fourth century they gave it a mixed reception. The Council of Laodicea (c.360) and Cyril of Jerusalem did not include it in their lists of canonical books,[3] and Chrysostom paid little attention to it. But Athanasius, Cyril of Alexandria,

Gregory of Nyssa, and Basil regarded it as scripture,[4] and by the end of the fifth century the Greek church granted it general acceptance. The Western church, however, was readier than the churches of the East to accept it. In 397 the Synod of Carthage officially recognized it as part of the New Testament, and its place in the scriptures of the West was secure. The reasons for its acceptance are not given, but it is likely that the decline of Chiliasm helped to overcome any opposition.

Chiliasm was on the wane but still had supporters. Apollinarius of Laodicea (d. c.390) may have been one of its advocates[5]; and at the end of the fourth century the African bishop Quintus Julius Hilarianus accepted Hippolytus's expectation that the millennium would begin about the year 500, which he believed to be 6,000 years after the creation.[6] But this viewpoint was not characteristic of writings at that time. An obvious sign of Chiliasm's decline was the silence of theologians about the millennium. Most fourth-century writers failed to mention it, but Eusebius (c.260–c.340), bishop of Caesarea, gave hints of a new kind of interpretation. Eusebius was a writer who changed his mind about the Apocalypse; in his earlier days his views were close to those of the Chiliasts,[7] but after Constantine's acceptance of Christianity, Eusebius revised his attitude. His effervescent account of the building of churches in the region of Tyre implies that the New Jerusalem is already present there. And a writing ascribed to Eusebius, though of uncertain authorship, suggests that a church built by Constantine in Jerusalem may be the New Jerusalem.[8] Such a viewpoint leaves no room for Chiliasm.

TYCONIUS

The interpretation that succeeded Chiliasm as the prevailing fashion was not that of Eusebius. Its pioneers lived in North Africa. They were a strange and unexpected combination. One of them was Tyconius, a lay member of the breakaway church of the Donatists. The other was Augustine, bishop of Hippo, one of the Donatists' leading opponents. Augustine, who for centuries dominated Western thought about both the millennium and many other matters, was greatly indebted to Tyconius and frankly recognized that debt. In spite of his disagreements with Tyconius, Augustine made use of both his ideas and his methods.[9]

Tyconius (late 4th cent.) laid down several rules of biblical interpretation, which he employed in his commentary on the Apocalypse. One of them was the principle of recapitulation, which had already been used by Victorinus, although Tyconius's statement of it is not the most familiar one. Another of his rules indicated that in prophecy a day can stand for a year or a month, and a year or a month for a day.[10]

Tyconius's rules have survived, but his commentary on the Apocalypse is lost. It is possible, however, to reconstruct some of his teaching about the book. He rejected the Chiliasts' expectation of a future millennium, for in his opinion the millennium had already begun. It was not the consequence of divine intervention at the end of history but extended from the first to the second advent of Christ.[11] Tyconius may have expected the millennium to end very soon, for, he explained, the three and a half weeks during which the two witnesses of Revelation 11 give testimony were 350 years, beginning with Jesus' crucifixion. If he took the 350 years literally, he must have expected them to end about 380, and he may have believed that the millennium would end about the same time. But it is not clear that he understood it in that sense.[12] Tyconius also rejected the Chiliasts' belief in two physical resurrections of the dead, one for the faithful at the beginning of the millennium and the other for the rest of human beings at its conclusion. The first resurrection, he said, is a spiritual transformation that occurs in baptism. Only the final resurrection will be physical, when all human beings will rise from the dead.[13]

According to modern reconstructions of his commentary, Tyconius made a contrast between the city of God and the city of the devil, both of which exist at the same time. The city of God is present in the church, but the devil's city is present in worldly power, symbolized by the beasts of the Apocalypse (Rev. 11:7; 13:1, 11).[14] If this contrast goes back to Tyconius, it foreshadowed Augustine's more famous teaching about the city of God and the earthly city.

Tyconius lived at a time when Donatists were in conflict with the mainstream church and with the Roman government. The Donatists refused to tolerate Christians who compromised with paganism in time of persecution, and they had formed a separate church. On several occasions they took part in armed conflict with the authorities, and many of their members won a questionable reputation for martyrdom by committing suicide. Since Donatists perceived themselves as a persecuted community, the Apocalypse was likely to appeal to them. It is easy, therefore, to understand why Tyconius devoted his energies to writing a commentary on the book. It is more difficult to know why he decided that the millennium had already begun. Perhaps he reacted against the materialistic pictures that the Chiliasts painted of their Utopia.

Later writers made use of Tyconius, but because he was a Donatist most of them were reluctant to express admiration for him.[15] He was a creative thinker who introduced a new theory about the Apocalypse, but it was Augustine's revision of his theory that had the more lasting effect.

AUGUSTINE

Tyconius's rules of interpretation and his claim that the millennium spanned the period between Christ's two advents won the support of Augustine (354–430). At first Augustine agreed with the Chiliasts, but in later years his views changed.[16] In the *City of God* he reproduced Tyconius's account of the two resurrections, one spiritual and the other physical.[17] The millennium, he said, is not literally a thousand years. Either it represents the rest of the sixth millennium of the world's history or it stands for the fullness of time. The binding of Satan, with which the millennium began, took place when the church spread beyond Judea into other nations of the world. "How can one," said Jesus, "enter a strong man's house and plunder his property, without first tying up the strong man?" (Matt. 12:29). Satan, argued Augustine, is the strong man of whom Jesus spoke. And the tying up or binding of Satan is repeated whenever men and women are converted to the Christian faith.[18]

Augustine refrained from speculating about the date of the final events. In the words of Jesus before his ascension, "It is not for you to know the times or periods that the Father has set by his own authority" (Acts 1:7). Even though the Roman Empire was in obvious danger of collapse, Augustine did not speak of the nearness of the second advent.[19]

Moreover, Augustine rejected the notion that a revived Nero would be the Antichrist. Rome is not the source of Antichrist but is the power that restrains his coming. As for the New Jerusalem, it is already present, descending from heaven, whenever grace enters into men and women and makes them citizens of the heavenly city. At the last judgment the New Jerusalem will appear with greater clarity, and the bodies of its inhabitants will receive incorruption and immortality. During the millennium people experience tears, grief, crying, and death. After the judgment, God will wipe the tears from their eyes, and there will be no more death, grief, crying, or sorrow (see Rev. 21:4).[20]

A striking aspect of Augustine's teaching is his contrast between the city of God and the city of the world, a contrast that may have a parallel in Tyconius. Augustine did not think that these cities were confined to any particular geographical location. They were two societies of people. One of them was to reign eternally with God and the other to suffer eternal punishment. In the city of the world love of self leads to contempt of God. In the city of God love of God leads to contempt of self. Even in the time of Cain and Abel the two cities were in existence. Cain belonged to the earthly city and Abel to the city of God. Augustine traced the history of the city of God in Abel, Noah, Abraham, Sarah, and the people of Israel until the coming of Christ.[21] He identified the city with the church. Its citizens are sinners, but they have repented and received forgiveness. By contrast, the citizens of the earthly city are doomed to eternal punishment with the devil. Augustine suggested that this godless city is the Apocalypse's beast from the sea (Rev. 13:1).[22] It is present in worldly empires, including those of Assyria, Athens, and Rome, and it will survive until the end of the millennium. The devil was put in chains at Christ's first advent, but although the devil's power is limited, he continues to seduce people. When he is set free at the end of the millennium, he will recover his power and initiate a final persecution.[23]

Augustine gave a vivid account of the last events in history. Antichrist will persecute the faithful Christians. Wicked nations, symbolized by Gog and Magog, will attack the city of God.[24] The dead will be raised and receive judgment from God. The wicked will receive eternal punishment and be thrown into a lake of fire, which will not cleanse and purge them but will punish them with everlasting torment.[25] Blessedness, however, is the destiny of the faithful. Their bodies will be both physical and spiritual, and will continue to be male or female, though they will be free from sexual desire. The life they enjoy in that blessed state will be an endless sabbath. "There we shall be at leisure, and we shall see. We shall see and love. We shall love and praise."[26]

For over seven hundred years Augustine's explanation of the millennium and the last days prevailed. Even after other interpretations entered the field, it continued to receive support and has persisted into the twentieth century. It is often described as *amillennial,* a term used in contrast with *premillennial* and *postmillennial.* The choice of the word *amillennial* is unfortunate. It gives the false impression that Augustine rejected a doctrine of the millennium. In fact, he affirmed it, and his viewpoint may be described as postmillennial, since he expected Christ to come again after the end of the thousand years. In practice, however, the term *postmillennial* has usually been confined to writers like Whitby, Vitringa, and Jonathan Edwards, who expected the thousand years to begin in the future as well as to precede the second advent. Since Augustine taught that the millennium had already arrived, he has not been classified with such interpreters. But if the term *postmillennial* is taken at its face value, it is true of his teaching. The term *amillennial* implies a rejection of belief in a millennium and is a misleading description of his thought.

Spiritual is a more appropriate description than *amillennial* for Augustine's interpretation, if *spiritual* is understood as the opposite of *literal.* He gave a spiritual account of the first resurrection, and he did not insist that the millennium would last for a literal thousand years. Yet his understanding of prophecy is partly literal. He expects a literal Antichrist to come. He believes in a literal second advent of Christ, a physical second resurrection, and a literal last judgment.

A remarkable feature of Augustine's interpretation was his refusal to affirm that the end of history was at hand. The Roman Empire was crumbling. The Franks had invaded Gaul, the Vandals had overrun Spain, and in his *City of God* Augustine expressly mentioned the recent sack of Rome by Alaric the Goth. The course of events invited the conclusion that the last days had arrived, but Augustine refused the invitation. He did not regard these disasters as a prelude to Christ's second advent, and he refrained from making any suggestion about the date of the world's end. By taking this cautious attitude, he charted the course for subsequent interpreters.

AUGUSTINE'S SUCCESSORS

Latin commentators perpetuated Augustine's account of the millennium, and one of the most famous of his contemporaries, the great biblical scholar Jerome (c.340–420), agreed with him in rejecting Chiliasm. Jerome made a revision of Victorinus's commentary and omitted the chiliastic interpretation. He explained the millennium as a symbolic reference to virgins who reign with Christ. In so doing he assumed that the period was already in existence and thought that it would come to a conclusion in the last days.[27] In one of his other writings, Jerome confirmed his rejection of Chiliasm. The saints, he said, will receive a heavenly, not an earthly, kingdom.[28]

It is not certain that Jerome depended on Augustine. Beyond doubt, however, Augustine was the inspiration for a succession of Western commentators. Primasius, bishop of Hadrumetum in North Africa (6th cent.), was the author of the first surviving full-scale Latin commentary in this tradition. Apringius, probably bishop of Béja in Portugal, was a contemporary of Primasius, but the surviving manuscript of his work deals only with the first five and last three chapters of the Apocalypse. Another sixth-century commentator in the same tradition was Cassiodorus, a senator in Ravenna, who withdrew from public life and founded a monastery. A commentary of the same period, traditionally ascribed to Augustine and often regarded as the work of Tyconius, may have been written by Caesarius of Arles.[29]

Bede, the renowned scholar of Anglo-Saxon Christianity, who lived at Jarrow in Northumbria, wrote an exposition of the Apocalypse in the early years of the eighth century, probably between 703 and 709. More concise than Primasius but more detailed than Cassiodorus, Bede relied heavily on his predecessors but made an original contribution by dividing the Apocalypse into seven parts. Many writers have agreed with his principle of a sevenfold division, although they have not always followed him in detail.[30]

In the middle of the eighth century, Ambrosius Autpertus (or Ambrose Ansbert), a monk of the monastery of St. Vincent in Samnium, Italy, and Alcuin, abbot of Tours, wrote commentaries in the Augustinian tradition, but Alcuin's work is incomplete, extending only to Revelation 12:12.[31] Another monk, Beatus of Liebana, Spain, who also wrote in the eighth century and relied heavily on earlier writers, belonged to the same tradition. Though unoriginal, he is an important source for reconstructing the views of Tyconius. Beatus's book is best known for the illustrations included in its numerous manuscripts. It was popular in Spain and France, where many copies of it survive.

Haimo of Auxerre, the ninth-century monk and commentator, who was largely dependent on Autpertus and Bede, continued the Augustinian style of interpretation,[32] as did the *Glossa Ordinaria,* a widely circulated collection of comments on the scriptures that relies mainly on previous writers.[33] The tradition of Augustine was still very much alive in the twelfth century, when its representatives were Bruno of Segni and Martin of Leon.[34] As well as accepting Augustine's account of the millennium, these writers regarded John the Apostle as the author of the Apocalypse. Most of them dated it to Domitian's reign,[35] but Apringius favored an earlier date, claiming that John was exiled to Patmos during the reign of Claudius, a viewpoint probably derived from the fourth-century theologian Epiphanius.[36]

Like Augustine, these authors refused to identify Antichrist primarily with Rome. They explained the Apocalypse's images of evil in terms of the totality of unrighteous people. According to Primasius, for example, the vast army of cavalry in the sixth trumpet vision includes all wicked persons (Rev. 9:16-17). The beast from the sea (Rev. 13:1-10) is the people who constitute the body of the devil, while the beast from the land (Rev. 13:11-18) represents men and women who do the devil's work in the name of Christ. The whore of Babylon (Rev. 17:1-8) stands for all human beings who are spiritually lost, and the seven heads of the beast on which she rides symbolize not only Rome but all ruling powers.[37]

In many points of detail these interpretations were similar to those of the Chiliasts. Primasius and Bede, in agreement with Tertullian and Methodius, described the 144,000 (Rev. 14:1-5) as literally virgins.[38] Moreover, they emphasized the worldwide nature of the church, a point already made by Victorinus. The seven churches of Revelation 2 and 3, the twenty-four elders (Revelation 4–5), the 144,000 (Revelation 7), the countless multitude (Revelation 7), and the woman of Revelation 12 symbolize the whole church.[39] And the two witnesses of Revelation 11 stand for the church in so far as it uses the Old and New Testaments in its preaching and prophesying.[40]

An important feature of these commentators is their tendency to be silent about historical events of their own times and to speak of history in a general rather than a particular sense. They explained the seal and trumpet visions as allusions to the time between the earliest church and the second advent. The white horse of the first seal vision stands for apostles and preachers, and its rider is Christ.[41] The four angels of Revelation 7:1 represent ancient empires from Assyria to Rome.[42] The scorpions and locusts of the fifth trumpet vision are heretical teachers.[43] This tendency to find general explanations for the prophecies continued until the twelfth century. Anselm of Havelberg (d.1158) explained the seven seal visions as predictions of seven stages of the church's history. Richard of St. Victor (d.1173), a native of Scotland, gave a similar account not only of the seal visions but also of the trumpet visions, the bowl visions, and the visions of the woman, the dragon, and the beasts.[44] Occasionally some of these writers were very specific. According to Primasius and Autpertus, the long hair of the locusts (Rev. 9:8) represents women supporters of heretics, in particular the Montanists Priscilla and Maximilla and the Donatist Lucilla. According to Bede, the pale horse of the fourth seal vision stands for the spread of the heresy of Arianism.[45] A writing thought to be the work of Quodvultdeus, bishop of Carthage (early 5th cent.), expected the holy city to be trodden down in the last days not only by Arians and other heretics but also by hostile nations, including Goths and Moors.[46] But most of the writers in Augustine's tradition avoided reference to particular individuals and events, especially those of their own time. They were equally reluctant to be specific about the future.

The monk Berengaud, who may have lived as early as the ninth or as late as the twelfth century, went much further than previous interpreters and explained the visions in terms of the whole of history from the creation until the second advent.[47] No commentator before him had given so panoramic an account of the book. He explained the description of Christ's tunic, girdle, hair, eyes, feet, voice, and sword (Rev. 1:12-16) as symbolic of groups of people at different stages of history.[48] Both the seal visions and the trumpet visions allude to periods before and after Christ's first advent,[49] and the seven heads of the dragon and the beast (Rev. 12:3; 13:1; 17:3) signify men and women who are reprobate in each of the seven ages of history.[50]

Rupert, abbot of Deutz (c.1075–1129 or 1130), also explained the book in terms of events before as well as after Christ's first advent. He did not trace the story back as far as the creation, as Berengaud did. The trumpet visions, he said, point to events from the destruction of Sodom and Gomorrah until the resurrection of the dead.[51] But in spite of their interest in history neither Berengaud nor Rupert was specific about the details of events during the Christian era, and neither of them mentioned events of his own day.

Commentators in this tradition were silent about natural disasters as well as political events. They often explained earthquakes and falling stars in symbolic rather than literal terms. Visions of earthquakes (Rev. 6:12; 11:13; 16:17-18), said Primasius, are descriptions of persecution; and visions of falling stars (Rev. 8:7-11) allude to the corruption of men and women by the devil.[52]

The silence of these writers, from Primasius until Rupert, about events of their own times is astonishing. They not only refrained from drawing attention to particular earthquakes or famines, but they had little to say about the great political changes that took place as well. During those years the map of Europe and North Africa was transformed. The western Roman Empire disintegrated. Arab armies conquered North Africa and Spain and penetrated into France. The Frankish army halted the Arab advance by its victory at the Battle of Tours (732), but many years elapsed before the Arabs were ejected from Spain. During the ninth and tenth centuries the Vikings ravaged the coasts of western Europe and even attacked North Africa. Charlemagne, king of the Franks, whom the pope crowned as emperor in 800, established a new Christian empire, including France, much of Germany, and a large part of Italy. Although Charlemagne's empire declined after his death, the German king Otto I, who became Holy Roman emperor in 962, brought it to life again and established control over a territory that included Germany and northern Italy. Yet Western commentators made no mention of these events. Their silence is specially worthy of note because many of them were living in close proximity to the scenes of action. Primasius lived in North Africa when the Vandals had overrun that part of the world. Beatus was an inhabitant of Spain when the Moors ruled over most of the country. Silence about these matters does not mean that the writers were oblivious to them. The Apocalypse attracted them because its assurance of God's power and justice was relevant for their times.[53] But their failure to make allusion to events is remarkable.

In fact, these writers showed a greater interest in ecclesiastical than in natural or political events. They readily mentioned the heresies of Montanism and Arianism. They were more concerned to point out the satanic influence of false teachers than to bemoan the occurrence of famines and earthquakes or to denounce the cruelty and savagery of secular leaders. Nearly all of these commentators were monks or bishops, and some of them were both. The preservation of pure doctrine was of primary importance for them, since they believed it to be essential for the salvation of souls.

EASTERN INTERPRETATIONS

The Apocalypse was not the subject of as many writings in the East as in the West. But two important commentators, Andreas (6th cent.) and Arethas (10th cent.), both of whom held the office of bishop of Caesarea in Cappadocia, gave an account of the millennium similar to Augustine's. They explained it as the period between Christ's first advent and the coming of Antichrist, and they described the first resurrection as spiritual.[54] While Western writers, however, freely acknowledged their debt to Augustine and grudgingly recognized their dependence on Tyconius, these Eastern commentators mentioned neither of them. Their silence may have been due to parochialism, a reluctance to recognize any dependence on Western Christianity, or it may have been because they derived their account of the millennium from elsewhere. In any case, there is no surviving evidence of this kind of interpretation before Tyconius and Augustine.

Opinions about the millennium were more varied in the East than in the West. According to Oecumenius (6th cent.), it stood for the brief period of Jesus' first advent, extending from his birth until his ascension.[55] The Syrian writer Dionysius bar Salibi (12th cent.) revived the belief in a future millennium.[56] And Bûlus al-Bûsi (13th cent.) of the Egyptian Coptic Church thought that the millennium lasted from 500 until 1500.[57] But Andreas was the Eastern writer with the greatest influence. Since Chrysostom had not written homilies on the Apocalypse, Andreas's work filled the gap and became the standard commentary in the Greek and Russian churches.

Although these writers were attracted to a symbolic interpretation of the Apocalypse's predictions of natural disasters, they were readier than Western writers to explain them literally. Oecumenius thought that the book described real earthquakes at the time of both Jesus' crucifixion (Rev. 6:13) and the last days (Rev. 11:13; 16:18); and Andreas explained the famine of the fourth seal vision as a literal famine during the reign of the emperor Maximin.[58]

Eastern writers were also more disposed than their Western counterparts to detect allusions in the Apocalypse to historical events. Oecumenius's interpretation of the six seal visions (Rev. 6:1–8:2) reflects his emphasis on Jesus' earthly life. The first five of them allude, he said, to events from Jesus' birth until his trial. The sixth tells of his crucifixion, resurrection, and ascension and extends to the war in which the Romans destroyed Jerusalem. The seventh deals with his second coming and the reward of the righteous. The vision of the woman, the child, and the dragon (Rev. 12:1-17) also refers to the life of Jesus. The woman is Mary; the dragon's attempt to destroy her child is Satan's activity in leading Herod the Great to plot against the infant Jesus; and her flight into the wilderness is Mary's journey with Jesus and Joseph into Egypt.[59] The harlot of Revelation 17 is Rome. The beast on which she rides is the devil. Its seven heads are the persecuting emperors Nero, Domitian, Trajan, Severus, Decius, Valerian, and Diocletian, and its eighth head is the devil himself.[60]

Andreas's historical allusions are different from those given by Oecumenius. The seal visions, he says, describe events from the earliest church to the end of the age.[61] The harlot of Revelation 17 is the universal, earthly kingdom that will flourish until the coming of the Antichrist, and the seven hills symbolized by the heads of the beast are the capital cities of the empires of Assyria, Media, Babylonia, Persia, Macedon, Rome, and Byzantium, empires that have exceeded all others in their aspiration to world dominion. The seven kings that the heads also symbolize are rulers of these empires, and the seventh of them is Constantine.[62]

Although these interpretations are similar to those of Augustine's successors, they are more specific in that they allude to the Christian empire of Constantine and the city of Constantinople. Moreover, although Andreas rejected the suggestion that Gog and Magog may symbolize the Huns, who invaded the Byzantine Empire, Arethas likened the beast from the sea to the Saracens, who attacked that empire from the East.[63]

The ninth-century *Apocalypse of Daniel*, a Byzantine writing, shows this tendency to allude to contemporary events. It takes sides in the controversy over the use of icons, the pictures that were frequently venerated in Eastern churches. It supports the iconoclasts, who advocated the destruction of icons, and it describes their opponent, the empress Irene, as the "foul and alien woman" who reigns in the seven-hilled city, an allusion to the Apocalypse's whore of Babylon. The king who comes to "the seven-hilled city" (see Rev. 17:9) is probably the emperor Constantine V, a supporter of the icono-clasts; and "Hagar's sons," who are reminiscent of the foul spirits of Revelation 16:13-14, are Arabs.[64]

THE END OF THE WORLD AND THE ANTICHRIST

Most writers from the fourth until the twelfth century shared Augustine's reluctance to be specific about the time of the final events, but there were exceptions to the rule. Tyconius probably thought that Antichrist's reign would end about 380. Quintus Julius Hilarianus, writing in 397, perpetuated the hope for a future mil-lennium, which he expected about 500.[65] Quodvultdeus (d.439) thought that the millennium would finish and the devil be let loose in the near future. Pope Gregory I (c.540–604), though he did not name the year, was convinced that the end of the world was drawing near.[66] Beatus, writing in 786, suggested that there were only four-teen years left before the end of the sixth millennium, which would take place in the year 800; but he refused to be dogmatic about the matter and drew attention to Jesus' affirmation that nobody, not even himself, knew the day or the hour.[67] When the year 1000 approached, people had growing apprehension about the future. But their tendency to expect the end of the millennium in that year has been exaggerated, and Abbo of Fleury, writing shortly before 1000, categorically rejected the idea.[68]

People did not expect the end until after the overthrow of Antichrist, a figure integral to apocalyptic thought. They saw him mainly as a demonic, supernatural being, active in various individu-als. Jerome preserved Victorinus's view that he was the wounded head of the beast that would be restored to life; and Sulpicius Severus (d. c.430) predicted that Nero would come back before the appearance of the Antichrist.[69] But the expectation of a resurrected Nero and the identification of Rome with the Antichrist declined in popularity. Primasius, for example, regarded Rome as only one of many forms of Antichrist. Interpreters gave strong support to the view that in the last days Antichrist would appear as a Jew of the tribe of Dan,[70] and the Greek writing known as Pseudo-Methodius said that Gog and Magog (Rev. 20:7-10) were the Jews.[71] These identifications fostered antisemitism. The Jews often experienced persecution, and during the First Crusade (c.1100) they were the victims of horrible massacres. Anti-Jewish interpretations of the Apocalypse helped to create the conditions that encouraged these atrocities.

* * *

Between the time of Constantine and the middle of the twelfth century, the Apocalypse had a growing impact on Christendom, especially in the West. Richard of St. Victor praised it as the culmination of the scriptural revelation. The Bible, he said, is like a tree. It begins on earth with the story of creation. In the writings of the prophets it rises to heavenly hopes and quests. In the Gospels it rises even higher, and in the Apocalypse it reaches the summit.[72] Not everyone regarded the Apocalypse as highly as did Richard, but the great extent of its influence is beyond doubt.

In many respects interpreters perpetuated the comments of earlier writers. Some of their views about the four living creatures, the twenty-four elders, the two witnesses, and the 144,000 have their origin before the time of Constantine. Most writers claimed that the twenty-four elders represented the twelve tribes or their patriarchs and the twelve apostles.[73] The four living creatures were usually the four Gospels or their authors. But commentators differed about the details. Some of them perpetuated Irenaeus's explanation that the lion stood for John's Gospel, the calf for Luke's, the human being for Matthew's, and the eagle for Mark's.[74] Others said that the lion was Matthew, the human being Mark, the calf Luke, and the eagle John.[75] Others argued that the human being was Matthew, the lion Mark, the calf Luke, and the eagle John.[76] Oecumenius, however, explained them as symbolic of the four elements. The lion stands for fire, the calf for earth, the human being for air, and the eagle for water.[77] Writers represented the 144,000 as the whole church, virgins in the church, or Jewish-Christians. Some commentators explained the two witnesses as Enoch and Elijah,[78] but others interpreted them as the two testaments,[79] the church preaching and prophesying through those testaments, the church of both Jews and Gentiles,[80] or confessors and martyrs.[81] Most of them were reluctant to relate the prophecies to specific events of their own times. And in explaining the millennium they broke away completely from the Chiliasts' belief that the thousand years would begin in the future.

Throughout this period Augustine was the dominant influence in Western interpretations of the millennium. Even in the East, where interpretations were more diverse than in the West, Andreas's became the standard commentary on the book, and an account of the millennium like Augustine's prevailed. At the end of the twelfth century Joachim of Fiore offered an interpretation that seriously modified Augustine's account, but Augustine's view continued to have supporters throughout the Middle Ages. During the Reformation and afterward it won adherents among both Protestants and Catholics, and several modern critical scholars are its advocates. Although it no longer overshadows all other viewpoints, it is still very much alive.

CHAPTER FOUR

THE APOCALYPSE
AS A CHART OF HISTORY

JOACHIM OF FIORE

In the late twelfth century a remarkable development occurred in the interpretation of the Apocalypse. Joachim of Fiore (c. 1135–1202) made one of the most distinctive of all contributions to the study of the book. An immediate result of his work was the rapid spread of the practice of treating the Apocalypse as a detailed prediction of the course of history. A later result was the widespread revival of the expectation of a future millennium.

Joachim wrote at a time of upheaval in church and state. Western European powers were organizing crusades to wrest the Holy Land from the Muslims. Conflict between popes and Holy Roman emperors was causing serious division in the church. And though he did not know it, Joachim lived on the threshold of the rise of two great religious orders, the Dominicans and the Franciscans. His interpretation of the Apocalypse reflected the turmoils that had already begun. It was also going to have an impact on the explanation of future events.

In both state and church Joachim was a man of influence. He was born in Calabria, Italy, and became attached to the court of the king of Sicily. In his mid thirties he entered the monastery of Corazzo, was soon appointed its abbot, and later founded a new monastic house in Fiore. He was highly esteemed during his lifetime and met both Richard I of England and the Holy Roman emperor Henry VI.[1] Joachim was both a theologian and a visionary. He recorded that during one of his nocturnal meditations he grasped something of the fullness of the Apocalypse and at the same time recognized the agreement between the Old and the New Testaments.[2] His two most famous works are devoted to these themes. They are his *Exposition of the Apocalypse* and his *Concord of the New and Old Testaments.*

Basic to Joachim's thought is the theory of three ages.[3] The first age (or "status," as he called it) was under the Jewish law and lasted until Christ's first advent. The second age is under the gospel, and it lasts until Joachim's own time. These periods had their origin at an earlier stage than might be expected. The first of them, though essentially an age of law, began with Adam, and the second, though an age of the gospel, started in the time of Uzziah, king of Judah. The third age is characterized by freedom of the Spirit. It had its origin with Benedict (c.480–c.550), founder of the Benedictine order, but it has yet to come in its excellence. The three ages belong respectively to the Father, the Son, and the Spirit, but in another sense each of them belongs to all three persons of the Trinity.[4]

In developing his views about the future, Joachim drastically revised Augustine's doctrine of the millennium, although he did not reject it outright. Satan, he said, was only partly bound in chains at the death of Christ. He will be bound completely when the beast and the false prophet are thrown into the lake of fire and all the beast's seven heads have been destroyed. At that time the millennium will arrive in its fullness.[5] Joachim probably expected the third age to begin soon, but he recognized that God alone knew the day and the hour.[6] Although Joachim retained the outward form of Augustine's teaching about the millennium, he in fact paved the way for a renewal of Chiliasm.

The originality of Joachim's contribution was not confined to his doctrine of the third age and the millennium. He made it fashionable to treat the Apocalypse as a detailed account of the course of history. He claimed that the book referred to specific events both before and after the first advent of Christ. He gave two interpretations of the seal visions. According to the first, they describe events in the first age, from the time of Jacob until the Roman conquest of Palestine. According to the second, they describe events in the second age, beginning with the lifetime of Jesus.[7] The rest of the Apocalypse deals mainly with the second age and predicts events until Joachim's own day. It alludes to persecutions inflicted by pagan Rome, to struggles against heresy, and to conflicts with Arabs and Turks. The evils endured by Christians approach a climax with the fifth and sixth heads of the beast. The fifth head is "one of the kings of new Babylon," a veiled allusion to the emperor Henry IV (1050–1106), who was in controversy with the church over the right to appoint the leaders of the clergy. The sixth head is Saladin (c.1137–93), the Muslim leader who recaptured Jerusalem from the crusaders.[8] There are many Antichrists, but the greatest of them has yet to come and will be like a universal pope with dominion over the whole earth.[9] The forces of evil will be opposed by a saintly pope, the angel that ascends "from the rising of the sun" (Rev. 7:2), who will be a prophet of the new age.[10]

Joachim showed great interest in people with a religious vocation, an interest to be expected from the founder of a monastic order. He explained the four living creatures (Rev. 4:6-9) as symbolic of pastors, deacons, doctors, and contemplatives. But the most remarkable of his references to ministry is his suggestion that the two witnesses (Rev. 11:3-12) not only have an affinity to Moses and Elijah but also stand for two religious orders.[11]

The writings of Joachim had a lasting impact on the interpretation of the Apocalypse. His doctrine of three ages shaped the thought of visionaries and prophets for many centuries to come and filtered through to philosophers. By drastically revising Augustine's account of the millennium, Joachim opened the door for the reemergence of Chiliasm. His detailed historical interpretation set a pattern for commentators. His description of Islam and its adherents as prominent forces of evil gave support to both the Crusaders and later Christian opponents of Islam. He was not hostile to the papacy, but his identification of Antichrist with a usurping pope gave strength to antipapal interpretations. Moreover, his explanation of the two witnesses as two religious orders had a special appeal to Franciscans and Dominicans, whose orders were founded soon after his death.

Circumstances made Joachim's interpretation of the Apocalypse appear timely and relevant. He lived during the age of the Crusades. Muslims had occupied Jerusalem since the seventh century, but for many years they had allowed the Christians to continue their practice of making pilgrimages to the city. In the eleventh century, however, the Muslims' policy changed. They persecuted Christians in the Holy Land and defiled the sanctuary of the Holy Sepulcher in Jerusalem. As a response to these actions, the Christians of the West launched the Crusades in an attempt to conquer Palestine. The first of these enterprises began in 1095 and four years later led to the capture of Jerusalem from the Muslims. At the time when Joachim wrote his commentary on the Apocalypse the Crusaders had failed to make any further progress, but there was still an air of anticipation. Very soon, however, after Joachim completed his commentary, the Muslim leader Saladin recaptured Jerusalem, and by 1192, at the end of the Third Crusade, the Christians were left with no more than a narrow strip of land along the coast of Palestine. Yet the hope for a Christian Jerusalem burned brightly in their hearts, and they focused their hostility to Islam on the great warrior Saladin. These events and these hopes contributed to the popularity of Joachim's interpretation.

Another series of events that made Joachim's views appear timely was the controversy over the investiture of clergy. The issue at the heart of the debate was the right to participate in the appointment of clergy to bishoprics, abbacies, and other leading ecclesiastical positions. Kings, princes, and especially the Holy Roman emperor claimed that right; but so did the pope. The dispute came to a head in the eleventh century when Pope Gregory VII (Hildebrand) excommunicated the emperor Henry IV. Several years later, in 1122, when Henry V and Pope Calixtus II reached a compromise, the terms of the agreement favored the church.

Crusades in the East and ecclesiastical controversy in the West played an important part in Joachim's interpretation. By describing Henry IV and Saladin as heads of the beast, Joachim made the Apocalypse an instrument for the defense of the church's policies. Like many other church—and world—historical interpreters,

Joachim assumed that the events predicted in the Apocalypse were reaching a climax in his own time.

Moreover, Joachim's doctrine of a third age suited the mood of dissatisfaction that prevailed in his day. Not only was Christendom threatened by Islam and shaken by the controversies between popes and emperors, but discontent with the church's doctrine and leadership also led to the formation of breakaway movements like the Waldensians. Unrest increased in a European society that included a large peasant class. For most people, life was harsh and unjust, and the promise of a glorious future on earth had a powerful appeal. These circumstances alone would not have produced an interpretation of the Apocalypse like Joachim's. In other generations equally momentous events and equally distressing conditions did not bring about drastic changes in the understanding of the book. It was a combination of events and conditions with the particular genius of Joachim that led to this new development.

The immediate result of Joachim's work was the emergence of interpretations that treated the Apocalypse as a detailed map of the course of history. Commentators argued that the book prophesied events from the time of Jesus until their own day, whether that day was in the thirteenth, fourteenth, or any other century. The need to revise the accounts given by their predecessors did not discourage them. Their ingenuity succeeded in bringing the predictions of the Apocalypse up to date.

AN ALTERNATIVE TO RECAPITULATION

Not many years after Joachim's death a new method of relating the Apocalypse to the course of history began to be popular. Joachim used the principle of recapitulation and argued that different prophecies in the Apocalypse referred to the same event. The new method discarded that principle and connected the prophecies with events in chronological sequence. The Franciscan commentator Alexander the Minorite (d. 1271), said to be from Bremen, was an early representative of this kind of interpretation. The letters to the seven churches, he explained, represent the life of the early church, and their angels were bishops.[12] Revelation 6–9 predicts the first five centuries of the Christian era,[13] chapters 10–14 prophesy events between 500 and 1000,[14] and chapters 17–20 describe the eleventh and twelfth centuries.[15] Alexander believed that each beast represented a separate individual. Belisarius, the Byzantine general during the sixth century, is the beast who persecutes the witnesses (Rev. 11:7). Chosroes, the son of a Persian king, is the beast from the sea (Rev. 13:1), and Mohammed is the beast from the land (Rev. 13:11). A Saracen king is the beast thrown into the lake of fire (Rev. 19:20), and Saladin is the beast mentioned in chapter 20.[16]

Alexander also identified the angels mentioned in the Apocalypse with different individuals. The angel "ascending from the rising of the sun" is Constantine (Rev. 7:2). The "mighty angel" and the angel "standing on the sea and on the land" (Rev. 10:1, 8) are the emperors Justin and Justinian, or both of them may stand for the monk Benedict. The angels in Revelation 14 represent church leaders and emperors between the eighth and eleventh centuries, including Boniface, missionary to the Germans (Rev. 14:6), and the emperor Charlemagne (Rev. 14:17, 19). The angel of Revelation 18:21 is Godfrey of Bouillon, ruler of Jerusalem after the city's capture by the Crusaders. Pope Calixtus II, under whom the investiture controversy was settled in favor of the papacy, is the angel of Revelation 20:1. The emperor Henry V, who took the opposite side, is Satan.[17]

For Alexander as for Joachim, the investiture controversy and the Muslim peril were events that heralded the beginning of a new age. Like Joachim, Alexander believed that the millennium came in stages. It began with the passion of Christ, but the devil was only partly bound in the time of Constantine and Pope Sylvester I. He was not completely fettered until the defeat of Henry V in the investiture controversy. The millennium was likely to end about 1300, a thousand years after Constantine. Antichrist would then arise to lead the nations that he had subverted against the "beloved city" (Rev. 20:9).[18] Alexander showed his Franciscan allegiance in his description of that city, which he identified with the New Jerusalem, as symbolic of the Franciscan and Dominican orders.[19]

The most distinctive feature of Alexander's commentary is its rejection of the principle of recapitulation and its development of a continuous-historical explanation. He set a fashion that persisted until the nineteenth century. During the later Middle Ages, Peter Aureolus and John Wycliffe adopted this approach to the book of Revelation, and its most famous exponent was the Franciscan Nicholas of Lyra (c.1270–1340).[20]

THE GROWTH OF HISTORICAL INTERPRETATIONS

From the fourteenth century onward the church-historical method, whether it accepted or rejected the principle of recapitulation, dominated the interpretation of the Apocalypse. Objections were raised by Dionysius the Carthusian (1402–71), but they did not stem the tide of fashion.[21] Not all subsequent interpreters, however, agreed with Joachim's revised view of the millennium. Some of them preserved Augustine's account of it. Others argued that it was already completed and had extended either from the first advent of Christ to about the year 1000 or from the reign of Constantine to about 1300. Luther said that it began about the time the Apocalypse was written and ended with the rise of the Turks. "Certainly," he wrote, "we have nothing to wait for now except the Last Day."[22] The Calvinist scholar Junius (16th cent.) thought that it extended from the time of Christ until Gregory VII, the pope known as Hildebrand (c.1021–85). The Anglican Arthur Dent said that it ended at the conclusion of the tenth century with Pope Sylvester II, who was reported to have sold his soul to the devil.[23] John Foxe, the celebrated historian of the martyrs, decided that it lasted from the time of Constantine until about 1300, when the Ottoman Empire began to be a threat to Europe.[24]

Some interpreters even suggested that the Apocalypse spoke of two distinct millennia. John Napier (1550–1617), the Scottish laird of Murchiston and the inventor of logarithms, argued that the first millennium, during which Satan was chained, extended from 300, the end of pagan Rome, to about 1300. The second millennium is the eternal reign of the saints, which is not to be measured by time.[25] Thomas Brightman (1562–1607), an Anglican clergyman of Calvinist persuasion, agreed with Napier that the first millennium lasted from 300 until 1300, but explained the second millennium as the life of the church on earth, beginning with the renewal of true Christianity (Rev. 20:5) in the ministry of Wycliffe, Hus, and others. In Brightman's opinion, Rome's dominion would be overthrown in 1686 and the second millennium would enter into a state of peaceful and growing prosperity.[26]

These writers, whether they spoke of one millennium or two, explained the Apocalypse as a prophecy of the course of church history. In the seventeenth century and afterward, when the belief in a future millennium became popular in Protestantism, many champions of that expectation continued to treat the Apocalypse as a synopsis of church history. Some of them agreed with Joachim that the prophecies recapitulated events. Others preferred Alexander's method and traced one continuous stream of history in the book. There is a tendency now to pour scorn on these kinds of interpretation, but in their day they had many distinguished supporters. It was only in the late nineteenth century that their popularity began to fade.

Most of the medieval and Reformation commentators explained the visions of natural disasters in a symbolic sense. Alexander, for example, described the famine of the third seal vision as the treatment of the Jews by Titus in the Jewish War. The famine and death of the fourth seal vision referred to Domitian's persecution. The earthquakes predicted in the Apocalypse were the persecution under Trajan (Rev. 6:12) and the invasion of Italy by the Goths (Rev. 11:13).[27] But sometimes a writer took prophecies of disaster literally. Luther, for example, affirmed that the third and fourth seal visions referred to literal famine, pestilence, and plague, although he treated several other allusions to disasters in a symbolic sense.[28] During the Middle Ages disease and famine often attacked the people of Europe. In the fourteenth century the bubonic plague known as the Black Death devastated the population, and in the fifteenth century a tragic famine struck France and other countries. Yet in spite of these horrors, interpreters of the Apocalypse concentrated on the turmoils of the churches rather than on natural calamities.

POPES AND EMPERORS

Although discontent with the papacy increased, Joachim's hope for an angelic pope had many supporters, including the English Franciscan Roger Bacon (c.1214–c.1297). Writers identified the angelic pope with a variety of angels in the Apocalypse. Ubertino of Casale (1259–c.1330), another Franciscan, described him as the angel descending from heaven (Rev. 18:1). As late as the 1520s Petrus Galatinus (Pietro Columna) affirmed that the coming saintly pope would be not only the angel of the sixth seal but also the angel of the Philadelphian church and the angel with the open book (Rev. 7:2; 3:7; 10:1-2).[29]

Notwithstanding these hopes for a saintly pope, the church-historical method of interpretation was a gift for critics of the papacy. Members of the Franciscan order found themselves in controversy with the Vatican during the thirteenth and fourteenth centuries. Division arose between the Spirituals, who believed in a strict adherence to Francis of Assisi's rule of poverty, and the Conventuals, who took a laxer attitude to the discipline. Spirituals who commented on the Apocalypse used it to exalt Francis and denounce hostile popes, and they identified Francis rather than an angelic pope with the angel of the sixth seal (Rev. 7:2). The most radical exponent of this viewpoint, Gerardo of Borgo San Donnino (13th cent.), contended that in 1260 the third age would dawn, the Christian church would cease to exist, and the writings of Joachim would supersede the Bible.[30]

Francis has a prominent role in the commentary on the Apocalypse by Peter Olivi (c.1248–98), a leader of the Spirituals. As well as identifying him with the angel of the sixth seal, Olivi said that the angel standing on the sea (Rev. 10:5) symbolized Francis's activity as a missionary to the Saracens. Although Olivi continued Joachim's prophecy of a future false pope, he did not attack the existing papacy. But he identified the beast from the sea with worldly Christians, among whom he included princes and leading clergy.[31]

After Olivi's death, his commentary on the Apocalypse was condemned by Pope John XII. Ubertino of Casale, one of the leading

Spirituals, went to greater extremes than Olivi in exalting Francis and attacking the church. He compared the coming of Francis with the advent of Christ twelve hundred years earlier.[32] The beast from the sea, said Ubertino, represents the life of the clergy, and the beast from the land symbolizes the whole mass of ambitious clergy: cardinals, archbishops, bishops, and others, striving for promotion. The mystical number 666 means *benediktos,* a Greek word taken from the Latin *benedictus,* the name of the pope whose reign ended only two years before the publication of Ubertino's book.[33]

Support for Olivi and opposition to the papacy were characteristics of some of the Beguins, who were an offshoot of the Spirituals. They held Olivi in great esteem and described him as the angel of the sixth seal. Moreover, they identified the Roman church with the whore of the Apocalypse. There were two Antichrists, they said, a lesser and a greater one. The first was Pope John XXII, who condemned the Beguins, and the second would appear in 1325 or no more than ten years later.[34]

Franciscan Spirituals and their sympathizers were not the only critics of the papacy. There was great anger at corruption in the church, and many people quarreled with the Vatican for personal, political, and doctrinal reasons. In the midst of controversy between church and state, Frederick II (1194–1250), one of the most famous of the Holy Roman emperors, led the chorus against Rome. He declared that Pope Gregory IX, who had excommunicated him twice, was not only the beast from the sea but also the red horse, the dragon, and the angel coming with bowls of wrath from the abyss. And one of Frederick's supporters explained that Gregory's successor, Pope Innocent IV, was the beast and that his name "Innocencius papa" had the numerical value of 666.[35] Members of the breakaway church of the Waldensians described papal Rome as the whore of Babylon.[36] Poets joined in the attack on the pope. Jacopone da Todi (1230–1306), a supporter of the Spirituals, associated the papacy with the dragon of Revelation 12. Dante (1265–1321), who depicted Joachim amid the blessings of Paradise and Pope Nicholas III in the torments of hell, identified the papacy with both the harlot and the beast of the Apocalypse.[37]

Some of the sharpest criticism came from Bohemia and England. In Bohemia John Milicz (d. 1374), Mathias of Janow (d. 1394), and John Hus (1369–1415) implied that the pope was Antichrist. Hus, who also associated the Roman curia with the synagogue of Satan (Rev. 2:9), provoked the church establishment beyond its limited capacity for toleration. He attended the Council of Constance under a guarantee of safe conduct from the emperor, but the guarantee was disregarded and he was burned at the stake.[38]

In England John Wycliffe and his disciples were equally vociferous in their opposition to the Vatican.[39] Wycliffe (1330–84) denounced the pope as Antichrist,[40] and his followers reiterated his message. One of them, John Oldcastle, who made an unsuccessful attempt at armed rebellion, was burned at the stake.[41] Eventually, the church unleashed its anger on Wycliffe's memory. His books were condemned, and in 1428, forty-four years after his death, his bones were dug up and thrown into a stream.[42]

Opposition to the papacy came to a head with the Protestant Reformation, and from then on antipapal interpretations were a matter of course for Protestant apologists. Writer after writer identified the papacy with one or more of the beasts. Luther described it as the kingdom of Babylon and as the Antichrist,[43] and he never departed from that viewpoint. The forces of evil, he believed, were incarnate in the papacy and especially in the pope. Philip Melanchthon and other Lutherans followed their leader's example, and Protestants outside the Lutheran tradition took a similar stance. Among them were the Zwinglian Bullinger, the Calvinists Knox and Junius, and the English theologians Bale, Foxe, and Dent.[44] In Scotland the antipapal writers included not only Knox but also Napier and James VI, the young king who later became James I of England.[45]

No one expressed the Protestant viewpoint more colorfully than the Anglican bishop John Bale (1495–1563). In his youth he was a zealous Catholic, but after his conversion to Protestantism, he transferred his zeal to his adopted cause. Known as "bilious Bale," he vented his spleen on both the Roman church and Islam. "The beast of the bottomlesse pitte," he explained in his comment on Revelation 11:7, is "the cruell, craftye, and cursed generacion of

Antichrist, the pope with his bishoppes, prelates, priestes, and religiouse in Europa, Mahomete with his dottinge doucepers [i.e. knights] in Affrica, and so forth in Asia and India, all beastlye, carnall, and wicked in their doinges." According to Bale, the beast from the sea is "the universal or whole Antichrist," and its names of blasphemy are the unscriptural titles assumed by leaders of the church: "Pope, Cardinal, Patriarche, Legate, Metropolytane, Primate, Archebishop." One of the beast's heads was wounded at the Reformation but was healed when Mary I restored Catholicism in England.[46]

Joachim had unwittingly helped to fuel these attacks on the papacy by his remarks about a wicked pope. Some opponents of the papacy also enlisted his doctrine of the three ages in the service of their cause. According to the Italian Protestant Giacopo Brocardo, the third age had already begun, the church hierarchy would soon cease to exist, and people would rely on the Holy Spirit.[47] Michael Servetus, whom the Calvinist government of Geneva burned at the stake for his views on the doctrine of the Trinity, said that the seventh of the seal visions predicted the third age, which would begin during the late sixteenth century.[48] Servetus's interpretation of the four horsemen is completely antipapal: On the white horse is seated the pope, the rival of Christ; the riders on the red, black, and pale horses stand respectively for the college of cardinals with their red hats, the Dominicans, who were known as black friars, and the Franciscans, who were known as gray friars.[49]

The papacy was not the only candidate for the role of Antichrist. The belief also persisted that he would be a Jew from the tribe of Dan, and it led to increasing persecution of Jews. The Crusades were campaigns to free the Holy Land from the Muslims, but instead of attempting to resettle the Jews there, the Crusaders made a habit of massacring them. Islam was another Antichrist figure. Pope Innocent III described Mohammed as a false prophet.[50] Joachim said that one of the beast's seven heads stood for Saladin; Alexander called Mohammed the beast from the land, and Luther identified the Saracens with the army of the sixth trumpet vision and the Turks with Gog and Magog.[51] Holy Roman emperors were also depicted as the powers of evil, mainly because of their controversies with the papacy. Joachim implied that Henry IV was the beast's fifth head, while Alexander the Minorite regarded Henry as Satan (Rev. 20:1).

Of all the emperors, Frederick II aroused the most sustained hostility. While his admirers described him as a messianic figure, his enemies identified him with Antichrist. This identification was approved by high authority. In 1239, when armed conflict broke out between the emperor and the papacy, Pope Gregory IX excommunicated Frederick and in his letter "Ascendit de mari bestia," denounced him as the beast from the sea. Protestants were also ready to condemn the empire as the temporal arm of the papacy. Luther said that while the papacy was the beast from the land, the empire was the beast from the sea. But the pope, he argued, had control over the empire.[52] Within Protestantism the pope and the papacy remained the favorite candidates for the role of beast, and even in the nineteenth century learned treatises upheld this interpretation.

CATHOLIC REACTIONS TO ANTIPAPALISM

So insistent was the antipapalism of sixteenth-century Protestant accounts of the Apocalypse that the Roman Catholic Church was in urgent need of answers. The answers soon came. One approach was to launch a direct counterattack on Protestants, identifying them with the forces of evil. Bertold Purstinger, bishop of Chiemsee, explained that the locusts of the sixth trumpet vision were Lutherans. Serafino da Fermo described Luther as the star falling from heaven and the beast from the land. According to the Jesuit Osorius, Ignatius Loyola was the angel of the fifth trumpet vision and the Jesuit order that Ignatius founded was the person like the Son of Man (Rev. 9:1-3; 14:14).[53]

A more lasting and effective answer to Protestants was known as Futurism. Its advocate was Francisco Ribera (1537–91), a Jesuit priest in Salamanca. He resisted the temptation to identify Protestants with demonic powers and devised a cogent method of refuting their arguments. Instead of trying to turn the church-historical interpretation against them, he developed an alternative strategy. Most of the prophecies in the Apocalypse, he said, are still awaiting fulfillment. The first five seal visions are an exception; they deal with events until the time of Trajan. But the sixth seal vision and everything that follows it point to events that have not yet taken place. Hence, the treading down of the temple (Rev. 11:1) describes the assault of Antichrist on the church in the last days; the two witnesses are two individuals who will be put to death in Jerusalem; the forty-two months of persecution are literally three and a half years, and the seventh trumpet vision is an anticipation of the last judgment; the birth-pangs of the woman in Revelation 12 are the travail of the church before the emergence of Antichrist; and the seven-headed beast in Revelation 13 and 17 is not the Rome of Ribera's day but a future Rome under the sway of Antichrist. In those final days the church will commit apostasy, but the pope himself will not fall from the faith, although the forces of Antichrist will drive him from Rome.[54]

Ribera maintained the Augustinian theory of a millennium that extends from Christ's first advent to the last days. The beloved city under siege in the final conflict is the church. When the New Jerusalem descends from heaven, it will not be established in a particular place on earth, for it is a heavenly Jerusalem, an eternal state of blessedness, and its descent is not a literal descent. In symbolic language the Apocalypse is asserting that the heavenly city comes from God.[55]

The Italian cardinal Robert Bellarmine (1542–1621) joined in the attack on Protestant interpretations and exposed their inconsistencies. He condemned their readiness to explain days as years and pointed out the variety of meanings that could be attached to the number 666. Luther's own name, for example, could be made equivalent to that diabolical number. Bellarmine dismissed the Protestant calculations that explained the 1,260 days as 1,260 years of papal oppression. He argued that they must be days rather than years because Antichrist will be an individual Jew and no individual will live for 1,260 years.[56]

The Futurist theory soon became popular in the Roman Catholic Church. Among its advocates were the Portuguese Blasius Viegas

(1554–99), the Belgian Cornelius of Lapide (1567–1637), and the Spaniard Thomas Malvenda (1566–1628).[57] It was attractive to Catholics because it dissociated the pope from Antichrist. It was cogent because it recognized the connection of the beast and the harlot with Rome, although it was a Rome of the future. Futurism challenged both the antipapal interpretation and the assumption that the Apocalypse provided a survey of church history.

Another important Catholic interpretation, known as Preterism, was put forward by John Hentennius in 1547,[58] but the Portuguese Jesuit Luis de Alcazar (or Alcasar) (1554–1613) developed it more fully. While Futurists contended that most of the prophecies in the Apocalypse were still unfulfilled, Preterists argued that most of them had been fulfilled already. Revelation 4–11, Alcazar explained, deals with Jewish persecution of early Christians and with the overthrow of the Jewish nation. Revelation 12–19 outlines the foundation of the church, the fall of pagan Rome, and the conversion of the empire to Christianity. Pagan Rome is the beast, and Constantine is the angel who binds Satan. The millennium began in the reign of Constantine and will extend until the coming of Antichrist; and the New Jerusalem is already present in the Roman Catholic Church.[59]

Preterism was congenial to Catholics because it rejected the suggestion that the pope was Antichrist and it gave honor to the Roman Catholic Church. Its advocates, however, were not limited to Catholics. It won the support of the Protestants Hugo Grotius (1583–1645) and Henry Hammond (1605–60). Grotius, the famous Dutch theologian and jurist, expounded his position in his *Annotations on the New Testament*; and Hammond, a leading English commentator, repeated that viewpoint with minor modifications. Grotius and Hammond followed Alcazar in explaining the prophecies in terms of the fall of the Jewish state and the demise of pagan Rome. They differed from him in limiting the millennium to the years from the accession of Constantine until 1300. Satan was set free, they argued, with the rise of the Ottoman Empire, and Gog and Magog symbolize the Turks and Syrians. Grotius and Hammond believed themselves to be living in the era between the millennium and the last judgment, but they did not indicate whether the end would come soon or late.[60]

The refusal of these Protestant thinkers to identify the beast with the papacy was consistent with their political and religious sympathies. Grotius was eager for reconciliation between the warring factions of Christendom. Hammond was a loyal supporter of the Stuart monarchy and for that reason lost his position as a canon of Christ Church, Oxford, during the English Civil War. English opponents of the Stuarts identified Antichrist with the king and the Anglican episcopacy as well as with the papacy. Hammond deplored the "raising and fomenting of commotions" that was a consequence of these speculations, and he removed the beast to the distant past of pagan Rome. Moreover, both Grotius and Hammond agreed that the Turks, whom they identified with Gog and Magog, were the main threat to Christianity.

Jacques Bénigne Bossuet (1627–1704), the celebrated French Catholic preacher and bishop, was another advocate of Preterism. His commentary on the Apocalypse was an answer to the millenarian and antipapal comments of the Huguenot Pierre Jurieu.[61] Bossuet differed from early Preterists in his explanation of details. He parted company with them by treating the Apocalypse as a prediction of historical events until the fifth century. The trumpet visions depict the period from Titus's conquest of Judea in the year 70 to the time of Constantine, who is the male child of the woman of Revelation 12.[62] Revelation 13 foretells the revival of paganism under Julian the Apostate. The reaping of the grapes (Rev. 14:19) alludes to the invasions by Attila the Hun. The seven bowl visions depict events from the second century until the capture of Rome by Alaric the Goth, and Armageddon is the defeat of the emperor Valerian by the Persians. Like Alcazar, Bossuet regarded the millennium as the period of the church's supremacy, beginning with the ministry and passion of Christ and ending with the last judgment.[63] In a secondary sense the millennium ended with the resurgence of heresy after 1000. Heretics like Luther partially fulfill the prophecy about Gog and Magog, but the ultimate fulfillment is reserved for the end of time.[64]

According to Bossuet, there are two ways of understanding the Apocalypse. The first is the general, moral sense, found in Augustine. Such an interpretation is edifying and encourages faith and endurance in times of persecution. But it does not rank John among the prophets. Only when the Apocalypse is understood as a prediction of particular events does it merit the name of prophecy. Bossuet believed that it satisfied that condition by predicting the course of history in the first few centuries of the Christian era.[65]

Preterists looked at the Apocalypse in the light of the situation in which it was written. Although they did not dominate the study of the Apocalypse in the seventeenth century, they had a lasting impact. Bossuet's lead was followed by French Catholic scholars of the eighteenth century. Grotius was often discussed by subsequent writers on the Apocalypse. Hammond's works went through several editions in the seventeenth century, and Jean Le Clerc, the Swiss Protestant who settled in Holland, translated Hammond's New Testament commentary into Latin, adding his own critical notes.

Futurism and Preterism did not dampen the ardor of Protestant opponents of the papacy. In the early years of the seventeenth century the Anglican Thomas Brightman (1562–1607) wrote in answer to Ribera, and shortly afterward the Calvinist David Pareus (1548–1622), a professor at Heidelberg University, took aim at both Futurists and Preterists.[66] But although at first they did not make a powerful impact in Protestant circles, Futurism and Preterism had an enduring legacy. In a revised form, Futurism appeared in those nineteenth- and twentieth-century forms of millenarianism that believed the Apocalypse to consist mainly of predictions about the last days. And Preterism had a clear connection with the historical criticism of the eighteenth and subsequent centuries that attempted to understand the Apocalypse in the light of the experiences and expectations of early Christians.

In spite of the challenges made by Futurists and Preterists, the identification of the papacy with one or more of the beasts remained a standard part of Protestant interpretation; and the majority of Protestant interpreters continued to trace the course of history in the Apocalypse's predictions. The church-historical interpretation that came into fashion in the Middle Ages was still in vogue until the middle of the nineteenth century, when its popularity began to fade. Several factors contributed to its decline. Historical criticism, which was the heir of Preterism, banished it from academic circles. The adoption of forms of Futurism by many conservative Protestants made the church-historical approach less acceptable in popular Christianity, and the growing secularization of Western Europe meant that Protestants had less reason than before to use the Apocalypse for invective against the Vatican.

CHAPTER FIVE

THE REVIVAL OF MILLENARIANISM

CHILIASM IN A NEW DRESS

Although Joachim did not reject Augustine's account of the millennium, he opened the door for a renewal of the expectation that it would begin in the future. In the early church this expectation was known as Chiliasm, but in recent times it has more often been described as millenarianism or millennialism. By asserting that the millennium would not begin in its fullness until the third age, Joachim challenged Augustine's contention that it began with Christ's first advent. Yet commentators were reluctant to commit themselves to an outright rejection of Augustine. The explicit renewal of Chiliasm began with fanatical leaders, like Müntzer and Bockelson, whose beliefs and activities will be mentioned in the next chapter. The new Chiliasm, or millenarianism, also obtained the service of more sober advocates. Even in the sixteenth century, theologians moved in that direction. Bibliander, a follower of Zwingli, was a millenarian.[1] John Bale admitted the possibility that the millennium was still to come,[2] and Brocardo and Servetus announced the advent of a third age.

The growth of Chiliasm was opposed by Lutheranism. The Lutheran Augsburg Confession (1530) denounced those "who are now spreading Jewish opinions to the effect that before the resurrection of the dead the godly will take possession of the kingdom of the world."[3] Moreover, Calvin rejected the doctrine, and in its Second Helvetic Confession (1566) the Reformed Church of Switzerland condemned "Jewish dreams that there will be a golden age on earth before the Day of Judgment."[4]

In the seventeenth century, however, at the time of the Thirty Years War, one of the most influential of millenarian treatises appeared. Johann Heinrich Alsted (1588–1638), a German Calvinist who went to Transylvania to escape the war, combined a church-historical with a millenarian interpretation of the Apocalypse. In Alsted's opinion, the seal visions trace the history of the church until 606. The trumpet visions continue the story from 606 until 1517, when Luther made his protest against papal indulgences. The visions of the woman, the child, the dragon, the beast, and the Lamb recapitulate events from Christ's birth to 1517, and the bowl visions deal with the years between 1517 and 1694. Alsted calculated 1694 as the year for the collapse of papal Rome and the beginning of the millennium, which would include the resurrection of the martyrs and the conversion of the Jews. But although Christ would reign during the millennium, his presence would be invisible.[5]

Other writers on the European Continent followed Alsted's example and predicted a future millennium. Johann Amos Comenius (1592–1670), who won fame for his educational writings, associated it with the development of a new system of education and expected it to begin in 1672.[6] Ludwig Crocius (1585–1655), who regarded the Apocalypse as "the princess among the New Testament writings," thought that the millennium would be a time for the renewal of the church and the conversion of the Jews.[7]

In England Joseph Mede (1586–1638), Fellow of Christ's College, Cambridge, who acknowledged his debt to Alsted, argued that the millennium was to come within a hundred years. Since a thousand years are as a day in God's sight, said Mede, the millennium will be none other than the day of judgment, an idea put forward five centuries earlier by Dionysius bar Salibi. It will begin with the judgment of Antichrist and the conversion of the Jews and will continue until the resurrection and judgment of the dead is completed.[8] Mede was not certain of the precise dates of future events, but he connected them with the overthrow of the papacy. The

1,260 days mentioned in the Apocalypse are 1,260 years of papal oppression that started in 365 with the death of the emperor Julian the Apostate, in 410 with the sack of Rome, or in 455 with the death of the emperor Valentinian. Those years of oppression are, therefore, likely to end between 1625 and 1715.[9]

Mede developed a theory of "synchronisms," which was in fact a form of recapitulation. The term *synchronism* indicates that different passages in the Apocalypse refer to concurrent events. The 1,260 days are mentioned in different places (Rev. 11:2-3; 12:6, 14; 13:5), and in each place they allude to the same period of history, the 1,260 years extending from the rise of the papacy to its overthrow. The New Jerusalem will coincide with the seventh trumpet vision, the countless multitude (Rev. 7:9), and the millennium.[10] This principle of synchronisms extends to the overall pattern of the Apocalypse. In Mede's opinion, the book contains two main overlapping prophecies, covering the same period of time. The first, in chapters 4–11, deals with the Roman Empire, both pagan and Christian, and the second, in chapters 10–22, with the church.[11]

The effect of Mede's interpretation was far-reaching in England. He kept away from the arena of political controversy, but his work gave intellectual respectability to millenarian speculation in the world of politics. The collected edition of his writings describes him as "the pious and profoundly learned Joseph Mede." His reputation for this combination of qualities gave his readers the assurance that he based his conclusions on devout faith, sober judgment, and expert scholarship. He spoke words that people wanted to hear, and he had a special attraction for opponents of the established order. Charles I ascended the throne in 1625. In the following years conflict arose between Parliament and the monarchy and reached its culmination in the execution of the king and the establishment of the Protectorate under Oliver Cromwell. Men and women looked to scriptural prophecies for guidance and inspiration, and Mede laid a scholarly foundation for the belief that the millennium was approaching. People who were restless and dissatisfied with the Stuart monarchy turned gladly to his works, and he received the accolade of official recognition in 1642, four years after his death, when the House of Commons authorized the publication of an

English translation of his *Clavis Apocalyptica*. But it was not only opponents of the monarchy who gave him approval. A wider circle of readers also appreciated his work, and for many years he continued to be the most respected of English writers on the Apocalypse.

Robert Maton and the Cambridge Platonist philosopher Henry More (1614–87) perpetuated Mede's account of the Apocalypse,[12] and an important commentary in Mede's tradition was that of the French Protestant Pierre Jurieu (1637–1713). In 1685 Louis XIV of France revoked the Edict of Nantes (1589), which had given a measure of civil liberty to Protestants. After the revocation of the edict, French Protestants suffered persecution. Many of them fled their country, and others ran into conflict with the authorities. Jurieu, a professor at the Huguenot seminary in Sedan who went into exile, first in Holland and later in England, responded to these events by publishing his reflections on the Apocalypse. His treatment of the book was similar to Mede's but differed in detail, since he drew attention to events after Mede's death. The final persecution, said Jurieu, began in 1655 with the massacre of the Waldensians by French and Savoyard troops in Piedmont, and it reached its climax with the revocation of the Edict of Nantes. The city where the witnesses are killed is France; it is part of the great city (Rev. 11:7,13), the Antichristian kingdom of the papacy, that will collapse in 1710 or 1714.[13]

Jurieu's book had a wide circulation. In France, Bossuet wrote his Preterist commentary in an attempt to refute it, and in Britain Jurieu's opinions were highly popular. France was the most powerful champion of the papacy and posed a continual threat to England's political and religious independence. And Jurieu encouraged British interpreters to include France among the forces of Antichrist.

In Protestant circles millenarianism had come to stay. By the end of the seventeenth century it was well established in England. It had taken hold among French Huguenots and was making headway in Germany and Holland. Biblical commentators combined it with a church—and world—historical account of the Apocalypse's prophecies. These interpretations maintained the antipapal emphasis of Protestant commentaries in the previous century.

Millenarian thought was attractive to Isaac Newton (1642–1727) in his younger days. His unpublished manuscripts indicate that he expected a millennium on earth and was indebted to Mede, though by no means strictly dependent on him.[14] Newton's only published work on the Apocalypse, which appeared in print after his death, does not give an account of the millennium. In this work Newton exercised caution in his approach to prophecy. He employed the church-historical method in explaining prophecies that he believed to be fulfilled, but he refused to conjecture about the future. God, he argued, did not intend people to reach a complete understanding of the prophecies until after the events they predicted.

> He gave this and the Prophecies of the Old Testament, not to gratify men's curiosities by enabling them to foreknow things, but that after they were fulfilled they might be interpreted by the event, and his own Providence, not the Interpreters', be then manifested to the world.[15]

Newton's book contains the startling assertion that the woman of Revelation 12 was identical with the whore of Revelation 17. The woman clothed with the sun was the primitive church. When Constantine obtained control of the Roman Empire, she became tainted, and her flight into the wilderness symbolizes her corruption. This interpretation may well be colored by Newton's sympathy for Arianism.

This interpretation of the woman was repeated by Edward Evanson (1731–1805), an Anglican clergyman of highly unorthodox views. The two basic tenets of the apostate church, Evanson said, were the doctrines of the Trinity and the atonement; and the Apocalypse calls on faithful Christians to come out from that church and wait for the second advent of Christ and the beginning of the millennium.[16] Evanson provoked a great deal of hostility, and resigned from his living in the Church of England. He founded no school and had no successor.

Protestants, whether they were millenarians or not, usually put forward an antipapal account of the forces of evil, but the pope was not the only target for attack. Radical groups in the sixteenth century pointed the accusing finger at Luther. And during the conflicts between the English king and parliament, both politicians and religious prophets took aim at a wide range of opponents.

Indeed, even before the conflicts arose, Thomas Brightman, who was not a millenarian, directed his criticism against two of the leading churches of Protestantism. Brightman was an Anglican with Calvinist views, and in his interpretation of the last three of the letters to the seven churches (Rev. 3:1-22) he attacked Lutherans and Anglicans but gave praise to Calvinists. "Hypocritical Sardis," a church that has the reputation of being alive but is really dead, symbolizes Lutheranism, which compromised its integrity by propagating the doctrine of consubstantiation. "Godly Philadelphia," with its untarnished reputation for faithfulness, stands for the Calvinist churches on the European continent and in Scotland.[17] "Lukewarm vainglorious Laodicea" specially captured Brightman's attention, and he gave a lengthy discussion of its shortcomings. He likened it to the Church of England, to which he belonged.[18] "We have," he complained, "such a mingle-mangle of the Popish Government with pure doctrine." It is a church typified by its "brave silken Ministers," who "glister as they goe" and "jet through the streets with troupes like Noble-men."[19]

Brightman's attack on the churches was mild compared with what came later. Puritans directed their wrath against the Anglican episcopacy and the Stuart monarchy. William Prynne, the parliamentarian, whose ears were cropped by order of a court under the control of Archbishop Laud, can be excused for suggesting that Laud was the Antichrist.[20] The Separatists Robert Browne and John Robinson condemned the episcopacy as Antichrist's supporter. Mary Cary linked the king of England with the beast. Radical Protestants accused Cromwell and Parliament of being the beast,[21] and the poet Andrew Marvell likened the Fifth Monarchists, who endeavored to inaugurate the kingdom of Christ by force, to the locusts of the sixth trumpet vision.[22] But these explanations of Antichrist were short-lived. They faded away when the crisis from which they arose had passed. Protestants continued to live in fear of Rome, and the papacy was their favorite choice for Antichrist.

A new development at this time was a friendly interest in the destiny of the Jewish people, which has been described as philosemitism by contrast with antisemitism. During the Middle Ages the Antichrist had often been identified with a Jew from the tribe of Dan, and interpretations of the Apocalypse had fostered hostility to Jews. A change occurred in the seventeenth century, especially among millenarian interpreters. Christians had long paid attention to biblical predictions of the restoration of Jerusalem. At the time of the Crusades, they understood these prophecies to indicate that Jerusalem would become a Christian city, and some interpreters looked forward to the conversion of the Jews. In the seventeenth century this concern for the Jews came to the forefront of apocalyptic hope. The Apocalypse does not contain a clear statement of these expectations. They have their roots in the Old Testament and in Paul's Epistle to the Romans (Isa. 35:10; 61:4; Jer. 31:11-12; Zech. 8:1-8; Rom. 11:26), but the Apocalypse is a possible source of support for them. Many interpreters argued that the 144,000 of Revelation 7 and 14 are converted Jews, and that the prophecy of the treading down of the Jerusalem Temple (Rev. 11:1) implies that the oppression of the Jews will be for a limited period of time. Moreover, some writers understood the vision of the New Jerusalem as a prediction of the literal rebuilding of the old Jerusalem. These interpretations, which supported a belief in the conversion of the Jews and their restoration to Palestine, assumed a growing prominence in millenarian thought.

During the seventeenth century, millenarianism became a leading doctrine in many areas of Protestantism. Although condemned by official Lutheranism and some Calvinists, it had a large number of adherents in Britain, Holland, and the Protestant parts of France. Even in Germany it was surmounting the obstacle of official opposition. In England it was not as widespread at the end of the seventeenth century as during the Civil War and Cromwell's Protectorate, but it was still the most popular way of expounding the Apocalypse.

THE MILLENNIUM AND THE WORLD OF NATURE

The seventeenth century was an age of great scientific discovery, when new theories were developed about the nature of the universe and the movements of planets and comets. The most famous scientist of those times, Isaac Newton, was an avid student of biblical prophecy, but he did not make use of scientific discovery in interpreting the Apocalypse. It was left for two of his contemporaries to undertake that task. The first of them, Thomas Burnet (c.1635–1715), Master of Charterhouse, London, gave his views on the Apocalypse and other biblical writings in a treatise about geology that surveyed the history of the earth from its creation until the last days. He assumed that originally the earth's axis was untilted, all days were of equal length, and life was perpetually in the season of spring. God, because of human wickedness and degeneracy, arranged for the earth's crust to crack, its underground waters to overflow, and the planet to assume its present motions and appearance.[23] One day a great conflagration will occur, in accordance with 2 Peter 3:10. By that time the earth will have grown extremely dry, and its vegetation and cities will be highly combustible. A catastrophic fire will begin in the region of Rome, the seat of Antichrist, aided by volcanic eruptions from Vesuvius and Etna.[24] Burnet's own land of Britain will be specially flammable. "As to the *Brittish* Soyl, there is so much Coal incorporated with it, that when the Earth shall burn, we have reason to apprehend no small danger from that subterraneous Enemy."[25] At the time of this conflagration Christ will appear to establish new heavens and a new earth. In its restored state the earth will be a paradise, its axis untilted and its climate a perennial springtime. The righteous will rise from the dead to share in Christ's millennial reign. Christ himself will not be there in the flesh but will be celestially present, as the sun is present to the earth. Eventually a race of brute creatures will be "generated from the slime of the ground."[26] They will be the Gog and Magog of Revelation 20:8, who will go to war with the righteous. After their defeat will come the last judgment, when the saints will be transported to heaven. Burnet was not sure about the ultimate fate of the earth but thought that it would be changed into a sun or a fixed star and "shine like them in the Firmament."[27] In characteristically majestic language, he professed ignorance about the date of those events.

> He that does not err above a Century in calculating the last period of Time, from what evidence we have at present, hath, in my opinion, cast up his accounts very well. But the Scenes will change fast towards the Evening of this long day, and when the Sun is near setting, they will more easily compute how far he hath to run.[28]

Burnet mingled scientific theory with the acceptance of biblical revelation. He believed his explanation of the earth's history in terms of natural causes to be consistent with the idea of a God in control of the universe. "The Causes indeed are natural, but the administration of them is from an higher hand."[29]

The other writer who attempted to understand the Bible in the light of science was William Whiston (1667–1752), Newton's successor as professor of mathematics at Cambridge. Whiston is known for his unfortunate attempts to calculate the date of the papacy's downfall. In 1706 he said that it would be in 1716. In 1724 he suggested 1731, 1740, or even 1754. In 1744 he revised his prediction and settled for the safer date of 1866. Mathematician though he was, the chronology of the future was not his strong point.[30]

Whiston's more creative venture in apocalyptic thought was a treatise that took the scientific explanation of the Apocalypse a stage further than Burnet had done. Whiston thought that comets played an important part in the workings of divine providence. Like Burnet, he claimed that the earth's axis was originally untilted, but, unlike Burnet, he believed the tilting to have been caused by a passing comet. The tail of another comet produced heavy rains that brought about the flood. The final conflagration will break out when a third comet approaches the earth. After the millennium and the last judgment, the earth will probably sustain a direct hit from yet another comet. Deflected from its normal orbit, it will itself become a comet for all future ages.[31] Whiston's theory reflects the intellectual and scientific interests of his day. He was writing soon after 1682, the year when Edmund Halley calculated the orbit of the famous comet named after him. A cometary explanation of the last days was in tune with concerns of the times.

These writers received severe criticism from other scientists, but not every reaction was negative. John Locke said of Whiston's *New Theory of the Earth:* "I have not heard one of my acquaintances speak of it, but with great commendation, as I think it deserves."[32] John Wesley commended Burnet's theory as "highly probable" and regarded his account of the final conflagration as "one of the noblest tracts which is extant in our language."[33]

The attempts by Burnet and Whiston to explain the beginnings and the end of the earth's history in terms of scientific knowledge were a new development, but natural catastrophes had long been regarded as signs of the approach of the last days. Predictions of such disasters were a characteristic feature of apocalyptic literature, and people who experienced them were inclined to understand them as signs of the end. A large number of writers on the Apocalypse gave symbolic accounts of earthquakes, plagues, and famines, explaining them as descriptions of wars, persecutions, and church controversies. This style of interpretation did not die out with the revival of millenarianism. Many writers, including Priestley and Bicheno, explained the earthquake of Revelation 11:13 as the French Revolution,[34] while others took these prophecies of natural disaster literally. The Lisbon earthquake of 1755, which killed as many as 60,000 people, seemed like a prelude to the end of the world. It had a fearful impact on contemporaries. An article in *The Gentleman's Magazine* compared it with the earthquakes predicted in Luke 21:25-26. Its purpose was "to make way for the glorious kingdom of the millennium." It was like the voice of the angel in Revelation 14:6-7. The event was "seemingly supernatural, as if it came to pass by the direction of a *particular providence,* to confound the wisdom and silence the audacious infidels of the age."[35]

It was not only the disaster at Lisbon that aroused this kind of response. Charles Wesley (1707–88), always ready to express himself in verse, was led by an earlier earthquake to write of the imminence of Christ's return:

> Expect ye ransom'd ones,
>   A new-created earth.
> The ruin of the old is near
>   Look up, and see your Lord appear![36]

The darkening of the sun and the appearance of meteors were other signs that awakened the expectation of the last days. In North America unusual darkness on May 19, 1780, and showers of meteors in 1803 and 1833 provoked speculation about the end of the world.[37] Millenarian writers of the twentieth century have laid great emphasis on earthquakes as a proof that the last days are drawing near.[38] But even when they draw attention to natural disasters, most interpreters concentrate on explaining the prophecies in terms of human events. Natural catastrophes have put people in a frame of mind to study the Apocalypse but have not played the major part in its interpretation.

POSTMILLENNIALISM

One of the best known versions of millenarian thought is post-millennialism, the theory that asserts that Christ will not appear visibly until the thousand years have ended and that the resurrection before the millennium will be spiritual, not physical. The word *post-millennialist* could, strictly speaking, be used of interpretations like Augustine's, who dates the beginning of the millennium at the time of Christ's first advent. But it is normally used to describe theories that expect the thousand years to begin in the future. Postmillennialists expect the millennium to be a period of growth and prosperity for the church and do not think that it will begin with a spectacular supernatural event. The difference between them and other millenarians must not be exaggerated. Neither Alsted nor Mede expected Christ to reign visibly on earth during the millennium. Their most conspicuous difference from the postmillennialists was their expectation of a physical resurrection of the dead at the beginning of the thousand years.[39]

Although postmillennialism became popular during the eighteenth century, earlier examples of it occurred in the writings of

John Cotton (1584–1652) of Boston, Massachusetts,[40] and in a volume of annotations by members of the Westminster Assembly.[41] In his *Pia Desideria* the German Pietist Philip Jacob Spener (1635–1705), although he did not mention the millennium, expected the conversion of the Jews and the fall of the papacy and asserted that these events would lead to "a more glorious and blessed condition of the church." In a later work, Spener predicted a thousand-year period of prosperity for the church, at the end of which Christ would visibly return to earth.[42] These interpreters believed that the millennium would be a work of divine grace, but they did not expect its arrival to interfere with the natural order of the world. The theory had many advocates in the eighteenth century. Daniel Whitby (1638–1726), precentor of Salisbury Cathedral, wrote a treatise in support of it.[43] The resurrection of saints and martyrs in Revelation 20 is, in Whitby's opinion, an allegorical reference to "the Return of the Church from her Obscurity and Thraldom to a glorious State."[44] The millennium, Whitby explained, will be "a Reign of the Converted Jews and of the Gentiles then flowing in to them."[45] The theory's supporters included the Dutch scholar Campegius Vitringa (1659–1722)[46] and the English commentator Moses Lowman. The views of Lowman were specially influential in English-speaking circles. He believed that the Apocalypse predicted the course of church-history in chronological order. The first five bowl visions had already been fulfilled, and Lowman thought that he was living during the time predicted by the sixth of those visions. He expected the millennium to begin in 2016, when the papacy would be ruined, 1,260 years after its assumption of temporal power.[47] Lowman, a well-known opponent of the Deists, was also critical of enthusiasts who expected the return of Christ in the immediate future. He regarded the Apocalypse as a safeguard against their excesses. "The whole Scheme of this prophecy then," he wrote, "is so far from being an Encouragement for Enthusiasm that it is a wise Preservative against it; for the general Doctrine of the whole Book is this, that the Patience of the Saints is the Way to Victory."[48]

In eighteenth-century England and America the postmillennial interpretation had influential advocates. Among them were the

English commentators John Guyse (1680–1761), Philip Doddridge (1702–51), and Thomas Scott (1747–1821).[49] In America, Jonathan Edwards (1703–58) adopted the theory, and thought that the millennium would be brought about by "a gradual progress of religion."[50] Samuel Hopkins (1721–1803), a Congregational minister in Newport, Rhode Island, and a friend of Jonathan Edwards, gave a glowing account of the ideal society that would flourish during the millennium.[51] The Utopian dreams of many subsequent writers were in harmony with the postmillennial tradition, even though they did not all claim to be interpreters of the Apocalypse.[52]

An unusual variation of postmillennialism was put forward by the German Pietist Johannes Albrecht Bengel (1687–1752), who held high office in the Lutheran Church and was a leading New Testament scholar. The most distinctive feature of Bengel's work was his expectation of two separate millennia. By a series of complex and dubious calculations, he predicted the overthrow of the papacy in 1836. The first millennium would begin in that year and be a period of glorious prosperity for the church. At its conclusion in 2836 Satan would be set free, and in the second millennium, which would last from 2836 until 3836, the saints would reign in heaven and the church on earth would enjoy a false sense of prosperity. Thereafter would follow the judgment and the New Jerusalem.

The beginning of the first millennium would be the occasion for the appearance or prelude of Christ's second advent. But Christ would come in glory at the end of the second millennium, when the dead would be raised.[53]

John Wesley (1703–91) had a high opinion of Bengel's interpretation and incorporated it into his *Explanatory Notes on the New Testament,* one of the basic documents of Methodism. Wesley did not commit himself to Bengel's views but merely put them forward for consideration.[54] The notion of a thousand years of church growth and prosperity was congenial to his evangelistic and perfectionistic concerns. Later, however, Wesley professed to be ignorant about the precise meaning of the prophecy of the millennium.[55] It was a fortunate admission both for him and for his followers, since the year 1836 came and went without any sign of the collapse of the papacy that Bengel had predicted.

Bengel's influence was greater in Germany than in Britain, but not all his disciples adhered rigidly to his opinions. Michael Hahn, for example, expected only one millennium and did not accept 1836 as the date of its beginning. And Friedrich Christoph Oetinger blended Bengel's apocalyptic expectation with the dream of a golden age in which human beings would acquire immediate, intuitive knowledge of truth and everyone would share in a community of goods.[56]

Although Bengel's supporters did not agree with every detail of his exposition, his millennial views made a difference to German Protestantism. The Augsburg Confession had put Chiliasm out of bounds for Lutherans. Several people had already crossed the boundary, and when Bengel entered the forbidden territory, others summoned the courage to follow him.

Postmillennialism had many supporters in the nineteenth century. It has survived into the twentieth century, and some of its fruits will be mentioned in a later chapter.[57] It has obvious attractions for advocates of evangelism and missionary work. Moreover, in some of its forms a desire for social change accompanied the concern for evangelism. Postmillennialism is congenial to both the missionary movement and the cause of social justice.

Typical postmillennialism expected the millennium to begin in the future. But strictly speaking, the term *postmillenial* could be applied to thinkers like Augustine, who believed that the millennium began with the first advent of Christ and would extend until his second coming. Augustine did not regard the present time as a period of progress. The city of God and the city of the world were in a perpetual state of tension with each other. But some writers combined the optimism of the postmillennialists with Augustine's belief that the millennium had already begun. Such was the opinion of the philosopher David Hartley (1705–57).[58] The millennium, which began at the time of Christ's first coming, was a period in which the church was growing. Before the return of Christ, he said, the gospel would be preached to all nations and the Jews would return to Palestine. Hartley regarded these expectations as reasonable because of the progress of the church's missionary work and the present condition of the Jewish people.[59]

Frederick Denison Maurice (1805–72) also combined a belief in progress with an Augustinian view of the millennium. A "moral change" came over the earth with the birth of Christ, and the "millennial state" is "that new kingdom into which we have been brought," and in which the idea of self-sacrifice is established in human minds as the principle "which can accomplish what no other accomplishes."[60] Although he understood the loosing of Satan and the emergence of Gog and Magog in terms of the invasions of the Roman Empire by Huns, Avars, and Tartars, Maurice believed that the millennium still continued.[61] "The new life of the thousand years affects government, education, manners, the cultivation of the soil. But it proceeds silently, mysteriously, in defiance of all appearances. You must study it by the lapse of centuries to know how complete it is."[62] There is a twofold meaning in the prophecies. They are true not just for the time of John but for all ages. Babylon does not just stand for Rome. It represents "an evil principle of society which manifested itself again and again in the old world, and has manifested itself again under more fearful and complicated conditions in the new." The holy city is "the Christendom of which we and of which all the baptized nations are members."[63] Not only is the millennium already here, but in a sense the new creation has already taken place as well. The earth is new because separation between nations is no longer necessary. Baptized Christians are citizens of the New Jerusalem.

THE NEW FUTURISM

Many forms of postmillennialism were linked with a church-historical interpretation of the Apocalypse. Premillennialists, like Joseph Priestley, Edward Bickersteth, and Thomas Birks, all of whom expected Christ to return at the beginning of the millennium, also treated the book as a prediction of the course of history. But the church-historical interpretation was dealt a severe blow by a renewal of Futurism, the theory put forward by the Spanish commentator Ribera, who affirmed that most of the Apocalypse's visions concerned the future.

From its beginnings in the sixteenth century, Futurism was essentially a Catholic interpretation, but in the nineteenth century Samuel Maitland (1792–1866), librarian at Lambeth Palace, provided a Protestant version of it. Maitland strongly attacked the attempt to trace the course of human history in the prophecies of Daniel and the Apocalypse. He argued that the 1,260 days of oppression (Rev. 11:2-3; 12:6; 13:5) predicted in the Apocalypse were not 1,260 years but literal days, which had not yet taken place, and he rejected the identification of the beast with the pope.[64]

Another variation of Futurism has become greatly popular in the twentieth century. It is known as Dispensationalism because of its belief that God's activity in history is divided into seven dispensations. Its champion was John Nelson Darby (1800–82), a clergyman of the Anglican Church of Ireland, who broke away to become one of the leaders of the Plymouth Brethren. Darby believed in the inerrancy of the scriptures. Unfulfilled prophecies in the Apocalypse, he said, must predict events that will actually happen. Darby made a concession to the church-historical approach. He argued that the Apocalypse's letters to the churches give an outline of church history, describing "the things that are." But most of the book refers to the "things which will be hereafter"; and among them are the millennium.[65] In this respect, Darby differed sharply from Ribera, who accepted Augustine's view that the millennium had already begun.

Darby recoiled with horror from the secularism of mid–nineteenth-century France. The first beast, he predicted, will be a renewed Roman Empire. It has not yet arrived, but Louis Napoleon (later to become Napoleon III of France) is an evil figure. His activities are a sign of "the rapid approach of the final scenes," but he is only the seventh head of the beast. The eighth and worst head is yet to come.[66]

Great emphasis was laid by Darby on the Jewish people's role in the divine plan. He argued that they were symbolized by the 144,000 of Revelation 7 and the woman of Revelation 12.[67] But his most distinctive teaching is about the rapture described in 1 Thessalonians 4:17, when Christians who are still alive will be caught up into heaven to meet the Lord. Most interpreters have assumed that this event coincides with the resurrection at the last day, but Darby argued that it will occur before the final resurrection. Indeed, it will be followed by a seven-year period of tribulation, after which the millennium will begin. The rapture, he contended, is implied in the promise to the church at Philadelphia, "I also will keep thee from the hour of temptation" (Rev. 3:10 AV).[68]

This teaching about the rapture was not entirely new. Mede had mentioned the possibility of a rapture before the tribulation but had not committed himself to the doctrine.[69] In the nineteenth century, William Cuninghame accepted the doctrine, and it was put forward at the Albury Park Conferences (1826–30) in which Henry Drummond and Edward Irving participated. But it was Darby who made it a central part of his theological system.[70]

The Plymouth Brethren, to whom Darby belonged, did not become a large denomination, but Darby's teachings have had a wide currency. Members of many churches accepted his theory, and during the twentieth century it reached new heights of popularity. C. I. Scofield, in his notes to the Scofield Bible, first published in 1909, preserved the general pattern of Darby's interpretation.[71] Scofield did not specifically relate the prophecies to his own times, but he expected two powers of evil to emerge, and described them as two Babylons. One will be ecclesiastical, the whore of Revelation 17, who is "apostate Christendom, headed up under the Papacy." The other will be political, "the last form of Gentile world-dominion," symbolized by the beast (Rev. 17:15-18). Political Babylon will destroy its ecclesiastical counterpart and will itself be destroyed by Christ at his second coming.[72] When Christ returns, he will save the Jewish remnant by overthrowing their Gentile enemies at Armageddon (Megiddo in Israel). He will destroy the beast and the false prophet, judge the nations, and reign for a thousand years.[73]

Dispensationalism grew in popularity during the second half of the twentieth century. A thorough presentation of the approach of this school to the Apocalypse is given by John F. Walvoord.[74] In his commentary, Walvoord is cautious about relating the prophecies to specific events in the twentieth century. In a more popular work he shows less caution. Writing in the early 1970s at the time of the great oil crisis, he predicted conflict in the Middle East leading to the emergence of a world dictator, a third world war, and the battle of Armageddon, all of which would be followed by Christ's second coming and the millennium. He expected that the battle of Armageddon would be fought in the plain of Megiddo in Israel. But before that battle and even before the emergence of the world dictator, the rapture will occur. "Our generation," Walvoord observes, "may well be the last before Christ returns to remove believers from the earth."[75]

In the second half of the twentieth century, the most popular statement of the Dispensationalist viewpoint has been that of Hal Lindsey, whose works have sold millions of copies. The seal visions, he says, predict the outbreak of a war in the Middle East, involving Arab states, Israel, and the Soviet Union (Dan. 11:40; Ezek. 38:8-17). They tell of economic distress, shortage of food, and the death of a quarter of the human race as a result of these disasters. They depict the persecution of believers, when nobody will be able to buy or sell or keep a job without the identification number 666, the number of the beast (Rev. 13:18). The sixth seal vision may describe the beginning of nuclear war,[76] and the trumpet visions may foretell the disasters in that war. The mountain falling into the sea may symbolize a hydrogen bomb. The poisoning of a third of the world's fresh water and the darkening of the sun, moon, and stars are the effect of pollution from the explosion of nuclear weapons. The 200 million cavalry are an army from the People's Republic of China that will wipe out a third of the world's population.[77]

The bowl visions describe the fearful punishment that will be inflicted on those who reject the Christian gospel. The Chinese army will do battle with the armies of the West at Armageddon (Rev. 16:12-16), and the earthquake of unprecedented magnitude (Rev. 16:17-21) symbolizes the destruction of cities in a nuclear conflict. These disasters will occur during the seven-year tribulation, symbolized by the seventieth week mentioned in Daniel 9:27.[78]

The beast from the sea, says Lindsey, is the Antichrist, who will emerge from the European Economic Community, whose member nations are symbolized by the ten horns. The beast from the land exercises religious power, seeking to unite all religions in a counterfeit faith.[79]

Like Scofield, Lindsey explains the letters to the seven churches as prophecies of periods of history, extending from the time of the apostles to the present day. In his comments on the letter to Laodicea, he gives a frank assessment of twentieth-century church life and castigates the churches for their corruption and decay and for the radical theology of their seminaries, which bears fruit in liberal preaching.[80]

Lindsey does not predict the rapture's exact date, although he expects it soon. The times, he thinks, are ripe for it. The decline in religious and moral life and worldwide political tensions are signs that the end is near.[81]

The Apocalypse as interpreted by Lindsey is a book for the nuclear age. Never before in human history was it so clear that war could destroy vast tracts of the earth. It is, of course, highly disputable whether the author of the Apocalypse thought of the prophecies as Lindsey does. And if Lindsey understands John rightly, then some of John's views were erroneous. Events have already shown some of Lindsey's claims to be mistaken. He has run into difficulty with his identification of the beast's ten horns with the nations of the European Common Market, since the membership of that organization rose from nine nations to twelve, and with the break-up of the Soviet Union his prophecies about that country's participation in the final events have suffered shipwreck. Only the passage of years will show whether Lindsey's prediction of a nuclear war is correct.

In the twentieth century the advocates of a rapture that precedes the tribulation have received great publicity. On more than one occasion groups of people have been convinced that on a particular day they would be snatched up into heaven and thereby avoid the final agonies that the human race would suffer. It is sufficient to mention one example. Edgar C. Whisenant, whose work received publicity in September 1988, calculated that Daniel's seventieth week started with the establishment of Israel as an independent nation in 1948 and would end forty years later on the Day of Atonement (Yom Kippur), September 21, 1988. At the Jewish New Year

(Rosh Hashanah), between September 11 and 13, 1988, the rapture would occur. During the subsequent period of tribulation, two world wars would devastate the United States and the Soviet Union, and Satan would conquer the world. The battle of Armageddon would occur on October 4, 1995, the day of Christ's physical return to earth. In the millennium, which would begin on December 23, 1995, the church would live in the heavenly New Jerusalem and commute to earth. At the end of the millennium there would be further conflict, followed by the last judgment, and on January 1, 3000, the New Jerusalem would descend to earth.[82]

Whisenant's calculations caused a brief sensation in parts of the United States. Some people sold their homes in preparation for the rapture, and others had their dogs destroyed to save them from being left on earth without their raptured owners. But September 1988 came and went without the predicted divine intervention. Whisenant admitted that he had made erroneous calculations and attempted to revise his scheme. He is only one of many prophetic writers and preachers whose attempts to predict the dates of events have come to grief. However, their failure has not deterred others from renewing the quest.

Although Dispensationalists have achieved great popularity, many premillennial interpreters reject the view that the rapture precedes the tribulation and expect it to occur after the tribulation, either shortly before the battle of Armageddon or at the second advent of Christ. Yet others think that it will occur halfway through that period, and link it with the vision of the seventh trumpet or with the picture of the 144,000 on Mount Zion (Rev. 11:15-19; 14:1-5). These interpreters agree with the Dispensationalists in rejecting the church-historical explanation of the Apocalypse.[83] Like the Dispensationalists they are Futurists, but they see no clear evidence for the time scheme that places the rapture seven years before the beginning of the millennium.

* * *

Millenarian teaching came back into fashion in Protestant circles after the Reformation and has continued to thrive ever since that time. It has many rivals, and in the academic world it has often been treated with disdain. At a popular level, however, it has had an immense appeal. It thrived amid the conflicts of the seventeenth century. In its postmillennial form, from the eighteenth century onward, it has exercised a powerful influence not only in church life but also in the secular world, where it has assisted in the growth of utopian and revolutionary theories about society. In its premillennial form, it has a large popular following in the twentieth century.

CHAPTER SIX

PROPHETS AND
PROPHETIC MOVEMENTS

Even before Alsted and Mede gave new life to Chiliasm, people claimed to have received special revelations from God and were spreading millennial teaching in Western Europe. They were prophets because they believed that God had communicated with them by special revelation. Many of them also predicted future events, and many of them claimed to have experienced visions. Such individuals have appeared in every generation. Most of them speak of a millennium or a New Jerusalem, and often they make no clear distinction between the two. Either they announce that the new age has already begun or they predict its arrival in the near future. Many of them have a strong popular appeal, especially among victims of poverty, pestilence, and persecution. Prophets were claiming to fulfill the predictions of the Apocalypse long before the Protestant Reformation. In 1300 Fra Dolcino of the Apostolic Brethren, a movement that had arisen forty years earlier, claimed that he was the angel of the church of Thyatira (Rev. 2:18).[1] Prous Boneta of Montpellier (c.1325) announced that she was the giver of the Holy Spirit and the angel with the key of the abyss (Rev. 20:1).[2] The flagellant leader Konrad Schmid made messianic claims for himself and predicted that the millennium would begin in 1369.[3]

The career of a prophet in those days was a perilous one. Dolcino was burned at the stake in 1306. Boneta probably met a similar fate in 1325, and Schmid died in prison.[4] But prophets continued to emerge. During the early sixteenth century, various individuals claimed to be the angelic pope,[5] and such activity alarmed the leaders of the church. As a result, the Fifth Lateran Council (1512–17) decreed that no cleric should publicly predict the date of future events without official church approval.[6]

Vigorous prophetic activity occurred among the first generation of Protestants. Fanatical millenarianism emerged in militant forms. The German preacher Thomas Müntzer (c.1488–1525) announced the approach of the end of history. He did not record his views in commentaries and scholarly treatises but put them into practice by revolutionary actions. After a turbulent ministry in other cities he gathered together the elect in the town of Allstedt, Thuringia, intending to lead them into combat against the forces of Antichrist. He advocated the common ownership of goods, as practiced by the first Jerusalem Christians. Large numbers of peasants attached themselves to him, but he ran into conflict with both Luther and the local princes. While Luther's aim was the overthrow of papal Rome, Müntzer opposed the whole of the existing establishment: princes, bishops, and other feudal overlords, as well as the papacy. He condemned Luther as the beast and the whore of Babylon because of his support for the princes. Eventually Müntzer established himself in Mühlhausen and, when the Peasants' War broke out, gave it his full support, until in 1525, after his capture by Philip of Hesse, he was beheaded.[7]

Other Anabaptists as well as Müntzer had dreams of the millennium. Most of them were peace-loving people, but the persecution they suffered in the aftermath of the Peasants' War led some of them to offer violent opposition to the established authorities. One of them, Hans Hut, a follower of Müntzer, prophesied that Christ would return to earth at Pentecost in 1528 and inaugurate a millennium in which people would share their goods and enjoy sexual freedom. But Hut's ministry was short-lived, since he was arrested and died in imprisonment.[8]

The prophet Melchior Hoffmann provided the prelude to one of the most bizarre of Reformation events. He regarded himself as one of the witnesses of Revelation 11:3-13 and about 1530 claimed that he and his adherents fulfilled the prophecy of the woman clothed with the sun (Rev. 12:1-17). Rome was the spiritual Babylon. Strasbourg was to be the spiritual Jerusalem, from which 144,000 evangelists would set out on their mission. The millennium would begin in 1533, fifteen hundred years after the death of Christ.[9]

Hoffmann, who had joined the Anabaptists, created a powerful sensation but soon found that his views were uncongenial to the authorities in Strasbourg. They arrested him and locked him in a cage, where he spent the rest of his life.

Hoffmann's message won acclaim from the inhabitants of Münster in Westphalia. A few years earlier the bubonic plague had ravaged the area, and its citizens, especially the poorer ones, resented the tax imposed by the ruling bishop for the defense of the empire against the Turks. There was an air of anticipation as men and women waited for the millennium. Since Hoffmann was behind bars, a Dutch baker, Jan Matthys, became the movement's inspiration. In 1534 Matthys sent apostles from Haarlem to Münster, and the people received two of them as Enoch and Elijah, the witnesses in the Apocalypse. One of these apostles, Jan Bockelson, also known as John of Leyden, eventually became the absolute leader of the movement.[10]

The Anabaptists soon acquired control of Münster's council, and Matthys arrived to join Bockelson. It was their plan to establish a New Jerusalem in the city. They drove from the town any Catholics and Lutherans who refused to accept rebaptism, and they prepared to defend the city against the army of the bishop of Münster. When Matthys was killed in a sortie against the besieging forces, Bockelson became the city's ruler. In place of the old council he appointed twelve elders, symbolizing the status of Münster as Israel, and he drafted people for military and civilian service. At first he enforced a strict code of ethics, punishing adultery and fornication with death. But he soon changed his mind and introduced polygamy, collecting as many as fifteen wives for himself and forcing women on pain of death to enter into polygamous relationships. He proclaimed himself king of the city, maintained a court of regal splendor, and imposed a reign of terror on the unfortunate inhabitants. A prophet who attached himself to the movement declared that Bockelson was king not just of the city but also was to be king of the whole world and inherit the kingdom of his forefather David. The fortunes of the New Jerusalem, however, were soon reversed. The bishop of Münster's army captured the city. Bockelson was taken prisoner and finally, in 1536, tortured to death. The Messiah perished with his New Jerusalem after a reign of less than two years.[11]

These extremists interpreted the Apocalypse in action. They tried to bring about the realization of its visions of the millennium and the New Jerusalem. But they did not rely exclusively on prophecies from the past. Believing themselves to be directly guided by the Spirit, they claimed the liberty to speak with divine authority.

Lutherans and Calvinists took a stand against this kind of extremism. The Augsburg and Second Helvetic Confessions pronounced their condemnation of Chiliasm. But official denunciations did not stop the spread of the doctrine. In the seventeenth century, when the Thirty Years War devastated much of Europe, the Continent was the scene of vigorous prophetic activity. Paul Felgenhauer (1593–c.1660) claimed that in 1617 the angel with an open book (Rev. 10:1-2) appeared to him in a dream. The harvest of the earth and the gathering of the vines (Rev. 14:14-20) would take place in 1655. All kings and nations who were not Jews or "philadelphically" minded would be overthrown.[12] Both heathens and Jews would be converted. The millennium would begin, the Messiah would reign with the saints, and the world would be renewed. The new heaven and earth, however, would not arrive until the end of the thousand years.[13]

Other prophets emerged during the Thirty Years War. Johannes Plaustrarius (or Wagner), in a commentary on prophecies believed to have been written by a Hussite priest, announced that the final fury of Antichrist would begin in 1621. Five years later, Rome would fall. In 1626 Christ would set up his kingdom on earth and rule through the agency of Frederick V of Bohemia. This kingdom would last for only thirty years but would fulfill the expectation of the millennium because of its great blessedness.[14] Christoph Kotter prophesied that in 1624 the Holy Roman Empire and the papacy would fall. By 1630, he predicted, the whole earth would share one religious faith.[15] The prophet Johann Warner had a vision of the city of Rome struck by lightning and set on fire. He heard a voice saying, "Now I have carried out my sentence on Babylon, and she has paid as she has earned."[16]

England, as well as the European Continent, was a breeding ground for prophets. During the conflict between King and Parliament and in subsequent years, Ranters, Levellers, Diggers, and Quakers proclaimed the coming of the millennium. Some of them tried to ensure the fulfillment of these expectations. Winstanley and the Diggers attempted to establish the common ownership of land, and the Fifth Monarchists tried to set up the Kingdom of Christ as the fifth of the kingdoms mentioned in Daniel 7. But these endeavors failed.

A characteristic of English prophets in the mid-seventeenth century was their favorable attitude toward the Jewish people. They predicted the return of the Jews to the Holy Land and their conversion to Christianity, and they tried to make these predictions a reality. The Ranter John Robins made a fruitless attempt to recruit an army of 144,000 to liberate the Holy Land from the Turks. Thomas Tany, another Ranter, who claimed to be a descendant of Aaron, announced that he was to lead the Jews back to Israel. Having been commanded in a vision to slaughter every member of Parliament, Tany drew his sword in the House of Commons. Nobody was killed, but Tany was committed to prison. He later drowned in an attempt to make the journey to the Holy Land.[17]

Prophets claimed for themselves other functions as well as that of restoring the Jews to Palestine. Mary Gadbury described herself as the bride of the Lamb (Rev. 19:7-8) and the woman of Revelation 12. Two weavers in Colchester set themselves up as the witnesses of Revelation 11. Lodowick Muggleton and John Reeve, who also described themselves as the witnesses, established a movement that lasted until the twentieth century. Others made more impressive claims for themselves. John Robins proclaimed that he was God the Father and that his wife was pregnant with the new Christ. James Nayler, a Quaker, who made a ceremonial entry into Bristol on a donkey, accepted the title of Christ from his followers; and William Franklin announced that he was both God and Christ.[18]

Some of the prophets were victims of persecution: Franklin was imprisoned, Gadbury was sent to prison and whipped, Nayler was branded and had a hole bored in his tongue, and the two weavers died in jail. These visionaries belonged to the extreme wing of millenarianism, but the movement touched a wide area of society. It included rich and poor, educated and uneducated, royalists and parliamentarians, soldiers and pacifists, members of the government and the people over whom they had authority. In those years of crisis, many people thought the last days had come or were fast approaching. The Apocalypse was in harmony with the mood of the times, and prophets who expounded it found a ready audience.

Millennial prophecy flourished in France as well as in Germany and England. In the aftermath of the Revocation of the Edict of Nantes, a remarkable movement arose in the Vivarais and Cevennes mountains of southern France. Prophetic speech and ecstatic behavior played a large part in Protestant worship in those regions, and in 1702 a group known as the Camisards took up arms against the government in reaction to persecution. The conflict was savage, with atrocities on both sides. In 1704 the rebel leaders made peace with the government, but sporadic fighting continued until 1710. Some of the prophets took refuge in England, and one of them, Elias Marion, traveled with his colleague Jean Allut as far as Constantinople. Marion predicted the imminent fall of Rome. Allut, prophesying in 1711, said that in the coming age of the Holy Spirit the New Testament would be abolished and external religion would cease. Christ would return to earth in 1717. Allut's logic was unusual. Since *J* and *I* are interchangeable, he argued, the first letter of the name "Jesus" is equivalent to the number 1. In the opening chapter of the Apocalypse Jesus walks among the seven lampstands and is 1 among 7, which, according to Allut, makes 17. When this number is repeated, it is 1717. The number, therefore, stands for Christ's return to be with the churches.[19]

Prophetic manifestations occurred among Catholics as well as Protestants. The Convulsionaries, a group of Jansenists, were Catholics noted for their ecstatic behavior. One of their number,

Jacques-Joseph Duguet (d. 1733), expected the second coming in the year 2000 and taught that it would begin after the conversion of the Jews and their return to the Holy Land. Convulsionaries tried to facilitate the coming of Elijah in order to obtain the restoration of the Jews, in accordance with Malachi 4:5-6 and Ecclesiasticus 48:10. Some of them regarded Pierre Vaillant, one of their leaders, as Elijah himself. Another Convulsionary, Sister Restant, described herself as the woman of Revelation 12, who would give birth to the leader of the new Israel.[20]

France continued to produce prophets throughout the eighteenth century. Catherine Théot (1716–94) announced that she was "the virgin who would receive the little Jesus," an allusion to Revelation 12. She described herself as the new Eve, who had produced the word of God.[21] Jean-Baptiste Ruer of Paris said he was a descendant of David and predicted the restoration of the Jews to the Holy Land, the rebuilding of Jerusalem, and the return of Christ to earth.[22]

Protestantism, however, proved itself to be more fertile territory than Catholicism for this kind of prophecy. The greater degree of tolerance in some Protestant countries made it possible for prophets to exercise their ministry with considerable freedom. As in former generations, the more venturesome of them made special claims for themselves.

Samuel Best (1738–1825) believed it to be his task to rebuild Jerusalem. Luckie Buchan (c.1738–91), the leader of a community known as Buchanites, claimed to be both the woman of Revelation 12 and the third person of the Godhead.[23]

One of the best-known prophets was Richard Brothers (1757–1824), who appropriated the Messianic title "Shiloh."[24] He described himself as "Collector of the Jews in the latter time of the world"[25] and "the predestinated king and restorer of the Jews."[26] Brothers, a retired naval lieutenant, born in Newfoundland, created a great sensation in England during the 1790s. Believing himself to be a descendant of James, the brother of Jesus, he announced that he was God's nephew, the Prince of the Hebrews. His mission was to lead the Jews to the Holy Land, and he predicted that on November 18, 1795, at about sunrise, he would ascend his throne in Jerusalem.[27] The angel of Revelation 17:1, he said, warned him that London was the Babylon that was about to be destroyed.[28] He prophesied that the earthquake of Revelation 6:12 would occur on June 4, 1795, George III's official birthday, and his prediction led many people to flee from London. Brothers was not dismayed when the prediction was unfulfilled. The Almighty, he explained, had postponed the punishment in response to Brothers's personal request.[29]

Brothers aroused intense curiosity. British aristocrats and French émigrés, as well as people of humbler station, went to visit him, and he won active support from Nathaniel Brassey Halhed, a member of parliament.[30] But his critics were more powerful than his supporters. In 1795 he was declared insane and sent to an asylum, where he remained until 1806.[31] Eventually he modified his attitude to George III, whom he had previously likened to the beast. He wrote in friendly terms to the king, requesting funds to buy seed and ploughs for the New Jerusalem.[32] After his release from the asylum, Brothers produced a detailed plan and constitution for the holy city, together with designs for the ceremonial robes of its leaders. Yet he no longer attracted as much attention as when he first issued his oracles. He retained a handful of admirers but left no prophetic movement to succeed him.

A fascinating aspect of Brothers is the mixed reaction he provoked. Government authorities treated him as a menace to the country, since his prophecies seemed to be seditious. But the general interest he aroused among the ruling classes suggests that some of them took him seriously.

The eighteenth century also saw the appearance of two noted women prophets in English-speaking countries. One of them was Ann Lee (1736–84), the leader of the Shaker movement, who emigrated from England to America. Even during her lifetime her followers described her as the woman clothed with the sun (Rev. 12:1).[33] In the early nineteenth century they went further and described her as the divine Wisdom.[34] According to Shaker teaching, Christ and Mother Ann were "the first Father and Mother of all of the children of regeneration," and Ann was Christ's second appearing.[35] The millennium had already begun with the rise of the Shaker movement.

The great millennium day has come,
The glorious work has now begun,
Which was in ancient days foretold
Wherein the saints should judge the world.

.   .   .   .

Christ's gospel now by Mother Ann
Is opened wide to fallen man,
And all who will may enter in
And purify their lives from sin.[36]

Another claimant for the role of the woman of Revelation 12 was Joanna Southcott (1750–1814), born in the village of Gettisham, near Ottery St. Mary, Devon. Having announced that she had received visions about the course of future events, she won numerous disciples.[37] In 1802 she began to give her followers a seal, indicating that they were heirs of God. Her intention was to give out 144,000 seals to make up the number in Revelation 7 and 14, but in 1809 she abandoned the practice after one of the recipients was executed for murder.[38] Southcott regarded herself as the seed of Eve, who would bruise the heel of the serpent in fulfillment of Genesis 3:15. She also believed herself to be the bride of the Lamb. Her most memorable pronouncement was in 1814. The Spirit told her, she claimed, that she was to give birth to a son, whose name was to be Shiloh. Since she regarded herself as the woman of Revelation 12, she probably expected her son to be the Messiah. Her claim to pregnancy was supported by her physical appearance. Twenty-one physicians examined her, and seventeen of them agreed that she was with child. She predicted that her offspring would become "the infant monitor of the Prince Regent, in whose palaces the bantling will pass its first six years and from whom the Prince will receive the lessons of reform and temperance."[39] Undoubtedly the prince was in need of such instruction. In November 1814, Southcott was secretly married in order to give Shiloh a legal father, but her hopes were unfulfilled. On the morning of December 27, she died. At her autopsy no child was discovered, nor was there any sign of a fatal disease.[40]

In spite of the failure of her most spectacular prophecy, Southcott continued to have supporters after her death, and her movement survived into the twentieth century. One of her leading disciples, John Wroe, broke away from the main body of Southcottians and formed a group who described themselves as Israelites and believed that Christ would reign on earth with the 144,000 for a thousand years. The members of Wroe's movement were concentrated in Ashton-under-Lyne, Lancashire, a town they treated as a prospective site for the New Jerusalem. "It was desirable," they said, "to have a city for the believers to dwell in, and of all other places Ashton was most favoured." They erected houses at the town's four corners and intended to build a connecting wall, but their plans never materialized.[41]

The prophetic spirit was manifested in England during the 1830s in the person of John Nichols Tom, who preferred to call himself Sir William Percy Honeywood Courtenay and designated himself Knight of Malta, Earl of Devon, and King of Jerusalem and the Gypsies. Tom first attained notoriety as an unsuccessful candidate for parliament. Afterward, in 1838, he set himself up as the Messiah who was to initiate the millennium. He rode around the countryside on a white horse, in fulfillment of the prophecy of Revelation 19:11-16, and prepared to lead an army to bring in his kingdom of justice. The streets, he announced, would "flow with blood for the rights of the poor." His messianic mission, however, came to an abrupt end when he was killed in an encounter with the military.[42]

The Apocalypse figured in the practices of a movement that established its headquarters in Somerset, England, in a settlement named "Agapemene" or "Abode of Love." Its founder, Henry James Prince (1811–99), was an Anglican clergyman who claimed to have been completely absorbed into God. He announced himself to be the founder of a new dispensation of judgment and glory and to be the herald of Christ's second coming. Instead of the Lord's Supper, his organization celebrated the Marriage Supper of the Lamb (Rev. 19:9), using milk, honey, and fruit as well as bread and wine. Two of his followers were the "anointed ones," whose function was to explain the meaning of the seven stars (Rev. 1:20). Prince did not set himself up as Messiah, but after his death his successor, John Hugh Smyth-Pigott (1852–1927), another Anglican clergyman, appropriated that title for himself.[43]

Numerous prophetic movements arose in the nineteenth century. George Rapp (1757–1847), a native of Württemburg, Germany, and an outspoken critic of the established church in his native country, emigrated in 1803 to the United States and two years later founded a community in Indiana at a place that he named Harmonie. Rapp and his community were preparing themselves for the return of Christ and the millennium. They expected to be instrumental in setting up God's kingdom on earth. To that end they pooled their material resources, worked diligently, and accumulated capital. They advocated celibacy, and husbands and wives lived together without sexual relations. In 1824 the Harmonie community moved to Pennsylvania and settled at a site they called Economy. The movement continued to exist until 1905, but before Rapp's death it was already in a state of decline.[44]

Three nineteenth-century movements won an extremely large following. The first, the Church of Jesus Christ of Latter-Day Saints (the Mormons), did not rely exclusively on biblical prophecies. Its members gave scriptural status to revelations given to its founder Joseph Smith (1805–44) and to other members of the church. But their teaching is greatly indebted to the Bible, and this blend of biblical prophecy with the pronouncements of their leaders has led them to expect both the rebuilding of Jerusalem in the old world and the erection of the New Jerusalem in North America. They look forward to the return of Christ to inaugurate his millennial reign over the earth.[45]

The second of these movements, Seventh-Day Adventism, relied on an unusual combination of biblical interpretations. Adventism had its origins with William Miller, who predicted that Christ would return in 1843. Because his prophecy did not come true, Miller changed his conjecture to 1844. When Miller's hopes were disappointed a second time, his followers, the main branch of whom are the Seventh-Day Adventists, decided that another divine event, invisible to human eyes, had occurred in 1844. Christ, they said, had entered the heavenly sanctuary (Heb. 9:24-28).[46]

The Seventh-Day Adventists grew into a thriving, expanding church and turned to the Apocalypse for support of some of their key doctrines. In arguing for the observance of Saturday as the holy day, they quoted the statement that those who do not keep God's commandments have the mark of the beast (Rev. 14:9-12).[47] The Adventist John Nevis Andrews (1829–83) identified the beast from the land with the United States, whose two horns were civil and religious liberty. The beast from the sea and the whore of Babylon represented the papacy. Andrews laid emphasis on the messages of the three flying angels in Revelation 14:6-11. The first announces that "the hour of his judgment has come." The second proclaims that Babylon is fallen, predicting the apostasy of the churches. The third is a warning of judgment on those who worship the beast, and an exhortation to keep God's commandments.[48]

Adventists have an unusual view of the millennium. They believe that during that period the earth will be desolate. At its beginning, Christ will visibly return to earth, unbelievers will perish, and the righteous will be raised from the dead and go to heaven; at its end the wicked will be raised and thrown into the lake of fire, where they will die. The fire, not the punishment, is eternal. After the judgment, the earth will be renewed, and the redeemed will descend there with the New Jerusalem to enjoy a life of endless bliss.[49]

A different version of the future was given by the Jehovah's Witnesses, who were founded by Charles Russell in the late nineteenth century and spread rapidly across the world in the twentieth. Conspicuous among their teachings is the belief that a special anointed class of 144,000 people will form the nucleus of God's new nation and will rule with Christ in the millennium. A much larger number of people, "the great multitude" (Rev. 7:9) or "other sheep" (John 10:16), will not share in Christ's millennial reign but will enjoy a blessed life on earth.

Jehovah's Witnesses have argued that the United Nations and the world's religious leaders will be on Satan's side in the Battle of Armageddon. Against them will be ranged the 144,000 and the other sheep, but Christ's heavenly army will actually win the victory, and the only survivors of the battle will be the Jehovah's Witnesses.[50]

Mistaken prophecies have not daunted the Jehovah's Witnesses. Joseph Franklin Rutherford, who succeeded Russell as their leader, predicted that Abraham, Isaac, Jacob, and other faithful Israelites would return to earth in 1925. More recent Witnesses have entertained the hope that the millennium might begin about 1975.[51] In spite of the failure of these expectations, the organization continues to thrive.

One of the most fascinating prophetic movements of the twentieth century is the Great White Brotherhood, which arose in the United States in the late 1950s. Its doctrines are a complex mixture of Christianity, Buddhism, and astrology, and it mingles the prophecies of Nostradamus with the visions of the Apocalypse. Its leader is Elizabeth Clare Prophet, who shared the leadership of the movement with her husband, Mark Prophet, until his death. The Apocalypse is the inspiration for some of their teaching. God is "the Alpha and the Omega" (Rev. 1:8). Alpha is "the personification of the God flame as Father in the core of consciousness we call life," and Omega is "the personification of the God flame as Mother." The twenty-four elders are cosmic beings, each of them twin flames that represent a quality of God. There are four aspects of the Godhead: the Father, the Christ, the Holy Spirit, and the Mother; and the dragon, the beast from the sea, the false prophet, and the great whore are perversions of them. Armageddon is a conflict between the forces of light and darkness in the universe.[52] Satan is already undergoing the imprisonment of a thousand years,[53] and the age of Aquarius has begun. The true church is the community of the Holy Spirit, the Church Universal and Triumphant under the leadership of Elizabeth Prophet,[54] who seems to imply that she and her husband are the two witnesses of Revelation 11.[55] Elizabeth Prophet has made her center in Montana a haven of refuge for the faithful. But although she expects the final events to take place soon, she does not believe that the fulfillment of prophecy is inevitable.[56]

The second half of the twentieth century has seen the growth of numerous cults with charismatic leaders. Some of these cults are clearly indebted to the Apocalypse, and Elizabeth Clare Prophet's church is one of them. Another is the Branch Davidians, whose leader, David Koresh, suddenly emerged from obscurity to capture the international headlines. Koresh proclaimed himself the Lamb of God and announced that the prophecies of the seven seals were in process of fulfillment. He seems to have decided that the number of the martyrs in the fifth seal vision was being completed; and he believed that the end of the world was at hand. Koresh, who exercised dictatorial control over the lives of his followers, amassed a large arsenal of weapons and ammunition in his compound near Waco, Texas. He became involved in armed conflict with federal agents who tried to search his premises. His compound, popularly known as Ranch Apocalypse, burned to the ground in April 1993, with tragic loss of life, and his body was recovered from the ashes. In his violence and his practice of wholesale polygamy, he was reminiscent of the sixteenth-century fanatic Bockelson. Koresh's behavior was far removed from the pattern of conduct commended in the Apocalypse. Koresh is evidence of the lethal potential of biblical interpretation when practiced by charismatic and violent leaders who exercise irrational control over the actions and beliefs of their disciples.[57]

The Apocalypse has awakened the imagination of the leaders of Bahaism, a movement that arose outside the Christian religion. Bahaism had its origin in a Muslim sect founded by Sayyid Ali Mohammad, who was known as the Bab. It proclaims the unity of all religions, and its chief propagator, Sir Abdul Baha Bahai, regarded both the Bible and the Koran as sources of revelation. When he gave his views of the Apocalypse in conversations during 1908, the influence of Islam appeared to be stronger than that of Christianity. The two witnesses of Revelation 11, he said, are Mohammed and Ali. The beast from the pit is the Umayyad dynasty of caliphs, regarded as oppressors by the Shiite Muslims. The resurrection of the witnesses is the revival of true religion under the Bab.[58] The woman clothed with the sun, the bride of the Lamb, the new Jerusalem, and the new heaven and earth are symbolic allusions to the spiritual law of God. The child of the woman in Revelation 12 is the Bab, and the dragon that lies in wait for him is the dynasty of Umayyad caliphs. The desert where the woman fled is the Arabian peninsula. It is after this period that the Bab, taken into heaven, is manifested.[59] In this interpretation, the prophecies of the Apocalypse took new roots in Muslim history.

Prophets and prophetic movements have thrived in most centuries, and it is likely that they will do so in the future. Prophecy catches the imagination most readily when it is presented in millenarian terms. Men and women feel the thrill of participating in the final act of the divine drama, and prophets who claim to have initiated the millennium or to be heralds of its arrival have attracted large numbers of followers. Millenarian ideas are found in other religions as well as Christianity, and they are present in cults like the Unification Church. But attention is here confined to those expressions of millennial hope that are indebted to the Apocalypse. It is remarkable how wide a cross-section of society has responded to this kind of interpretation of the book. In times of social unrest, millenarianism has attracted the poorer members of society. Konrad Schmid the flagellant had an attraction for the poor at the time of a deadly plague. But the appeal of millennial prophecy has extended to the rich as well as the poor, the powerful as well as the weak. During the English Civil War, many people from the middle classes accepted millenarian thought, and in twentieth-century America prophetic movements have included persons of wealth and power. It is obvious that the victims of poverty have cause for grievance and labor under a sense of injustice. But the rich and powerful can also feel threatened. In the struggle between the English king and parliament, members of the middle classes believed themselves to be unjustly taxed and feared that their prosperity would collapse. At the time of the French Revolution and during the Napoleonic Wars the upper and ruling classes throughout Europe felt threatened by those upheavals. And in the United States during the late twentieth century affluent people have lived in dread of nuclear war.

Men and women do not automatically turn to the Apocalypse in these circumstances. But the book has appealed to large numbers of them, and they have not been confined to one section of society. They have been hungry for assurances about the future, and although they have also made use of other biblical writings, the Apocalypse's warnings of disaster and judgment and its promises of a millennium and a New Jerusalem have been a staple part of their prophetic diet.

Part Two

Critical Approaches to the Apocalypse

CHAPTER SEVEN

AUTHORITY, AUTHORSHIP, DATE, AND SOURCES

Previous chapters have concentrated on theories about the millennium and the relationship of the Apocalypse's visions and prophecies to the course of history. Most of the interpreters mentioned have presupposed that the Apocalypse is a divinely given writing whose teaching is unquestionably true. The discussion now moves in another direction and examines questions characteristic of biblical criticism, a discipline that asserts the right to question everything.

Criticism is an umbrella world that covers a variety of activities that involve the analysis and evaluation of biblical books. One aspect of it is textual criticism, which is the attempt to establish the earliest attainable form of the text. Textual criticism of the Apocalypse is a skilled discipline that examines the evidence of manuscripts in the original language, early versions in other languages, and allusions to the Bible in writers of the first few centuries. While it is important to establish, as far as humanly possible, what was originally written, the textual differences are not serious enough to have had a great impact on controversy about the book. According to most of the later manuscripts, Revelation 1:5 describes Christ as one who "washed us from our sins." But the earliest and most reliable manuscripts say that he "freed us from our sins." Such a variation, however, does not seriously affect our understanding of the Apocalypse. Another textual difference concerns the number of the beast (Rev. 13:18). Most manuscripts, including the earliest, give it as 666, but an alternative reading is 616. This evidence has made a contribution to the discussion of the identity of the beast but has not had a major influence on the history of interpretation.[1]

More vigorous controversy has centered on other aspects of criticism of the Apocalypse, including its authorship, date, sources, and genre; its meaning for its author and earliest readers; its historical accuracy and artistic qualities; and its importance in the light of the social sciences. Not all critics question its authority, nor do they all discuss its authorship or ask who were its first readers. Not all of them evaluate its historical value, its artistic merits, or its relationship to the social sciences. But criticism occurs when thinkers raise some of these questions, weigh the arguments for and against possible answers, and reach reasoned conclusions.

The impression is often given that a critical approach to the Bible began in the eighteenth century. That impression is misleading. Although interpreters were looking at the Apocalypse critically from the second century onward, the eighteenth century is noteworthy as a time when scholars began to discuss these issues in greater detail and to challenge the authority of the scriptures with greater liberty than they had done before.

AUTHORITY

The most important critical question to be asked about a biblical book concerns its authority, and it was raised about the Apocalypse as early as the second century, when Gaius and the Alogoi condemned its teaching and refused to recognize it as scripture.[2] The slowness of Eastern churches to accept it into the Bible is evidence of division of opinion about the matter. In the West, however, these hesitations were dormant from the fourth until the beginning of the sixteenth century, when they were revived by several of the most prominent men in Christendom. In his comments on the Apocalypse, Erasmus (1469–1536) remarked that some biblical writings were more sacred than others. He implied that the Apocalypse was among the less sacred,[3] and although he included it in his edition of the Greek Testament, he omitted it from his New Testament paraphrase. Carlstadt (c.1480–1541) divided the New Testament into three groups. The first consisted of the four Gospels, "the brightest lights of the whole divine truth." The second included Paul's Epistles, 1 Peter, and 1 John, writings whose authorship Carlstadt believed to be definitely known. The third group consisted of James, 2 Peter, 2 and 3 John, Hebrews, and the Apocalypse—works whose authorship was disputed. These books, he said, had the least authority.[4] Ulrich Zwingli (1484–1531) held the Apocalypse in little esteem, regarding it as an unbiblical work that lacked the stamp of John's heart and mind.[5] It was Martin Luther (1483–1546), however, who made the most memorable criticism. In the preface to the first edition of his German translation of the New Testament (1522), although he retained the Apocalypse in his Bible, he pronounced a harsh verdict on it. The Holy Spirit, he said, had nothing to do with its composition. The book was neither apostolic nor prophetic, and Christ was "neither sought nor known in it." In later years, Luther changed his mind. He omitted these disparaging remarks from his 1530 edition of the New Testament and gladly used the book in his polemic against the papacy,[6] but the Apocalypse was never at the heart of his theology.

Eighteenth-century Deists and Rationalists renewed the challenge with great vigor. With their emphasis on the sufficiency of reason, they found it easy to free themselves from accepted views about scriptural authority. They believed it possible to discover religious and moral truth through the use of reason without revelation, and consequently did not hesitate to make negative comments about biblical books.

Matthew Tindal (1657?–1733), a fellow of All Souls' College, Oxford, and one of the leading English Deists, branded the Apocalypse as unreliable. Its author, he said, mistakenly expected a literal second coming of Christ in the near future. John shared this mistake with the other New Testament writers. He also shared it with Jesus himself, who gave the apostles every reason to believe that his second advent was near.[7]

Another Deist, Thomas Morgan (d. 1743), a dissenting preacher who eventually trained as a medical doctor, was equally severe in his judgment of the book. He believed it to have corrupted the true message of Christianity, and he agreed with Tindal that its author mistakenly expected the return of Christ in the near future. Morgan argued that the Apocalypse was a Judaizing work, and that John the Apostle, who wrote it, was an ally of James and Peter in opposition to Paul. He also argued that it contained the seed of the Catholic practices of prayers for the dead and invocation of the saints. In Morgan's opinion, the mere hint of these practices led to an automatic condemnation of the book.[8]

The Deist Henry St. John, Viscount Bolingbroke (1678–1751), gave even less friendly treatment to the Apocalypse than did Tindal and Morgan. Bolingbroke was a renowned parliamentary orator and a leading member of Queen Anne's cabinet. Early in the reign of George I, he joined an unsuccessful plot to overthrow the king and replace him with the son of James II. After receiving a royal pardon, Bolingbroke returned to England and, though forbidden to sit in the House of Lords, organized Tory opposition to the Whigs. He was the author of many political, theological, and philosophical works. His writings on theological subjects, which were published posthumously, were eloquent but not always closely or consistently argued. Bolingbroke was far from being a sympathetic student of the Bible. In his discussion of the scriptures, he employed the scathing language for which he was famed in politics. He dismissed most of the Old Testament as totally inconsistent with Christianity and wrote off Paul as a distorter of the gospel. At least he gave Paul serious consideration.[9] He was less generous with the Apocalypse. He admitted that, although the doctrine of the millennium did not go back to Jesus, it was "an apostolical doctrine, and taught as such by the immediate successors of the apostles."[10] But he regarded the Apocalypse as a "strange rhapsody of unintelligible revelations."[11] He suggested that it contained "the reveries of a mad Judaizing Christian," which found their way into the canon "under the apostle's name." It was the product of an age "when enthusiasm was the epidemical disease, and when one great revelation gave occasion and pretense to so many little ones."[12] If the Apocalypse had been lost, "there might have been some madmen the fewer, and Christianity would not have suffered so much."[13] Apocalyptic literature, as far as Bolingbroke was concerned, was the product of irrational enthusiasts.

Bolingbroke made a frontal attack on the Apocalypse. Voltaire (1694–1778) preferred the side thrust. In his *Dictionnaire philosophique*, he gave full weight to disputes about the book's authorship and to the tendency of interpretations to conform to the polemical interests of the interpreters. He was caustic about its prophecies. Since the walls of the New Jerusalem, he observed, will be 1,500 miles high (Rev. 21:16) and the houses will be as high as the city, it will be "rather unpleasant to live on the top floor." As for the comments on the Apocalypse by Bossuet and Newton, "the eloquent declamations of the one and the sublime discoveries of the other have done them more honor than have their commentaries." Evidently Newton "wanted by this commentary to console the human race for the superiority which he had over it."[14] Voltaire's observations about Bossuet and Newton were echoed by Denis Diderot (1713–84), who said that interpretations of the Apocalypse were "well suited to humiliate the human spirit."[15]

When Thomas Paine (1737–1809) called the Apocalypse "a book of riddles that requires a Revelation to explain it,"[16] he expressed the irritation that it caused among Deists. Of all the New Testament writings, the Apocalypse was least congenial to their frame of mind. They regarded the true religion as the religion of nature, which conformed to the law of reason, and most of them believed it to be inconsistent with the Apocalypse.

After 1750 the influence of the Deists waned, although their cause was maintained by writers like Paine. In biblical studies their successors were the German rationalist scholars, who shared their misgivings about the Apocalypse. Johann Salomo Semler (1725–91), professor of theology at Halle, found no "divine matters" in the book, had a low opinion of its moral and religious value, and regarded it as unfit for inclusion in the Bible.[17] He believed in the supremacy of reason and expected the scriptures to contribute to the moral improvement of their readers. With its prophecies of savage divine retribution, the Apocalypse did not meet Semler's standards any more than did large portions of the Old Testament.

Other rationalists modified their criticism with a recognition of the book's aesthetic qualities. Johann David Michaelis (1717–91), professor of oriental languages at Göttingen, questioned its divine authority because it mistakenly prophesied the imminent destruction of Rome.[18] He had a higher opinion of its literary than of its prophetic merits. Its language, he observed, "is both beautiful and sublime, is affected and animating." "The Author of the Apocalypse hurries us away to enchanted ground."[19]

Heinrich Corrodi (1752–94), the author of a history of Chiliasm, was a powerful critic of the book. Chiliasm, he said, is a "system of fantastic expectations," and the Apocalypse is chiliastic.[20] At the same time the book has redeeming features. It is like a "prophetic drama," and its core must be distinguished from its shell. It has value as poetry, and the trumpet and bowl visions are "poetic pictures."[21] But in so far as it tries to be prophetic, it is mistaken.[22]

Critics in the nineteenth century pronounced a similarly divided verdict. While they questioned the book's authority, they acknowledged that it had merits. Friedrich Lücke (1791–1855) thought it worthy of a place in the Bible but did not accord it the highest value. He recognized, however, that it must be taken into account in the formulation of Christian teaching. Without it the New Testament would have no complete example of an early Christian expression of prophecy.[23]

Friedrich Bleek (1793–1859) regarded it as a fitting conclusion to the New Testament but did not grant it "full canonical normative authority." It possessed "a more limited and subordinate authority," as a "supplementary treatise" of the New Testament canon. But it was not qualified to be a source of doctrine, except where it agreed with scriptures "of the first rank."[24]

The French scholar Ernest Renan (1823–92) complained that the author of the Apocalypse isolated himself from the world around him and was in many ways remote from the gospel of Jesus. Moreover, Renan regarded it as a dangerous book, capable of leading people astray. Yet he believed that it had a legitimate place in the Bible. Its style, he thought, is often coarse and crude, but it gives expression to human hopes for an ideal world and affirms the existence of God in both the present and the future.[25]

Lukewarmness about the worth of the Apocalypse was in harmony with the attitudes of leading liberal theologians in the nineteenth century. Friedrich Schleiermacher (1768–1834) regarded the doctrine of the last things as of secondary importance. He believed in an afterlife for individuals and a great consummation for the church in the future, but his main theological work, *The Christian Faith*, makes no reference to the Apocalypse.[26] The best-known liberal theologian of a later generation, Albrecht Ritschl (1822–89), explained the kingdom of God as "the organization of humanity through action inspired by love" and excluded any apocalyptic kind of expectation.[27]

The same tendency persisted in the twentieth century. The dialectical theologians who became fashionable after World War I did not give prominence to the Apocalypse. The pioneers of liberation theology in the second half of the century paid comparatively little attention to it. Some writers moved beyond neglect to open criticism. The New Testament scholar Rudolf Bultmann had little use for the book. In the tradition of Luther, he attached special value to Paul's Epistles and John's Gospel and regarded the Apocalypse as one of the least important parts of the New Testament. Bultmann, who was an existentialist, was primarily concerned about the present rather than the future. He believed that Jesus transformed apocalyptic thought by teaching that the kingdom of God was already breaking into the life of the world.[28] The Apocalypse was far removed from Bultmann's interests. He regarded its religion as inferior in quality and "a weakly Christianized Judaism."[29]

The American scholar Shirley Jackson Case was equally critical of the Apocalypse. Case represented the optimistic liberalism that was popular in the early twentieth century. He fervently believed in the gradual progress of the human race. "Scientific knowledge," he wrote, "leaves no room for the retention of primitive mythical fancies regarding a cataclysmic end of the world."[30] He dismissed the Apocalypse as irrelevant to the modern age. It had a message for its own times,[31] but its hope of sudden and final divine intervention was no longer tenable.[32]

One of the most hostile verdicts comes from the literary critic Harold Bloom. He regards the book as artistically inferior to the apocalyptic writings of the Hebrew Bible. "Resentment," he writes, "not love is the teaching of the Revelation of St. John the Divine. It is a book without wisdom, goodness, kindness, or affection of any kind. Perhaps it is appropriate that a celebration of the end of the world should be not only barbaric but scarcely literate."[33] Yet in spite of his strictures Bloom has edited a collection of essays about the Apocalypse. Whether they react with approval or disapproval, literary critics have taken the Apocalypse seriously.

Evaluation of the literary merits of the Apocalypse is by no means new. Deists like Bolingbroke and Voltaire passed a negative verdict on it, but others have highly esteemed its poetic values. Bossuet praised the book as a fitting climax to the Bible. "All the beauties of the Scripture," he wrote, "are gathered together in this book. All that is most moving, most vivid, most majestic in the law and the prophets receives there a new brilliance and passes again before our eyes to fill us with the consolations and graces of all the ages."[34] Herder described it as "a book for all hearts and all times." Carl August Auberlen (1824–64) affirmed that "in this book all the other biblical books end and meet."[35] In the twentieth century, H. H. Rowley described it as "first and foremost a vision of the glory of Christ, and of the eternal triumph over all the forces of evil which He is destined to achieve."[36] R. H. Charles said that the author displayed "a faith immeasurable, an optimism inexpungable, a joy inextinguishable."[37] G. B. Caird had no hesitation about its merits. John, he explained, "wrote as an artist, giving to ancient images new life and meaning by combining them in the unity of a great work of art." Caird also spoke of John's other qualities. "So vividly did he apprehend the presence of God that he was able to make that presence real to others, and this no doubt is the reason why Christians in every generation have come back and back to his book, even when they imperfectly understood its symbols and were not entirely sure that they ought to approve of them."[38]

In spite of these favorable verdicts, the Apocalypse has aroused misgivings even among those who esteem it highly. William Barclay was disturbed by its call to rejoice over fallen Babylon (Rev. 18:20). "We are here very far from praying for those who despitefully use us," he commented. While he recognized the strength of its author's faith in God, Barclay regretted that "this is not the more excellent way that Jesus taught."[39] Adela Yarbro Collins thinks that although the Apocalypse's images of violence may have been needed in the first century, they have their dangers. The book has "a partial and imperfect vision." Its text is "flawed by the darker side of the author's human nature, which we, like all the readers, share."[40]

The book's allusion to 144,000 "virgins" who have not "defiled themselves with women" (Rev. 14:4) has been a source of disquiet to many readers. It is probably a symbolic reference to members of the churches who have resisted the temptation to commit idolatry, which was often described as fornication or adultery in Jewish thought. But even if the words are symbolic, the Apocalypse's use of women as a metaphor for objects of idolatry causes offense. Charles attempted to solve the problem by assuming that an editor had added it.[41] Elisabeth Schüssler Fiorenza accepts it as part of the original Apocalypse but points out that we live in a different "rhetorical situation" from that of the early church. Metaphors that were appropriate and effective at that time can "perpetuate prejudice and injustice" in other situations.[42] Susan Garrett finds both the Apocalypse's use of female imagery and its descriptions of violence to be "disturbing and dangerous." Its images, she says, are the products of a patriarchal society, and even its positive image of the woman (Rev. 12:1) "remains subject to male control." Garrett recognizes the worth of John's claim that everybody will be accountable to God, and she applauds his desire to encourage faith and obedience. But the book's "implicit disparagement of women," she fears, may well hinder the accomplishment of that purpose.[43]

Criticism of the merits of the Apocalypse has a long history. It goes back to the early church. It was revived at the Reformation, and it is frequently practiced by modern scholars and theologians. But many who have misgivings about its violence and the nature of its imagery are captivated by its poetic power and beauty. They value its emphasis on the transcendence of God and its picture of churches faithful under the threat of persecution.

Under these circumstances a large number of theologians and scholars evaluate the Apocalypse by standards that are not wholly derived from its contents. They read it in the light of ideas of love, justice, and peace that are more clearly stated in other parts of the

115

Bible. When they examine the book in this way, they give it limited authority. They treat the teaching of other parts of the Bible or the dictates of their own consciences as a superior authority to the Apocalypse.

AUTHORSHIP

The issues of the authorship and authority of biblical books are closely connected. Early Christians were concerned to establish that either the apostles or their followers wrote the books of the New Testament. As long as they were convinced that John the Apostle wrote the Apocalypse, they were ready to accept its authority. Not everyone in the early church, however, agreed that John was the author. Gaius and the Alogoi said that it was written by the heretic Cerinthus; and Dionysius, bishop of Alexandria, suggested that it was the work of John the Elder.[44] Doubts about authorship subsided for many years, but in the sixteenth century Zwingli and Luther, who also questioned the book's authority, said that it was not apostolic. In the eighteenth century, Deists and Rationalists brought up the issue again. Bolingbroke and Semler rejected the traditional viewpoint, and Michaelis had serious doubts about it. In the nineteenth and twentieth centuries the number of scholars who denied apostolic authorship greatly increased. Some of them, like Ewald and Charles, ascribed it to an unknown John, not the apostle. Others, like Lücke, Bleek, and Bousset, preferred Dionysius's suggestion that John the Elder was the author. Hitzig made the unusual conjecture that it was written by John Mark. More recently, Josephine Massyngberde Ford put forward the equally unusual theory that much of the book was the work of John the Baptist and his disciples.[45] And B. W. Bacon has suggested that the author was one of Philip's daughters, who was endowed with the gift of prophecy (Acts 20:9).[46] By no means have all modern scholars, however, rejected the claim that John the Apostle was the author. The traditional view has had many supporters.[47] The main reason for questioning whether John the Apostle wrote the book is its obvious difference from the other writings ascribed to John. The Greek vocabulary and the style of writing are different. The thought is different. While the Gospel and Epistles emphasize that believers can have eternal life here and now, the Apocalypse concentrates on promises for the future; while the Gospel and Epistles speak of a present life in Christ, the Apocalypse focuses on the last judgment, the lake of fire, and the New Jerusalem. In both overall atmosphere and particular details, the Apocalypse is vastly different from the other biblical writings ascribed to John.

These considerations led Dionysius of Alexandria to reject the idea that the apostle was the author, and many recent writers have agreed with him for the same reasons. But, especially in the twentieth century, many scholars have decided that the apostle was responsible for none of the writings traditionally ascribed to him, and have therefore felt the need to explain why John was supposed to be their author. Some of them have reached the conclusion that the actual writers of these works were members of a school or community. In the opinion of C. K. Barrett, for example, John's Gospel, John's Epistles, and the Apocalypse were the work of three different followers of John the Apostle, and the Apocalypse was closest to the teaching of the apostle himself.[48] Schüssler Fiorenza thinks that the author of the Apocalypse was the leader of a group of prophets,[49] and Oscar Cullmann believes that he belonged to a Johannine circle that migrated from Samaria to Ephesus.[50] These are plausible theories, but there is no clear evidence for the existence of a Johannine school.

Several critics maintain the traditional theory that one person wrote all these books.[51] They account for the Apocalypse's difference in style and thought from the other works in various ways. Joseph Sickenberger suggests that John the Apostle himself was responsible for the rugged style of the Apocalypse and that someone else translated the Gospel and Epistles from John's original Aramaic.[52] Others argue that the Apocalypse has a different style because John was in a state of ecstasy when he wrote it. Yet others assume that John wrote these works at separate stages of his life. Herder took this last position. All these writings, he said, show the marks of "the same strong and gentle soul." Herder waxed lyrical over John's writings. "If the Revelation stands forth as a royal aloe, his gospel is a lily and rose, marked with the blood of love, his least epistle a forget-me-not, a flower of dear remembrance." Both the Gospel and the Apocalypse have the same spirit and character, but John wrote the Apocalypse "in the fire of his years" and the Gospel "in the calm of his age."[53]

DATE

The date of the book's composition is not as controversial a subject as its authorship. The majority of options suggested are within the possible lifetime of John the Apostle. Only a date in the second century seriously challenges the view that the apostle was its author. The most generally accepted date is 95 or 96 at the end of the reign of the emperor Domitian. The first person known to accept this viewpoint was Irenaeus, and most early writers agreed with him. In the early church two other suggestions were made. Epiphanius (4th cent.) and Apringius (6th cent.) dated it during the reign of Claudius (41–54), although they may have confused Claudius with Nero.[54] The other suggestion, found in a writing mistakenly ascribed to the third-century Dorotheus of Tyre, is that John the Apostle wrote the Apocalypse when Trajan was emperor.[55] For many centuries, however, Irenaeus's opinion prevailed, and most interpreters dated the book at the end of Domitian's reign.

In the eighteenth century, scholars began to question Irenaeus's opinion. Abauzit, Wettstein, and Herder thought that the Apocalypse was written in the sixties.[56] Their reason for adopting this viewpoint was that Revelation 11:1-2 seemed to imply that the Temple was still standing. Since the Romans destroyed the Temple in 70, they concluded that the Apocalypse must have been written before that year. Several nineteenth-century scholars, including Ewald, Lücke, Bleek, Baur, and Renan, also dated the book in the late sixties.[57] Edward Evanson argued that it was the earliest of the New Testament books and that it influenced Paul in his Epistles to the Thessalonians and Corinthians.[58] Züllig dated it between 44 and 47, during Claudius's reign, reviving the theory of Epiphanius. But by the end of the nineteenth century the date in

Domitian's reign was coming back into favor and was supported by Bousset.[59]

Most twentieth-century scholars accept the traditional date, but Hartenstein, J. A. T. Robinson, and Gentry argue that it was written between Nero's death in 68 and the destruction of Jerusalem in 70. Kraft thinks that it contains material written under Nerva and Trajan, and Farrer dates it in Trajan's reign.[60]

Those who date the Apocalypse after 70 usually give a spiritual interpretation of the passage about the preservation of the Temple's inner court (Rev. 11:1-2). They argue that the inner court symbolizes the faithful remnant of God's people,[61] although Charles suggests that John was reediting a document that in its earlier form referred to a literal temple.[62]

Critics are still divided about the date, and unless startling new evidence emerges, it is unlikely that a consensus will be reached. Most writers think that the book was written between 64 and 96, when John the Apostle is likely to have been alive. If it comes from that period, its date offers no serious challenge to the view that the apostle was its author, since it is conceivable that a disciple of Jesus could have lived until that time.

SOURCES

In the nineteenth and twentieth centuries, critics have devoted great energy to the investigation of possible sources of biblical books. The issue is related to that of authorship, since it often leads to the conclusion that an author incorporated a large amount of work by other writers. The first such account of the Apocalypse was of a modest kind. The seventeenth-century scholar Grotius suggested that John wrote the book at different stages of his life, first during his exile on Patmos and later after 70, when he had returned to Ephesus.[63] Modern scholars have developed similar theories. Marie-Émile Boismard says that the author merged two of his own works, the first written soon after Nero's persecution of Christians and the second after the fall of Jerusalem.[64] Kraft has a more complicated explanation. The Apocalypse, he says, underwent several revisions, all possibly by the same writer. The original version consisted of the seal visions. At later stages the author added the trumpet visions, the bowl visions, and finally the letters to the churches and the vision of the heavenly city, although Kraft recognizes that these final additions may be the work of other writers.[65] Most source theories, however, assume that someone other than the final author made a substantial contribution to the book's content. The heyday of these theories was the nineteenth century. They had an abortive beginning early in that century when Vogel argued that the book was an amalgam of works by two authors. Before 64, he said, the year when Nero persecuted the Roman Christians, John the Apostle wrote Revelation 4:1–11:19, predicting the destruction of Jerusalem. During the reign of Galba, who was the sixth of the seven kings in Revelation 17, another person wrote Revelation 12:1–22:20, prophesying the end of the Gentile world. After Galba's time, John the Apostle wrote 1:9–3:22. Finally, the second author joined these sections together and made some small additions to create the book in its present form.[66] Bleek espoused a simpler theory, arguing that John the Elder wrote the whole book at different times, first chapters 12–22, then 4–11, and finally 1–3. These theories had plausibility: The book would still have unity if the first three chapters were absent, and chapters 4–11 could stand on their own since they seem to reach a climax in a final catastrophe. Later, however, Bleek changed his mind and treated the book as a unit.[67] His turnabout was symptomatic of reactions to source criticism of the Apocalypse, which did not become a fashionable approach until the last two decades of the nineteenth century.

From 1880 onward critics renewed their interest in the book's sources. They produced many learned and ingenious theories but failed to attain substantial agreement. Some writers argued for a single written source. Daniel Völter thought it was Christian, but Eberhard Vischer claimed it was Jewish. Others postulated more than one source. According to the Dutch scholar Gerard Johan Weyland, its editor made use of two different Jewish documents, one written during the reign of the emperor Titus and the other under Nero. A Christian editor added the letters, the introduction, the final section, and other passages.[68]

Not everyone was content to argue for one or two sources. Friedrich Spitta opted for three, one from the reign of Caligula, a second from the early sixties, and a third from the century before the birth of Jesus.[69] Völter, who at first opted for only one main source, changed his mind. He still believed that the basic writing, which he ascribed to John Mark, was written in the early sixties, but he claimed that the present Apocalypse included an independent work written by Cerinthus in the year 70. An editor, who was responsible for chapter 13, brought together the works written by Mark and Cerinthus, and finally, during Hadrian's reign, a second editor added the letters to the seven churches.[70]

The vogue of biblical source criticism was at its height in the late nineteenth century. It had two remarkable successes. One of them was the theory about the sources of the Pentateuch. The other was the two-document hypothesis about the Synoptic Gospels. These theories, though at first highly controversial, won a large amount of support in the scholarly world. None of the hypotheses about the Apocalypse obtained that measure of assent, and source criticism of the book became less fashionable in the twentieth century, though it has not died out. Ford has put forward an intriguing theory. She suggests that the book contains two apocalypses, one (Revelation 4–11) from a John the Baptist community and the other (Revelation 12–22) from a Christian community. A Christian editor combined these works and added chapters 1–3 and parts of chapter 22.[71] For the most part, however, scholars in the late twentieth century have devoted their energy to other topics.

Variations on source theories were developed. Carl Weizsäcker and Wilhelm Bousset argued that the author of the Apocalypse introduced apocalyptic fragments and traditions into the work.[72] R. H. Charles developed a redaction theory, according to which the author, although he made use of sources, was responsible for most of Revelation 1:1–20:3. A redactor or editor, possibly a Jew of the Dispersion, wrote the bulk of chapters 20–22 and made several additions to the rest of the book, including the statement that the 144,000 had "not defiled themselves with women" (Rev. 14:4). The most controversial aspect of Charles's commentary, however, is his attempt to reorganize the contents of Revelation 20–22, which he believed to

121

contain serious dislocations of the text, caused by the redactor. He argued that the material in these chapters was at first written in a different order. In an attempt to reconstruct the original text of the chapters, Charles reshuffled the contents.[73] A few years later, John Oman, who was dissatisfied with Charles's solution, produced an even more complex and drastic reconstruction of the order of the text.[74] But dislocation theories have commanded little assent. They are highly speculative, and they operate on the assumption that an editor made the material more confusing than it originally was. In practice, editors usually try to make a text read more smoothly.

Many writers have treated the Apocalypse as the work of one person. Some of them, like Grotius, contend that it was written at different stages of the author's life. Others, like Lohmeyer, argue that it is coherent in its present form. Advocates of source—and redaction—theories have based their case partly on the lack of smoothness in the book's transition from one theme to another, but Lohmeyer claimed that lack of smoothness is characteristic of most human writings. It is not a sign of editorial interference or the presence of underlying sources.[75]

After centuries of discussion, no prospect of agreement is likely about the sources or redaction of the Apocalypse. The division is as wide as ever, and none of the proposed solutions has won general support. In these circumstances, many critics have preferred to concentrate on the text of the book as a whole rather than on hypothetical sources or possible stages of redaction.

* * *

From the point of view of traditional Christianity, the most serious question that can be raised about a biblical book concerns its authority. The question is complex and has many facets. In the early church, the rejection of a work's authority led to its exclusion from the Bible. Once the canon of the scriptures was fixed, the state of affairs changed. The Apocalypse could not be removed from the Bible when it was firmly rooted there. But, as Luther and subsequent critics showed, it was possible to reject its authority and still accept it as part of the Bible.

The challenge to authority led to further developments in biblical criticism. Scholars were able to approach the Bible without assuming that it was completely free from error. In dealing with the Apocalypse they recognized that its claims about the future might be mistaken. They did not feel obliged to explain away passages that implied that Jesus was coming soon, and they were prepared to pass unfavorable judgments on the book's theology and ethics. Not all scholars desired or ventured to do these things, and some of them defended the Apocalypse against criticism, but a climate developed in which they felt free to express opinions that disputed the accepted traditions. Challenges to the book's authority made it easier to raise questions about its authorship, and conversely the freedom to question its authorship made it easier to challenge its authority.

CHAPTER EIGHT

CONTEMPORARY-HISTORICAL CRITICISM AND MYTHOLOGY

THE APOCALYPSE AND
THE SITUATION IN WHICH IT WAS WRITTEN

A prominent feature of modern biblical criticism has been the attempt to understand the books of the Bible in relation to the times when they were written. In studying the Apocalypse, scholars consider how it reflects the hopes and fears of Christians in the first or early second century. They reject the notion that it predicts the whole of church history. They anchor the book's teachings firmly to events and expectations in the early years of the church. For this reason they are sometimes called Preterists. But while Preterists like Alcazar, Grotius, and Hammond thought that the Apocalypse gave a detailed and accurate forecast of the course of events as far as Constantine, many subsequent interpreters have made no such assumption. They are known as contemporary-historical critics because they explain the Apocalypse not in terms of the detailed events of several centuries but in terms of the concerns and immediate expectations of people at the time when it was written.

Some of the first contemporary-historical critics explained the prophecies exclusively in terms of the fate of Jerusalem and Judea. According to the Swiss writer Firmin Abauzit (1679–1767), the Apocalypse was written during Nero's reign and predicts the destruction of the Jewish state. It is based on prophecies by Jesus in Mark 13 and its parallels and deals mainly with events in the sixties.

The four horsemen are Roman governors of Judea: Felix, Festus, Albinus, and Florus. The vision of the destruction of a third of the earth's inhabitants (Rev. 8:7) is a prophecy of the death of a third of the Jews during the Jewish War. The beast from the sea is the Jewish Council, the Sanhedrin; and its seven heads (Rev. 17:9) do not symbolize the hills or emperors of Rome but seven hills of Jerusalem and seven high priests.[1] The beast from the land stands for the Pharisees, and Babylon symbolizes Jerusalem. Its fall is the destruction of that city by the Romans, and the New Jerusalem is the church after that event.[2]

A similar account was given by Johann Gottfried von Herder (1744–1803), general superintendent of the church in Weimar, who was a friend of Goethe and a leading literary critic. In his *Maran Atha* (1779), Herder interpreted the Apocalypse in the light of the defeat of the Jews and the fall of Jerusalem, but he differed from Abauzit in details. The beast from the sea, for example, was the rebel leader Simon ben Gurion in the Jewish War, and the beast from the land was his subordinate Johanan ben Levi.[3] In the nineteenth century, Züllig adopted the same approach to the book, although he differed from his predecessors in explaining the seven heads of the beast not as high priests but as rulers who belonged to the Herodian family.[4]

A weakness of these explanations is that the prophecies about the seven-headed beast seem more likely to refer to Rome than to Judaism. The Apocalypse explains the heads of the beast as seven hills (Rev. 17:9), and the tradition of seven hills is more clearly associated with Rome than with Jerusalem. Moreover, the vision of Babylon speaks of a city that rules over the nations of the world, a description that best fits Rome.

Another strand of contemporary-historical criticism that explains the book as a prophecy about both Jerusalem and Rome has achieved greater popularity. The fall of Babylon in Revelation 18 appears to allude to the fall of Rome. And Revelation 11:13 seems to point to a disaster in Jerusalem, since it speaks of an earthquake in the city where Christ was put to death.

Johann Jakob Wettstein (1693–1754), a native of Switzerland who became professor in the Remonstrant seminary at Amsterdam, was a pioneer of this approach. He believed that John wrote the Apocalypse just before the outbreak of the Jewish War in 66 and that he predicted events culminating in the Jewish leader Bar Cochba's revolt against Rome in 135. The Apocalypse, Wettstein said, contains two main prophecies. The first (Revelation 6–11) deals with the collapse of the Jewish state. The second (Revelation 12–22) speaks of Rome. It does not predict the fall of the Roman Empire, but the death of the emperor Domitian, an event that was the occasion for the imprisonment of Satan. The millennium was a period of only forty years (96–135) from Domitian's death until Bar Cochba, a Jewish claimant to messiahship, revolted against Rome. Gog and Magog are Bar Cochba's army, and the descent of the New Jerusalem from heaven is the rapid spread of Christ's teaching after the subjugation of the Jews.[5]

Wettstein's contention that the prophecies applied to both Jerusalem and Rome won many supporters, but his theory about the millennium did not prove to be popular. In the experience of Christians, the forty years after Domitian's death were far from the most blissful in history. Christians were victims of persecution, and the church was an oppressed minority. It seemed absurd to regard that period as the millennium.

Johann Gottfried Eichhorn (1752–1827) produced a more acceptable explanation. The purpose of the Apocalypse, he argued, was to predict the victory of Christianity over Judaism and paganism and to portray the blessedness of eternity.[6] He agreed that the prophecies in Revelation 8:6–12:17 referred to the Jewish War and the destruction of Jerusalem. He treated the subsequent chapters as predictions about Rome. The beasts symbolize the Roman emperors and the enforcers of emperor worship, and the fall of Babylon is the collapse of the Roman Empire.[7] The millennium is a period in which Christianity grows and flourishes. It will reach its conclusion in the last days of history, when Satan will be released and be given an opportunity for salvation, an opportunity that he will refuse, and the New Jerusalem refers not to the present state of the church but to the joy of the future life.[8]

Nineteenth-century German scholars Heinrich Ewald, Friedrich Bleek, and Friedrich Lücke followed in Eichhorn's footsteps and asserted that the Apocalypse's predictions about Babylon related to the overthrow of Rome. According to Ewald, although the letters to the churches referred to Jewish hostility to Christianity, the main opposition faced in the Apocalypse stemmed from Rome.[9] Bleek took a similar viewpoint: while the book prophesies Rome's utter destruction, it predicts a less savage fate for Jerusalem, which will be punished for its sins but not completely destroyed.[10] Lücke agreed that the Apocalypse alluded to the overthrow of both Judaism and Rome, although he did not think that it specifically predicted the destruction of the city of Jerusalem.[11]

The highly distinctive theory of Ferdinand Christian Baur (1792–1860) emphasized the Apocalypse's role in church controversy. Baur, who was strongly influenced by Hegel's philosophy, regarded the early church as a battleground for conflicting theological viewpoints, and he believed that the Apocalypse was written in opposition to Paul. On one side of the conflict were Paul and his supporters, who stressed grace and justification by faith. On the other side were the Judaizers, who emphasized justification by works. Paul's party claimed freedom from the law, but the Judaizers affirmed dependence on the law. Baur contended that the Apocalypse was written by John the Apostle a few years after Nero's persecution of Christians, and that John's Gospel was an attempt by a later Christian to give expression to the apostle's thought. The aim of the Apocalypse, he argued, was not only to encourage Christians in time of Roman persecution but also to support the Judaizers. Its attacks on false apostles, Balaamites, Nicolaitans, and Jezebel are attacks on Paul and his followers. The reference to twelve apostles in Revelation 21:14 implies a deliberate exclusion of Paul from the apostolate. In vivid contrast with Paul (1 Cor. 10:23-30), the Apocalypse (Rev. 2:14, 20) categorically forbids the eating of food sacrificed to idols. Its outlook is thoroughly Jewish. It implies that the beast came from the Gentile, not the Jewish world, and, according to Revelation 7, it promises blessing to Gentiles only if they become members of the people of Israel.[12]

Baur's account has obvious similarities to that of the eighteenth-century Deist Thomas Morgan. Both writers looked on Paul with favor and on the Apocalypse with disfavor. Both of them saw Paul and the Apocalypse as representatives of opposite poles of thought in the early church. But while Morgan regarded Catholicism as an extension of the Judaizing movement, Baur treated it as a synthesis of the two opposites. And although both Morgan and Baur affirmed that New Testament writings were in theological disagreement with each other, it was Baur who made it a central issue for debate among scholars.

Renan agreed with Baur that John was a Judaizer. He described John as "the most ardent of the Judaizing Christians," and he regarded the Apocalypse as a "symbolic manifesto," predicting the destruction of both Jerusalem and Rome. At the second advent Christ would establish the millennium on earth, and Jerusalem would be the capital city. In Renan's opinion, John mistakenly believed that these events would take place in the immediate future.[13]

Other scholars have emphasized the background of church controversy without assuming that there was a conflict between John and Paul. According to Paul Minear, the Apocalypse is not primarily concerned with persecution but is an answer to false teachers and their disciples.[14] Schüssler Fiorenza believes that the book was written at a time of persecution but that it was also the product of controversy between schools of prophets, one of which was led by John and another by the woman described as Jezebel (Rev. 2:20).[15]

Contemporary-historical critics have explained the details as well as the broad outline of the Apocalypse in relation to the events of the first century. One of the most intriguing discussions concerned the number of the beast, 666 (Rev. 13:18). Bleek and de Wette retained the older explanation that it stands for the Greek word *Lateinos,* whereas Ewald suggested that the original number was not 666 but 616, a number that in Hebrew can have the meaning "Caesar of Rome."[16] The most striking contribution to the investigation was by Fritzsche, Benary, Hitzig, and Reuss. The last three of these scholars disputed each other's title to be the originator of the theory, but it is possible that all four of them reached the conclusion independent of each other. Their theory is complex but attractive. The Greek equivalent of the Latin words *Nero Caesar* is *Neron Kaisar,* and these critics argued that when those Greek words are written in Hebrew letters, their numerical value is 666.[17] Their theory reinforced the belief that the Apocalypse identified the beast with a returning or resuscitated Nero.

Not everyone has agreed with them. Kraft claims that 666 signifies Nerva.[18] Gunkel argued that the number 666 represents the world kingdom,[19] and some scholars argue that it represents a trinity of evil, either because the number six falls short of the perfect seven or because 666 contrasts with 888, the numerical value of Jesus in Greek.[20]

Discussion of the identity of the beast goes beyond the task of deciphering the meaning of the number 666. Georgi makes the interesting suggestion that the false prophet of the Apocalypse represents the advocates of the religion of Caesar, in particular the poets Horace and Virgil, who used their genius to glorify the Roman state.[21] Other scholars think that the number seven is symbolic of completion and that the seven heads of the beast indicate either the whole series of emperors[22] or, in a general sense, the enormity of the power of evil.

Critics have also pointed out similarities between the visions of the Apocalypse and events of the first century. Some of them have drawn attention to earthquakes, volcanic eruptions, and famines that occurred in the eastern Mediterranean area in the century when the Apocalypse was written.[23] But scholars have been reluctant to pay too much attention to these events. They have pointed out that earthquakes and volcanic eruptions were part of the standard apocalyptic expectations.[24]

Interpreters have laid special emphasis on the presence of Parthian armies on the eastern boundaries of the Roman Empire. The Parthians were a source of terror to the inhabitants of the eastern parts of the Roman Empire. Twice they had destroyed a Roman army, and they posed a constant challenge to Rome's reputation for invincibility. Scholars argue that these armies, noted for their mounted cavalry, were the source of the vision of the rider on a white horse, armed with a bow (Rev. 6:2). They also argue that the Parthians are behind the visions of the two hundred million cavalry from beyond the Euphrates and the warrior kings from the East, although the visions speak of demonic rather than human beings (Rev. 9:16; 16:12).[25]

Not all critics give this kind of explanation. Beasley-Murray, for example, is more cautious and complains about the "lust for identification" displayed by commentators.[26] He argues that John may not have had any particular events of his own time in mind. Yet although, as Beasley-Murray says, caution is needed, both John and his readers were likely to be affected by the memory of earthquakes that had devastated the cities of the province of Asia within the past thirty years. Nor were they likely to forget that Parthians had destroyed Roman armies in the past and were capable of doing so again.

Contemporary-historical critics have attempted to relate the book's allusions to particular acts of persecution initiated by the Roman government. They believe that the visions of the martyrs under the altar and of the two witnesses who die for their faith (Rev. 6:9-11; 11:3-13) are inspired by the experience of the early church. But they do not agree about the date of the persecution that the author had in mind. Some of them identify it with Nero's savage treatment of Christians in Rome in the year 64, when he blamed them for the fire that devastated part of the city. Others argue that it is the persecution in Bithynia, when Trajan was emperor and Pliny was governor of the province. But the most frequent identification is with oppression by Domitian. The chief problem about this explanation is that there is no early Roman record of a persecution in Domitian's reign, although Christian writers of the late second century attest to it. Others, however, argue that the Apocalypse was not written in the midst of persecution, and that it reflects the fear rather than the experience of such an event.[27]

The seven cities to which the Apocalypse was addressed have been the object of research. Evidence from ancient historians and geographers together with archaeological remains provide a picture of the life and history of those cities. William M. Ramsay contended that the letters to the seven churches contained allusions to the religion practiced in those regions and the industries and trades that flourished there. "Satan's throne" in Pergamum (Rev. 2:13) may be the temple of Augustus. When John advised the members of the church in Laodicea to buy "gold tried in the fire," he was contrasting the spiritual riches of Christ with the wealth of the city's bankers. When he told them to buy "white raiment," he was alluding to the clothing of righteousness by contrast with the woolen products manufactured in Laodicea. When he instructed them to anoint their eyes with eye salve, he was contrasting the gift of the Spirit with the eye ointment for which the city was noted (Rev. 3:17-18).[28] Colin Hemer has done further investigation, collecting new information. For example, Hemer suggests that the allusion to the lukewarm condition of the church of Laodicea (Rev. 3:15-16) may have its origin in the presence of lukewarm water in the city's water supply.[29] Such details give an insight into the author's mind and his gift for communicating with his audiences.

The meaning of the allusion to Armageddon, or Harmagedon, (Rev. 16:16) has long perplexed interpreters. Popular writers, like Scofield, Walvoord, and Lindsey, have taken the view that it means "mountain of Megiddo" and predicts a great battle that is yet to be fought near Megiddo, where Barak and Deborah defeated Sisera and Pharaoh Necho was victorious over Josiah (Judges 5:19-21; 2 Kings 23:29-30).[30]

Many modern scholars are inclined to the view that it means "mountain of Megiddo" but that John used it symbolically. Herder, for example, who believed that the fall of Babylon (Rev. 18) was the destruction of Jerusalem in 70, regarded Armageddon as a symbolic reference to the siege of Masada. Many scholars, of whom Bleek is an example, argue that John uses it to refer to a great battle without implying that it must be in a particular place.[31] Others point out that there is no mountain at Megiddo and look for other meanings. Early Greek interpreters thought that it meant "mountain of cutting."[32] Grotius thought that it referred to "mount of assembly" (Isa. 14:13), and explained it as a prophecy of the defeat of Maxentius by Constantine at the Milvian Bridge in 312.[33] The nineteenth-century scholar Gunkel suggested that it referred to the site of a mythical conflict between the gods and demons.[34] And Bousset thought that John may have used the myth with reference to the danger of attack by Parthians.[35] A further possibility is that the word means "fruitful mountain."[36] With all this diversity of opinion, it is not surprising that many modern commentators conclude that we cannot be sure of the meaning, but that it is a symbolic allusion to a great battle in the last days.[37]

Contemporary-historical criticism flourished in the nineteenth and twentieth centuries, but its underlying principle and basic method were well stated by Wettstein, one of its eighteenth-century practitioners. He categorically rejected the idea that the Apocalypse contained a detailed prophecy of the course of church history. He poured scorn on the notion that it was primarily intended for later generations. "Whoever heard of any book being written and issued for the purpose of being understood so late?" "If my hypothesis is true," he affirmed, "the Apocalypse was written specially for the benefit of certain people who were living at that time, and for the purpose of being understood by them."[38] Wettstein exhorted interpreters to pay attention to the context in which the book was written. They should examine the author's vocabulary in the light of first-century usage. They should explain difficult words and phrases in language that is clear and easy to understand. They must try to read the scriptures from the perspective of the first readers or hearers, and they need to become acquainted with the customs and opinions of those times.[39]

Wettstein displayed the strength and the weakness of contemporary-historical criticism. He surpassed his contemporaries and many of his successors in the diligence of his attempt to interpret the Apocalypse in relation to the first century. At the same time he neglected the message's relevance for later generations. Few commentaries are more technical and formidable in appearance than Wettstein's. On each page there is the Greek text with detailed notes about textual criticism under it. Beneath the notes are lengthy quotations of Latin and Greek parallels, with rabbinic parallels given in Latin translation. Then follow Wettstein's own concise comments on the biblical text. He designed his commentary for teachers and argued that by detailed study of the New Testament they would have a clearer grasp of the subject, but he admitted that people can reach an understanding of the scriptures by other means than technical commentaries. By reading or hearing translations of the New Testament in their own language, they can discover all that is necessary for salvation and learn about their moral obligations.[40] Wettstein, however, did not deal with moral and doctrinal issues in his commentary. He possessed great learning and a simple faith, but the two traveled on separate roads. He did not confront the task of showing the relevance of his investigations; while many scholars have attempted that task, contemporary-historical criticism by its very nature concentrates on the Apocalypse's meaning for a past age rather than on its relevance for the present.

An examination of the views of Wettstein and Herder shows how fine a line divides contemporary-historical critics from Preterists. Wettstein thought that John was an accurate prophet whose millennium was fulfilled in the events between Domitian's death and the revolt of Bar Cochba. Herder regarded the Apocalypse as correct in its predictions of events in the late sixties,[41] but beyond the year 70, he admitted, its accuracy is open to question. The Apocalypse links the fall of Jerusalem with the end of the world and the beginning of the millennium.[42] Its author expected all these events in the near future, but although the world did not end and the millennium did not begin after the destruction of Jerusalem, the message of the Apocalypse continues to be relevant. Jerusalem's fate is a symbol and pledge of the final events in history.[43] In different ways Wettstein and Herder moved beyond the limitations of the Preterists. Wettstein clearly stated the need to understand the book in the light of the situation in which it was written. Herder confronted the reality that John's predictions were not all fulfilled as he had expected.

By the end of the nineteenth century, contemporary-historical criticism dominated scholarly approaches to the book and had pushed the church-historical interpretation into the background. The church-historical approach did not go out of fashion abruptly. It had a variety of adherents with differing views about the millennium. Augustine's interpretation had support from Protestants as well as from Catholics, and the Anglican Christopher Wordsworth, nephew of the poet, was in this tradition.[44]

But many of the Protestant church-historical interpreters expected a future millennium. They numbered postmillennialists like Vitringa, Lowman, Edwards, and Bengel. They also included writers who expected a physical resurrection to precede the millennium, among whom were the Anglican bishop Thomas Newton, the Unitarian minister and scientist Joseph Priestley, the Scottish preacher Edward Irving (1792–1834), the former Spanish Jesuit Manuel de Lacunza (1731–1801), as well as the Seventh-Day Adventists.[45]

In the mid-nineteenth century, a group of German scholars mounted a rear guard action in defense of the church-historical approach. Their theory, sometimes known as kingdom history, treated the Apocalypse as a prediction of the main periods of history and understood it as a prophecy of the triumph of God's kingdom. Johann Christian Konrad Hofmann (1810–77), Carl August Auberlen (1824–64), Johann Heinrich August Ebrard (1818–88), and Ernst Wilhelm Hengstenberg (1802–69) were leading exponents of this approach. They attempted to salvage the church-historical interpretation by concentrating only on the great epochs in history and refusing to identify the visions with the detailed course of events. While Auberlen, Hofmann, and Ebrard looked forward to a future millennium, Hengstenberg preferred the Preterist point of view and equated the millennium with the Germanic ascendancy that he dated from 800 until about 1800.

All these writers explained the Apocalypse's visions as prophecies about the whole period between the first century and the arrival of the New Jerusalem. They varied in their attitude to Germanic ascendancy. According to Hengstenberg, it coincided with the millennium, but Hofmann and Auberlen regarded it as the period of the seventh of the kings of Revelation 17. It was an era, Auberlen explained, when the beast was absent from the earth.[46]

Moses Stuart (1780–1852), a professor in the theological seminary at Andover, Massachusetts, adopted a similar position to that of the kingdom-historical scholars. He argued that "it is the great and leading concerns of the church, and those only, which are sketched in the Apocalypse."[47] The book's message is centered around three great catastrophes: the overthrow of the Jewish persecutors (Revelation 6–11); the overthrow of the Roman persecutors (Revelation 12–19); and the overthrow of Gog and Magog, who symbolize barbarous nations that will threaten God's people at the end of the millennium (Rev. 20:1–22:5).

Stuart and the writers in the kingdom-history school were opposed to the rationalism and secularism of their day, and they were convinced of the prophetic accuracy and divine inspiration of the Apocalypse. But their efforts did not stop the decline of the church-historical interpretation. Nor did they halt the advance of contemporary-historical criticism.

THE APOCALYPSE AND MYTH

The eighteenth century saw the beginnings of another development: the attempt to relate the Apocalypse to ancient mythology. Although this treatment of the book did not become well known until the end of the nineteenth century, it was practiced by Charles-François Dupuis (1742–1809), a leading supporter of the French Revolution, who at one stage presided over his country's national assembly. The second edition of his *Origine de tous les cultes* is appropriately dated in year three (1795) of the revolution and describes its author as Citizen Dupuis. Dupuis believed that traditional religions, including Christianity, corrupted the true philosophy of life, which was based on reason. The first religion, Dupuis contended, was the worship of nature, and later religions distorted it. Christianity is a product of human imagination. It does not matter whether Jesus Christ was a real person or not. The religion named after him is a variation of an ancient solar myth, which is at the root of Zoroastrianism, Judaism, Etruscan religion, and the mystery cults. Jesus' function as savior is like that of Heracles, Osiris, Adonis, and Bacchus in other religions.

Dupuis singled out the Apocalypse for special treatment. He described it as a Phrygian manual of instruction for initiates into the mysteries of the light and the sun. It was used at the spring equinox under the symbol of the lamb or the ram, the first of the twelve signs of the zodiac. The festival for which it was designed took place at the same time of year as the Phrygian festival of Attis. Each of the seven churches to which it was addressed was a "lodge" of the cult. Christ is the angel in the sun (Rev. 19:17) and holds in his hand the seven stars that symbolize the planets (Rev. 2:1). The four living creatures are four constellations: the Lion, the Bull, Aquarius, and the Eagle. The twenty-four elders stand for the twenty-four hours of day and night. The seven eyes of the Lamb (Rev. 5:6) represent the seven planets. The open door that John saw in heaven (Rev. 4:1) corresponds to the eighth gate of the religion of Mithra, giving access to the heaven of fixed stars. And the battle between the Lamb and the powers of evil reflects the myth of conflict in Persian religion. Dupuis attempted to peel away from the Apocalypse what he regarded as layers of superstition that encrusted the philosophy of reason. He rejected the hypothesis that it is an inspired book. No book, he said, is inspired. They all bear the stamp of human wisdom or human folly.[48]

Dupuis' theory received recognition in some intellectual circles but did not have an immediate impact on biblical scholarship.[49] In the late nineteenth century, however, a general upsurge of interest in mythology led to further attempts to uncover the myths behind the Apocalypse. The discussion focused on the vision of the woman, the child, and the dragon (Rev. 12). Albrecht Dieterich argued that it was derived from the Greek myth about the monster Python's attempt to kill Leto, who was about to give birth to Apollo.[50] Hermann Gunkel (1862–1932) contended that Revelation 12 was probably translated from a Semitic original that was based on a Babylonian creation myth about the conflict between Tiamat the seven-headed dragon and Marduk the god of light.[51] Völter claimed that the Apocalypse derived its vision from the Persian myth of a dragon that assisted Ahriman in his struggle with Ormuzd. Bousset emphasized its similarity to the Egyptian story of the dragon Typhon, which pursued Isis when she was about to give birth to the sun god Horus.[52] Since none of these myths provides an exact parallel to Revelation 12, it is difficult to trace the vision to one particular origin, and eventually Gunkel, who was joined by others, decided that the Apocalypse made use of an international myth.[53]

In the twentieth-century, Franz Boll went further and traced the origins of the Apocalypse to an astral myth, as Dupuis had done many years earlier. According to Boll, the dragon of Revelation 12 corresponds to the constellation of the Hydra; the woman clothed with the sun is the queen of heaven and the virgin of the zodiac.[54] Nicolas Morosow produced a theory that was considerably more venturesome than Boll's. He not only explained the book in terms of astrology but also regarded it as a tract against rulers of the Byzantine Empire, which he identified with the beast from the sea.[55] Morosow was even ready to oblige with the Apocalypse's date and authorship. It reflected the state of the heavens above the isle of Patmos on the night of September 30–October 1, 395.[56] Its author was the fourth-century bishop John Chrysostom, who was a "revolutionary and a republican," strongly inclined to socialism.[57] This description hardly fits Chrysostom. Morosow, a Russian revolutionary who suffered imprisonment for his political views, was echoing his own experiences and beliefs. Morosow's work achieved popularity for a short time and was translated into German, but it made no serious mark in the world of scholarship.

Although twentieth-century commentators on the Apocalypse have taken mythology into account, they have been skeptical of attempts to specify the place where the myths behind the Apocalypse originated. Charles pointed out that not all features of the Babylonian myth reconstructed by Gunkel were present in Babylonian traditions. The author, he concluded, was using a myth from Jewish sources, but much of it was similar to myths from other cultures.[58] Adela Yarbro Collins is equally reluctant to speak of a single place of origin for the myth. She argues that the visions of Revelation 12 reflect a combat myth that is to be found in many parts of the Mediterranean and the Middle East.[59]

Some advocates of a mythological interpretation reject the contemporary-historical approach to the book. Dupuis was one of them. And Gunkel declared that the method was bankrupt.[60] Although he was prepared to admit that the whore of Revelation 17 represented the city of Rome, he argued that for the most part the Apocalypse did not refer to particular people or regimes. Ernst Lohmeyer, another advocate of a mythological interpretation, asserted that the book was concerned with eternal truths rather than particular historical events. He believed that although the first of the seal visions may be a historical allusion to Parthians,[61] the Apocalypse as a whole has a timeless message. Its aim was not to attack the Roman Empire. The beasts and the whore are demonic powers, not human rulers, and the martyrs are from every age, not just from the first century.[62] It is a book about eternal truths, extolling the eternal worth of Christ, who is the beginning and the end, the first and the last. It expresses "the meaning of all faith," whether past, present, or future.[63]

In spite of Lohmeyer's assertions, the recognition that the Apocalypse has a mythical background does not inevitably lead to a rejection of the historical-critical method. Many scholars, including Bousset and Charles, have combined the mythological approach with an attempt to understand the Apocalypse in the light of the first-century situation. Indeed, most modern scholars agree that the book contains mythical themes. To this extent they have achieved a greater consensus about myth than about sources, redaction, date, or authorship. Hardly any of them has gone as far as Dupuis, who argued that Christianity was unrelated to historical events, but many of them believe that ancient Near Eastern myths provided the author of the Apocalypse with some of the most important means for expressing his message.

CHAPTER NINE

LITERARY CRITICISM, THE SOCIAL SCIENCES, AND THEOLOGY

LITERARY CRITICISM

The term *literary criticism* describes a variety of activities. It may refer to matters discussed in earlier chapters: the inquiry into a book's authorship, date and sources; the attempt to understand it in the light of its own times; and the evaluation of its artistic qualities, a matter briefly mentioned in the section on the Apocalypse's authority. But literary criticism includes other forms of research as well. Among them is the discussion of a book's relationship to other literature. In the case of the Apocalypse, it may be its relationship to books of the Old Testament writings and to later Jewish apocalyptic writings.[1]

Literary criticism may also take the form of examining the characteristics of literature both in the past and in more recent times. Frank Kermode, for example, stresses the presence in modern literature of apocalyptic features such as a sense of terror, decadence, renovation, and transition.[2] At the same time, he argues that a sense of tragedy is more characteristic of the modern world than a sense of apocalypse.[3]

Northrop Frye examines "apocalypse" in relation to the Bible as a whole. He describes it as the last of seven phases of biblical revelation. Five of them—creation, revolution (or exodus), law, wisdom, and prophecy—have their center in the Old Testament. The last two, gospel and apocalypse, have their center in the New. But all of them lead to the Apocalypse.[4]

Twentieth-century scholars have shown an interest in the rhetorical techniques of the book. Even in the sixteenth century Junius examined it in the light of ancient rhetoric,[5] but modern study of the book's rhetorical techniques has moved in other directions. David Barr, in his discussion of its oral presentation, argues that it is organized in such a way as to demonstrate the presence of God's kingdom.[6] John Erwin examines the relationship between the text of the Apocalypse and various readers that it mentions. By readers, Erwin means those who hear as well as those who actually read, some of whom are the audiences who first heard the message of the book. Others are the church leaders who read it to them (Rev. 1:3), and yet others are the angels, the four living creatures, and Jesus himself, all of whom read or hear messages that come from God.[7]

The author, Yarbro Collins observes, uses rhetorical techniques to affirm the validity of his statements. He frequently mentions the heavenly origin and truth of the visions, a repetition that serves to confirm the genuineness of the revelation (e.g., Rev. 1:1-2, 10-11; 22:6-10, 16). The book's use of the Old Testament serves as a reinterpretation of the Hebrew prophecy, and the very use of that prophecy is intended to confirm the message in the mind of the audience.[8]

Schüssler Fiorenza draws attention to the author's "visionary rhetoric," which he uses to motivate people to right action. By placing visions of heaven and visions of evil alongside each other, he confronts his audience with a choice. The vision of the 144,000 followers of the Lamb with "his name and his Father's name" on their foreheads is in contrast with the vision of the beast with two horns and of the men and women with the mark of the beast (Rev. 14:1-5; 13:11-18). The vision of the New Jerusalem, the bride of the Lamb, is in contrast to the vision of Babylon, the whore. These contrasts confront the audience with the need to choose between worship of God and worship of Rome. Within this situation the references to the faithful as male virgins, who have not defiled themselves with women, is rhetorically effective, since it refers to their refusal to commit idolatry. But in the modern situation it has a different impact and is no longer appropriate.[9]

GENRE

Discussion of genre is a tantalizing aspect of literary criticism. Critics have often attempted the task of classifying literature and dividing it into genres, such as comedy, tragedy, biography, and history. Aristotle wrote about the differences between comedy and tragedy, and both he and other ancient writers classified the different kinds of rhetoric. The genre of the Apocalypse, however, was not a matter for controversy until the seventeenth century. For many centuries, it was generally regarded as prophecy, but from the seventeenth century onward several scholars categorized it as drama. Richard Bernard called it a tragicomedy.[10] David Pareus described it as a tragedy and a dramatic prophecy.[11] Pareus divided it into seven visions, each of which is a drama in itself, and all but two of which have four acts.[12] Pareus's theory won the approval of Milton, who wrote, "The Apocalyps of Saint John is the majestick image of a high and stately Tragedy, shutting up and intermingling her Solemn Scenes and Acts with a sevenfold *Chorus* of halleluja's and harping symphonies: and this my opinion the grave authority of Pareus commenting that booke is sufficient to confirm." Pareus did not actually mention a sevenfold chorus, and Milton was more accurate when in another work he remarked, "*Pareus* commenting on the *Revelation,* divides the whole Book as a Tragedy, into Acts distinguisht each by a Chorus of Heavenly Harpings and Song between."[13]

The dramatic nature of the Apocalypse was the subject of interest in the eighteenth century. Eichhorn treated the book as a drama in three acts, each of which is concerned with a city: Jerusalem, Rome, and the New Jerusalem.[14] He contended that drama was a form of art well known to the Jews and that dramatic performances were staged in Jerusalem and Caesarea in theaters built by Herod the Great.[15] But he regarded the Apocalypse as a "description of a drama" rather than an actual play.

Twentieth-century scholars have continued the tradition of Pareus and Eichhorn, and they argue that the Apocalypse has the form of a drama.[16] Frederic Palmer divides it into five acts,[17] Alfred Wikenhauser into three,[18] and John Wick Bowman into seven.[19]

James L. Blevins takes the matter a step further by treating the Apocalypse as a drama that can be produced on a stage. He thinks that the seven windows in the theater at Ephesus provided a background for the book's emphasis on the number seven.[20] Yet, although these writers are convinced that the book is organized like a drama, none of them thinks that it was actually intended for performance in a theater.

Not everyone was satisfied with the suggestion that the work was a drama. Moses Stuart, the nineteenth-century New England scholar, regarded it as an epic. It has the main qualities of epic, "continued action of the deepest interest, wonderful actors, great events, much display of imagination and fancy, poetry in respect to its conceptions and diction, a general unity of design, and catastrophes of higher import and more thrilling interest than all the catastrophes of other epics united."[21] But intriguing though Stuart's opinion is, it did not prevail.[22]

The theory that commanded most assent had its origin in the mid-nineteenth century with Friedrich Lücke (1791–1854). Writers were already exploring the relationship between the Apocalypse and similar literature, both biblical and nonbiblical.[23] But Lücke made the most important contribution to the discussion when he made use of the term *apocalyptic* to describe the genre of literature to which the Apocalypse belonged.[24] He demonstrated the points of similarity between the book of Revelation and other apocalyptic writings. He dismissed Eichhorn's theory that it was a drama. The Jews, he said, did not normally write such works.[25] Some Jewish literature, including the Apocalypse, contains dramatic elements. But drama and epic arose in a culture that showed more interest in aesthetic matters than did the ancient Jews, whose primary concerns were religious and practical. Moreover, Lücke contended, Eichhorn's statement that there were theaters in Palestine is misleading. Palestinian theaters were used for athletic contests and for fights with wild animals. No evidence exists that plays were performed there. It was only later that the dramatic qualities of apocalyptic literature bore fruit in Christian drama and epic.[26] Although he rejected the notion that it was a drama, Lücke regarded the Apocalypse as a poetical book. Its style, he said, is not that of classical

Greek poetry. It is neither dramatic nor epic. Nor is it the style of Hebrew prophecy. Nevertheless, it needs to be interpreted as poetry, and much of it is to be understood symbolically.[27]

Apocalyptic literature, Lücke observed, is the outcome of a union of objective and subjective elements. The objective element is the manifestation of the activity of God and Christ in the outward expansion of God's kingdom. The subjective element is the inspiration of individuals by the Spirit. This combination of divine manifestation and individual inspiration gives rise to apocalyptic literature.[28] Lücke's discussions led to a widespread agreement that the Apocalypse was an example of apocalyptic literature. Not everyone accepted his conclusions, and in the second half of the twentieth century the issue of the book's genre became highly controversial. Scholars have failed to obtain consensus about the meaning of *apocalyptic*. They have discussed the difference between prophecy and apocalypses. They tend to regard prophecy as being concerned with the present condition of the world and God's activity in history, while apocalyptic literature looks forward to a transcendent mode of existence beyond history. But they do not find it easy to make a precise distinction between the two.

The discussion has been complicated because of the large amount of literature, both Jewish and non-Jewish, that is regarded as apocalyptic. One way of defining *apocalyptic* is to list its characteristics.[29] But a striking feature of most of these writings is absent from the Apocalypse. Other apocalyptic writings, like the Similitudes of Enoch, are pseudonymous. They claim to be written by somebody who was not the author. The book of Revelation, however, does not share this characteristic. Even if its author was not the apostle, his name was probably John.

Scholars have, therefore, tried to define an apocalypse without reference to pseudonymity and have produced definitions of varying complexity. According to a group of scholars under the leadership of J. J. Collins, an apocalypse has a narrative framework and an otherworldly mediator, and it discloses a transcendent reality that is both temporal and spatial.[30] David Hellholm expands Collins's definition by adding that the purpose of an apocalypse is to exhort and console "a group in crisis."[31] Other scholars have contributed to the discussion. Paul Hanson describes *apocalypse* as a literary genre that incorporates "the revelation of future events by God through the mediation of an angel to a human servant."[32] And David Aune provides a complex definition that pays attention to the form, content, and function of apocalypses. In form they are autobiographical prose narratives. In content they communicate "a transcendent, often eschatological, perspective on human experience." And their function is to "legitimate the transcendent authorization of the message."[33]

In addition to controversy about the meaning of apocalyptic writings, critics dispute whether the book of Revelation is in fact an apocalypse. Some scholars, already mentioned, regard it as a drama or an epic. David Hill and F. D. Mazzaferri think that it is akin to Hebrew prophecy.[34] Jacques Ellul, while not denying that it is an apocalypse, stresses its difference from other apocalyptic writings.[35] Austin Farrer is even more explicit than Ellul about the uniqueness of the book. The Apocalypse, he says, belongs to a genre of its own. Apocalyptic literature does not have the same form as the book of Revelation.[36] Other apocalypses are "mostly formless as wholes," but the biblical Apocalypse has a complex structure that builds up to a climax. "St John was making a new form of literature: it happens that he had no successor."[37]

In spite of the difficulty of establishing its genre, most scholars treat the Apocalypse as an example of apocalyptic literature. But some of them regard it as an instance of more than one genre. Wikenhauser pointed out that although it is closely related to Jewish apocalyptic writings, its spirit is prophetic, its form is like that of a circular or pastoral letter, and its outline is like that of a drama with three acts.[38] In fact, however, Wikenhauser's observations give support to Farrer's theory. If the book is a blending of several genres, it cannot be confined within any one category and is a candidate for uniqueness.

LITURGY

The Apocalypse's hymns and descriptions of heaven are evidence of its author's interest in worship, and scholars have speculated about the book's relationship to liturgy. These speculations are of interest for the investigation of the situation in which the book was written. But they also have a bearing on the question of genre. Dupuis, for example, argued that it was an initiation document for a Phrygian cult of sun worship.[39] Biblical scholars have paid little attention to Dupuis' theory, but twentieth-century theosophists have claimed that the Apocalypse represented a rite of initiation into secret knowledge.[40] Indeed, interest in the book's relationship to worship revived in the twentieth century, although there was division of opinion about the nature of that relationship.

Many scholars claimed that the book was influenced by liturgical practices, though they hesitated to say that it was intended as a religious rite. Touilleux argued that it attempted to deter Christians from accepting the Phrygian cult of Cybele and Attis. He contended that Christians in Asia Minor were under pressure to worship the goddess Cybele as well as the Roman emperor, and the Apocalypse encouraged them to resist these enticements. Instead of the ram of the Cybele cult, it depicts Christ as the triumphant Lamb, and instead of the mother-goddess Cybele, it presents the church as both mother and bride (Rev. 12:1-2; 19:7-8). In place of the initiation rite, it concentrates on the participation of Christians in the blood of the Lamb and their marriage to the Lamb, and it replaces the great processions of the Cybele cult with visions of the celestial liturgy before God's throne.[41]

In a vastly different theory from Touilleux's, Ethelbert Stauffer argued that the outline of the Apocalypse reflected the ritual of the imperial games in Ephesus. It is a protest against enforcement of the imperial cult and "a weapon against Domitian's myth of the emperor." It portrays a festival of Messianic games by contrast with the imperial games. Its opening chapter presents the Son of Man as both emperor and high priest, and the letters to the churches replace the decrees with which the games begin. The four horses reflect the four teams that competed in the chariot races, and the visions of disaster recall the fights in which gladiators took part.[42] An obvious weakness of Stauffer's theory is that the Apocalypse offers no clear clue to the analogy with games. In the Pauline Epistles metaphors connect the life of discipleship with wrestling, boxing, and racing, but no such images appear in the Apocalypse.

Dupuis, Touilleux, and Stauffer explained the Apocalypse by relating it to pagan rituals. Austin Farrer, however, stressed its debt to Jewish worship. The Apocalypse, he said, follows the pattern of the Jewish liturgical year. Its visions recall particular festivals. The seven lampstands symbolize the feast of Dedication, the Lamb is a symbol of the Passover, and the trumpets suggest the New Year Festival.[43] The lampstands, the elders, the sacrificial lamb, and the offering of incense are all features of temple or synagogue worship (Rev. 1:12; 4:4; 5:6, 8; 8:3).[44] Though Farrer's explanation aroused lively discussion, it won little support, and in a later book Farrer ceased to uphold it in any detail.[45]

While these scholars connect the liturgical emphasis of the Apocalypse with paganism or Judaism, others argue for its dependence on Christian patterns of worship. Massey Shepherd claims that it follows the order of the paschal liturgy, reaching its climax in the eucharist, which is reflected in the allusion to the marriage of the Lamb.[46] Pierre Prigent contends that a Passover Eucharist underlies the visions of Revelation 4 and 5, and notes that the words "Holy, holy, holy" (Rev. 4:8) and "Come, Lord Jesus!" (Rev. 22:20) are part of a eucharistic liturgy.[47] M. D. Goulder suggests that the book was constructed according to the pattern of readings appointed in a Christian lectionary. His theory, admittedly speculative, assumes that during their weekly Saturday evening worship the churches used readings from the Old Testament in a sequence beginning with Easter, which Goulder identifies with the Lord's day (Rev. 1:10). John, according to this theory, experienced his visions during these services, and after seeing them repeatedly for several years he recorded them in the Apocalypse.[48]

A less speculative theory is that the book was read in public worship. On the basis of the allusions to "the one who reads" and "those who hear" (Rev. 1:3), David Barr argues that the book was read aloud in early Christian assemblies. It was a lengthy service, in which the whole of the work was read to the congregation.[49]

Although theories about liturgy are largely conjectural, the visions of heavenly worship and the inclusion of hymns in the text suggest a liturgical setting, and the book was probably intended to be read aloud at worship. But it cannot be proved that the Apocalypse was related to the paschal liturgy, planned for lectionary use, based on the Jewish calendar, or designed in opposition to pagan cults. Neither can it be proved that it was planned as an initiation rite. There may be some truth behind these theories, but there is no clear evidence to support them. They are matters for speculation.

OUTLINE AND STRUCTURE

Bede was the first person to divide the Apocalypse into seven parts, and his division was popular for many centuries. In the past three hundred years, theories about outline have multiplied. Advocates of the drama theory reach diverse conclusions about the number of its acts; some say that it has three, others five, and others seven. Scholars who do not accept the book as drama have equally varied opinions.[50] Kraft, on the other hand, maintains that the author had no clear outline in mind.[51] In a matter where so much uncertainty prevails, Kraft's conclusion is attractive. But even though it is difficult to establish a precise outline, the book is not formless. It is far more orderly than most apocalypses. It has repeated patterns of seven: seven letters to the churches, seven seal visions, seven trumpet visions, and seven bowl visions; and it intersperses its predictions of disaster with visions of heaven. Yet its precise outline, if it has one, is elusive.

At any rate, it is clear that John had given thought to the organization of his material. But the presence of order in the book does not mean that his claim to have seen visions is fictitious. The majority of scholars agree that his work is a record based on vivid and memorable experiences. Yet the structure of the book, though it may be difficult to determine with exactness, gives the impression that he reflected on his experiences before he wrote them down.

THE SOCIAL SCIENCES

In the twentieth century, biblical scholars turned to methods practiced in other fields of research and used them to interpret both Old and New Testaments. The social sciences of psychology, sociology, and anthropology spread across the academic world. Along with students of other disciplines, biblical scholars looked to these sciences for help; and at the same time scholars in those fields devoted attention to the Bible.

With its visions and its strange images, the Apocalypse is an attractive subject for psychologists. Carl Gustav Jung examined it in terms of his own theory of a collective unconscious. He argued that John the Apostle, whom he believed to have written the Gospel and Epistles of John as well as the Apocalypse, underwent a psychological change after he wrote the Epistles. In the Epistles, John proclaimed the message of love but was "a bit too sure" and ran "the risk of dissociation." By the time he wrote the Apocalypse a "counterposition" had arisen in his unconscious.[52] In the vision of the woman, the child, and the dragon John's unconscious used the Greek myth of Leto, Apollo, and Python to describe the birth of a second Messiah who is no longer a savior but "a savage avenger."[53] John was not giving expression to personal resentment, since his visions arose from the collective unconscious. Being aware of the dark side of God, he supplemented the gospel of love with the gospel of fear. Although the "brutal impact with which the opposites collide in John's visions" is characteristic of severe psychosis, John was not a psychopath. He thought that his destiny was to separate himself from the dark side and identify with "the bright pneumatic side of God."[54]

Adela Yarbro Collins offers other psychological explanations of the Apocalypse. She argues that it can be understood as "part of a process of containing aggressive feelings."[55] Early Christians desired vengeance against the Romans and even felt hostile to Christians with whom they disagreed. The Apocalypse deals with these feelings by transferring the aggression to another subject. Christ becomes the aggressor on the Christians' behalf and makes war on the heretics (Rev. 2:16, 22-23). Another way in which the book restrains aggression is by internalizing it and making demands of abstinence in relation to money and sex.[56] Yarbro Collins compares the psychological effects of the Apocalypse with those of Greek tragedy. Both have the power of effecting "catharsis" (purging). In Aristotle's opinion, tragedy purges the emotions of fear and pity, and according to Yarbro Collins the Apocalypse has a similar effect on the emotions of fear and resentment. It does not totally eliminate these emotions but removes their "painful or disquieting elements."[57]

Attempts have been made to look at the Apocalypse in the light of sociology and social history as well as of psychology. Sociologists and social historians often concentrate on apocalyptic thought in general rather than on the Apocalypse itself. Norman Cohn has examined apocalyptic movements, especially in the Middle Ages, and has argued that millenarianism flourished among people on the margin of society: peasants with little or no land, migrant and unskilled workers, beggars and vagabonds, people who had no regular support from social groups and who gladly followed the leadership of charismatic prophets. Although Cohn's book is mainly about the Middle Ages, he points out that in the twentieth century apocalyptic ideas have attracted people in technologically backward societies that are overpopulated and in a process of social transition.[58] Michael Barkun, however, argues that disaster is the key to the rise of millenarian movements. When a sequence of disasters occurs and a charismatic figure arises, millenarianism is likely to flourish, especially in agrarian regions comparatively isolated from other currents of thought.[59] Paul Hanson offers a different explanation. He claims that apocalyptic movements come to birth as a result of disappointments in history when the conditions of life call into question traditional worldviews.[60] These theories, different as they are from each other, agree in their assertion that apocalyptic literature arises in situations of upheaval and tension when people are the victims of injustice or disaster or when they feel their whole understanding of life to be challenged.

While Cohn, Barkun, and Hanson look at apocalyptic thought in general, other writers have given a sociological account of the Apocalypse itself. They have argued that it was the product of a situation in which there were acute tensions between the rich and the poor or between the strong and the weak. Yarbro Collins stresses the discrepancy between wealth and poverty in first-century Asia Minor and argues that it explains the Apocalypse's hostility to Rome.[61] Schüssler Fiorenza focuses on the contrast between power and weakness. The Apocalypse emphasizes the power of God and the Lamb over all other powers and authorities. In a world in which the Roman government appeared to have supreme power, the Apocalypse's promise of Rome's destruction and Christ's triumph offered an alternative power-structure, in which Christ is supreme.[62]

Leonard Thompson considers the Apocalypse from the viewpoint of the sociology of knowledge and stresses the diversity of people whom it attracts. Its appeal is not confined to the persecuted and oppressed but extends to people who are discontented with the existing order of society. It was probably produced by a group that regarded itself as a minority in the church, and it presents an alternative perspective on life, different from that embraced by people in power. It comes from a "cognitive minority," with its own way of looking at life. For these people it provides a "deviant knowledge" by contrast with the "public knowledge" embodied in the traditional institutions of Greece and Rome.[63]

Closely linked with sociology is the discipline of anthropology. One of its best-known representatives, Claude Lévi-Strauss, argues that myth is a means of overcoming contradictions. His theory has had an impact in many fields of research, and J. C. Gager has applied it to the Apocalypse. Gager claims that the Apocalypse functions in the same way as myth. It is a book produced by an oppressed community that seemed to have no hope of justice under the regime of Rome. The goal of the Apocalypse is "to transcend the time between a real present and a mythical future." It performs this function by the use of symbols that overcome the contradiction between the hope for life in God's kingdom and the present reality of persecution. The Apocalypse, in Gager's opinion, contains two kinds of symbols. The first kind are symbols of victory and hope: the throne, the Lamb, the elders, the book of life, the new heaven and earth, and the New Jerusalem. The second are symbols of oppression and despair: the beasts, the plagues, Babylon, and Satan. The Apocalypse makes a contrast between these two groups of symbols, using the first of them in descriptions of the courts of heaven and the second in pictures of disaster and despair. Its message is a "form of therapy." By giving people an experience of a blissful future, it fortifies them to endure persecution in the present.[64]

In making use of the social sciences, scholars have endeavored to show how the Apocalypse and apocalyptic ideas bring about change in people during times of tension. They have not made a judgment on the accuracy of the book's prophecies or the correctness of its theological beliefs. Instead, they have shown its effectiveness in helping men and women to deal with crises. It does not follow, however, that the psychological, sociological, or anthropological interpretations are the only correct ones. The Apocalypse can be effective in the ways described by the social sciences and at the same time have theological significance. The two approaches do not exclude each other.

Many works in the field of social sciences and literary criticism are concerned with apocalyptic ideas without giving special attention to the Bible. In these writings, the words *apocalypse* and *millennium* have acquired a general meaning that is only loosely connected with the thought of the book of Revelation. *Apocalypse* has come to refer to any drastic change in the fortunes of societies or individuals. It is used to describe not only writings that focus on destruction, judgment, and catastrophe but also the catastrophic events themselves.[65] The word *millennium* has acquired as general a meaning as *apocalypse*. It denotes utopian expectations of a better world and can describe movements that have no connection with Christianity and no dependence on the Apocalypse. Yet the use of these terms in a general sense is evidence of the Apocalypse's impact. They have entered into everyday vocabulary to give expression to human hopes and fears and human aspirations and tragedies. In an age of upheaval and transformation, they evoke a vibrant response in the minds of men and women.

153

THEOLOGY

Amid all the varied approaches to the Apocalypse, the book's theology often appears to be of least concern. But that appearance is deceptive. Its theology is often discussed. The millennium and the last judgment are theological topics, and they have never lacked attention.

The Apocalypse does not set out to be a theological treatise, but a theology underlies it. It gives a memorable account of God's heavenly presence. Its pictures of the divine court with celestial beings around the throne convey a sense of God's transcendent majesty. Moreover, it emphasizes the activity of God in history. Whether it predicts the course of history or not, it clearly speaks of God's activity in human affairs, and it tells of God's ultimate purpose for the nations of the world.

The book's picture of Christ is also one of majesty. He is the Alpha and Omega, the beginning and the end. He is dressed as the high priest (Rev. 1:13) and will rule the nations with a rod of iron (Rev. 19:15). His exalted appearance is like that of God Almighty, for he has the hair white as wool of the Ancient One (or "Ancient of Days"), who is none other than God (Rev. 1:14; see also Dan. 7:9). As the Lion of Judah he is the victorious Messiah, and as the Lamb he is both triumphant and put to death (Rev. 5:5-14). He is the faithful witness and the one "who loves us and freed us from our sins by his blood" (Rev. 1:5).

The allusions to the Spirit are tantalizing, since the Apocalypse speaks not only of "the Spirit" (Rev. 1:10; 22:17) but also of "the seven spirits" (Rev. 1:4). And its description of the members of the church as a kingdom and priests recalls the language used of Israel in the Old Testament (Rev. 1:6; see also Exod. 19:6).

One of the Apocalypse's most prominent theological themes, that of the Last Judgment, has provoked sharp disagreement between interpreters. The dead, it says, are judged according to their works (Rev. 20:12). Morgan and Baur regarded this as evidence of the Judaizing nature of the book, and contrasted its works-righteousness with the message of grace taught by Paul. They pointed out John's insistence on avoiding food sacrificed to idols by contrast with Paul's greater openness on the issue (Rev. 2:14, 20; 1 Cor. 8:1-13; 10:14–11:1). And they claimed that the 144,000 whose names are sealed are all Jews.[66] Charles takes a very different approach. The works are never said to be the works of the Jewish law. They are "love, faith, service, and patient endurance" (Rev. 2:19). Although the Apocalypse emphasizes works, it does not require adherence to a code of rules but stresses the importance of moral character; and although Paul did not think that food sacrificed to idols was evil in itself, he discouraged members of the church from eating it.[67] Moreover, in addition to these comments by Charles, it should be noted that Paul has a place for judgment according to works (2 Cor. 5:10).

Controversy has ranged around the book's statements about everlasting punishment in the "lake of fire." The devil, the beast, and the false prophet, says the Apocalypse, will be thrown into this lake to suffer eternal torment. At the last judgment, those whose names are not written in the book of life will also be thrown into the lake (Rev. 20:10, 14). The traditional understanding of the passage, supported by Augustine, is that these people will share the agonies of the demonic powers.[68] Critical scholars are uncomfortable in dealing with this aspect of the book; many of them pass it over as briefly as possible, and their views about it are not always clear. Some of them reject the notion of everlasting torment. Long ago Origen affirmed that punishment in hell will be of limited duration and that God's love will prevail in every heart.[69] In the opinion of the modern scholar Rissi, the Apocalypse expects everybody to be saved; the gates of the New Jerusalem are always open (Rev. 21:25), and ultimately everyone will pass through them.[70]

Thomas Hobbes (1588–1679) accepted neither the idea of universal salvation nor that of everlasting torture. The fire of which John speaks, he said, is everlasting and has an everlasting potential for torment, but it will totally destroy the wicked instead of torturing them forever. Their fate, the "second death" (Rev. 20:14-15), is total annihilation.[71] Caird is not as definite as Hobbes but inclines in the same direction. John, he points out, describes the lake of fire as the place of torture for demonic powers (Rev. 20:10) but does not indicate that it serves that purpose for human beings. At the same time, "there would be no point in a last judgment unless the final decisions lay in the hands of the Judge."[72] Another view, expressed by Eugene Boring, is that the Apocalypse sustains a tension between the expectation of universal salvation and the recognition of the possibility of total rejection by God. John wishes to affirm both the ultimate triumph of a loving God and the responsibility of human beings for their actions.[73]

Twentieth-century scholars have devoted much thought to the effects of the "Delay of the Parousia" on New Testament writers. They use the term *parousia* (Greek for "presence" or "coming") to allude to the second advent of Christ. Their thesis is that many early Christians mistakenly expected Christ to return to earth in the very near future. When he did not appear, the church had to adjust to the fact that his coming was delayed. And André Feuillet argues that the author of the Apocalypse made the adjustment by maintaining a tension between the expectation that the end is near and the recognition that many events must precede Christ's coming.[74]

Modern criticism has not removed the ancient disagreement about the book's attitude to the millennium. The most unusual theory about the matter is that of Corsini, who places it mainly in the period before Christ and explains it as the years between the fall of the angels at the time of creation and the destruction of Jerusalem by the Romans.[75] Allo, Prigent, and others, following Augustine, regard it as the time between Christ's first advent and the last days.[76] Warfield agreed with Augustine about its duration but thought that it referred to the life of the redeemed in heaven. He described it as the "intermediate state" of the faithful dead between their physical death and the final resurrection.[77] Many scholars think that John expected the millennium to begin in the future, but they express it in different ways.[78] Ladd argues that John took a premillennialist position, expecting a physical resurrection of the martyrs and other faithful Christians before the resurrection.[79] Lilje suggests that the millennium may refer to "a final spiritual possibility of the church on earth" and not to the establishment of an "external world-power."[80] As far as Caird is concerned, the advent of Christ that John expected was not his final coming but a private presence in the church. "The time is near" (Rev. 1:3) does not mean that the final crisis in history is soon to begin, but it refers to the persecution of the church.[81]

Others understand the millennium symbolically. Boring claims that although John expected a future millennium, he primarily used the idea to portray the Christian life as royal existence.[82] William Milligan, however, thought that it did not refer to a period of time at all but was an ideal picture of the results of Christ's life, death, and resurrection.[83] Abraham Kuyper argued that it symbolized the fullness of God's action in the last days,[84] and Ellul thinks that it stands for the time of human life and activity "outside the presence of Satan." He understands it as the work of love and reconciliation, expressed in "the great modern historic efforts to express fraternity, solidarity with the poor and weak, the movement toward a pure and idealistic socialism."[85] For these writers, the basic issue is not whether the millennium is past, present, or future but the way in which it symbolizes a new kind of life.

Interpreters have divergent views about John's teaching on the New Jerusalem. One view is that he expected it to begin after the millennium,[86] another that he thought it was present during the millennium.[87] Whereas Milligan thinks that it is symbolic of the church,[88] Caird combines several interpretations of the prophecy. The New Jerusalem comes down from heaven, "not only before and after the millennium, but wherever the martyr wins his crown."[89]

These scholars do not regard the theology of the Apocalypse as a matter of merely historical interest. They treat it as relevant for their own times, and integrate its teaching about God, Christ, morality, the judgment, the millennium and the New Jerusalem into their own understanding of the Christian faith.

THE QUESTION OF RELEVANCE

The emphasis on the theological relevance of the Apocalypse provides an important corrective to the tendencies of critical interpretation. In earlier times most scholarly writers on the Apocalypse were clergy or leaders of reform movements, and they were eager to show that the book spoke to the issues of their own times. But in the nineteenth and twentieth centuries the bulk of critical work has been done in universities and colleges. That world has a life of its own. Its fashions rise and fall, and scholars deal with questions asked by their colleagues. The danger of this situation is that it may make biblical study seem irrelevant to the general concerns of the world.

This danger has been specially evident in the work of historical critics. Their chief interest has been to understand the Apocalypse in terms of the early church's situation, not to demonstrate its relevance for the modern world. In their methods of interpretation and in the detailed points they make, they are indebted to trends of scholarship that acquire a life of their own. The changing fashions of the academic world chart the course of scholarly interpretation, and that world has its own momentum.[90] Nevertheless, as will be shown in the next two chapters, some contemporary-historical critics have spoken of its relevance for their own time. Moreover, interpretations in the light of the social sciences have demonstrated how the book may function effectively in other ages besides that in which it was written. And when interpreters believe that the book was not just intended for a particular age but has a message for all generations, they have no difficulty in asserting its importance for their own time.

Part Three

The Apocalypse and Human Experience

CHAPTER TEN

CHURCH, STATES, AND NATIONS

In the nineteen centuries since the Apocalypse was written, most interpreters have given prominence to its relevance for their own day. Their explanations of the book have covered a wide area of human experience: They have related it to the corporate life of the church and to the affairs of states and nations; they have used it to express their dreams for the transformation of human society; they have interpreted it with reference to the inner life of individuals; and they have appropriated its words in worship. Moreover, its images have fired the imagination of writers and artists and have become part of the general cultural means of expression. These matters are the theme of this and the three subsequent chapters. The first issue to be addressed is the way in which writers have explained the Apocalypse in relation to the life of the church and the affairs of states and nations.

CHURCH

The Apocalypse was written at a time when the church was not only threatened with persecution from outside but was also divided on the inside. The letters to the seven congregations in Asia show that one of the reasons for writing the book was to deal with disputes between Christians. John sought to maintain unity in the churches, and he condemned the false teachers who were active

161

among them. Most early interpreters followed his lead and used the Apocalypse to confront the divisions and tensions in the church. In the second century, Irenaeus cited the four living creatures as evidence that there were only four genuine gospels and as grounds for rejecting any other such writings. Interpreters in the tradition of Augustine showed more interest in ecclesiastical disputes than in conflicts with foreign armies. They claimed that the Apocalypse was evidence of divine hostility to Montanists and Arians. They explained the scorpions, the falling stars, and the frogs that came out of the beast's mouth as symbols of false religious teaching.

Neither the collapse of the western Roman Empire nor the assault of the Muslims or attacks by Vikings deterred these writers from their preoccupation with heresy. They said little about political changes or natural disasters. Comets fell. Earthquakes and volcanic eruptions took their toll. Plagues cut off the lives of large numbers of people. But these were not the central theme for commentators on the Apocalypse. Their chief concern was purity of doctrine, and in their eyes the greatest disaster was the triumph of heresy. The church-historical school, which flourished from the time of Joachim onward, paid much closer attention to political events than did the style of interpretation that preceded it. Its adherents believed that the prophecies of the Apocalypse were fulfilled in wars with Goths, Persians, Arabs, and Turks. But they still gave precedence to church affairs. This school was concerned with church authority and correctness of doctrine, and it even regarded the wars with Islam as wars against heresy. The conflicts that made the greatest impression on these interpreters were between popes and emperors or between popes and reformers, in short, ecclesiastical as well as political conflicts.

At the time of the Reformation, church concerns continued to have primary importance in the interpretation of the book, although they were, as before, thoroughly mixed with political issues. Catholics upheld the authority of the pope. Protestants were equally concerned to denounce him, and antipapalism remained one of their central themes until the nineteenth century. Often the Apocalypse became an instrument of propaganda in disputes between groups within Protestantism. Furthermore, during the

French Revolution and in the nineteenth century interpreters employed the book as a weapon not only against the papacy but also against the growing secularism of the age. They treated Napoleon himself and in later years Napoleon III as embodiments of evil. They leveled against both of them the charge that they had secularized the culture. But in the first three and a half centuries after the Reformation the quarrel with the papacy dominated Protestant commentaries on the book. In the twentieth century the attitude changed. Protestants were reluctant to use the Apocalypse to display hostility to the pope. But the antipapal theme did not vanish, although Lindsey, one of its best-known advocates, combined it with hostility to the mainstream Protestant churches.

Interpreters linked the Apocalypse with the church's mission as well as with its conflicts. Early commentators explained the first of the seal visions as an allusion to the spread of the gospel in the age of the apostles. By identifying the age of the church with the millennium, Augustine drew attention to the success of the church's mission even in the midst of its struggle with evil forces. Church-historical interpreters laid emphasis on the conversion of unbelievers to the Christian faith. They highlighted the missionary activities of preachers such as Boniface and Francis. Postmillennial interpreters described the millennium as a period of unprecedented church growth. They regarded missionary and evangelistic movements as a prelude to that blissful era. The American evangelist Charles Finney (1792–1875) believed it to be the church's task to advocate "a universal reformation of the world."[1] In the twentieth century, the French Catholic H.-M. Féret treated the Apocalypse as a prediction of the course of history and expected the future to be a time of great progress, reaching its climax in the millennium.[2] The German Protestant Karl Hartenstein believed that the establishment of the World Council of Churches foreshadowed the millennium, which he expected to be a period of unprecedented missionary expansion. He looked upon the council's assembly at Amsterdam in 1948 as a prefiguration of the countless multitude that gave glory to God in heaven (Rev. 7:9-17).[3]

STATES AND NATIONS

The first writers to devote attention to the Apocalypse were concerned with political events as well as with the church. The persecutions initiated against Christians by the Roman Empire belong to both political and church history. Until the time of Constantine, interpreters used the Apocalypse to condemn Rome's oppression of Christianity and to prophesy the empire's ultimate doom. Moreover, Lactantius and Commodianus made unmistakable allusions not just to the persecution of the church but also to civil wars and attacks by foreign invaders.

From the fourth century onward the emphasis shifted. Although commentators identified Daniel's four wicked kingdoms with empires of the past, including pagan Rome, they were reluctant to mention events of their own day. The Eastern writers Andreas and Arethas made allusions to such events. But although the successors of Augustine in the West knew of the turmoils in which their civilization was involved, it was not until the twelfth century that they made a sustained attempt to explain the book in terms of historical occurrences. From that time on interpreters had a tendency to emphasize the special role of a particular monarch, empire, nation, or city-state.

Two ideas led to this emphasis. The first was the belief that God had chosen a particular state or nation above all others to be the agent of the divine purpose. The idea of a chosen state or nation was not new; the Jews were convinced that they were God's people. The Greeks, even though they were divided into many city-states, regarded themselves as superior to other nations, and the Romans thought that the gods and goddesses looked with special favor on Rome.

The second influential idea was the expectation of a last emperor. This idea did not have as long a history as that of the chosen people, becoming popular only during the Middle Ages. The legend, which was popular in both East and West, foretold that in the last days a righteous emperor would set up a kingdom in Jerusalem. In some forms of the tradition, the emperor ultimately prevails over Antichrist, and in other forms Antichrist overthrows him. The different accounts agree that his reign will be a time of unparalleled peace and happiness.[4] The prophecy became an important part of apocalyptic hope. It is indebted to the expectation of a power that will restrain the coming of the Antichrist or "lawless one" (2 Thess. 2:6-7). Its hope for a period of bliss on earth belongs to the same tradition of thought as the Apocalypse's prediction of a millennium, although it expects the emperor to reign for a much shorter period than a thousand years.

This expectation fanned the flames of national pride. Although the Holy Roman empire transcended national boundaries, many people hoped that the last emperor would be a German. Since most of the Holy Roman emperors were of German origin, this desire was understandable. A favorite for the part was Emperor Frederick II (1194–1250), who led a crusade to the Holy Land and crowned himself king of Jerusalem. After his death, the expectation persisted that Frederick or one of his descendants would appear in the last days.[5]

The most fiercely partisan of these accounts arose at the beginning of the sixteenth century. It was an anonymous German treatise that treated the last emperor as a fulfillment of the Apocalypse, predicting that his name would be Frederick and that he would come on a white horse (Rev. 19:11) as a savior of the poor and would reign for a thousand years. The treatise, whose author became known as the Revolutionary of the Upper Rhine, predicted the supremacy of Germany and branded France, England, Spain, and Italy as the four evil empires of the book of Daniel.[6]

Other writers, like Adso (10th cent.) and Martin of Leon, hoped for a Frankish emperor in the last days,[7] and Jean de Roquetaillade (c.1310–c.1377) predicted that the emperor would be a French king, who with the aid of a virtuous pope would bring unity to the Christian church, heal the warring factions in Europe, and overthrow the forces of Islam.[8] A prophecy attributed to Telesphorus of Cosenza (14th cent.) went as far as to affirm that this future emperor would be a second Charlemagne. In the closing years of the fifteenth century, apocalyptic hopes centered on Charles VIII of France, and in the sixteenth century supporters of France associated the prophecy with the French king Henry IV. The French version of the expectation was still alive in the seventeenth century when Tommaso Campanella greeted the birth of Louis XIV in terms that suggested that he was its fulfillment.[9]

As well as Germany and France, Spain had its candidates for the last emperor. Arnald of Villanova (c. 1240–1311) assigned the role to Frederick II of Sicily, who was a native of Spain.[10] Peter of Aragon (14th cent.) and John Alamany (15th cent.) predicted that Spanish kings would exercise worldwide dominion. Christopher Columbus quoted a prophecy that "the restorer of the House of Mt. Zion would come from Spain."[11] One of the rulers linked with the prophecy, Charles V, Holy Roman emperor from 1519 to 1556, had the qualifications to satisfy at least three constituencies. As a member of the Austrian house of Habsburg, he was Germanic. As king of Spain, he pleased those who wanted their last emperor to be Spanish, and since the name "Charles" qualified him for consideration as a new Charlemagne, he had attractions for those who prophesied the coming of a French king.[12]

Use of the Apocalypse in the service of a state or nation was not confined to interpretations that exalted a particular nation. In Italy, which was divided into many city-states, civic pride took the place of national ambitions. The Dominican friar, Girolamo Savonarola (1452–98), drew large crowds to the cathedral in Florence to hear his eloquent warnings about the corruptions of the church and society. He preached on the Apocalypse and similar texts, and predicted renewal of the church and divine punishment for Italy. Rome was Babylon, and Florence was the New Jerusalem, the city blessed by God. He foretold a period of great prosperity for Florence and regarded Charles VIII of France as a new Charlemagne, who would be the city's benefactor. Savonarola's popularity did not last for long. When the French king failed to support the city, the friar's power collapsed, and he was tortured and burned at the stake.[13] During his brief period of power, he gave supreme expression to the pride and ambition of Florence.[14]

In England, although they did not introduce the legend of the Last Emperor, interpreters used the Apocalypse to emphasize the special role of the British or English nation in the unfolding of divine providence. John Foxe followed the example of Bede,

Wycliffe, and Brute, and gloried in the knowledge that Constantine was born in Britain of a British mother. Under this "British" emperor, Foxe said, Satan was put in chains and the thousand years began.[15] Foxe's vision, however, extended beyond his own nation, and he insisted that Christ's kingdom was to be found wherever the spirit of truth flourished.[16] In this way he transcended the narrow vision that could have easily developed from his remarks about Constantine. That was not the case, however, with John Aylmer, who eventually became bishop of London. "We live in Paradise," Aylmer wrote. "God is English."[17]

In the seventeenth century, according to their political preferences, English interpreters chose Oliver Cromwell or one of the Stuart monarchs for a special role in the Apocalypse. The poet Andrew Marvell expressed the hope that Cromwell's triumphs would hasten the advent of the final day. Rulers of other countries "sing Hosanna to the Whore," but "Angelic Cromwell" fights against the beast that retreats to its "Roman den."[18]

Messianic terms were applied to members of the British royal family. Arise Evans said that Prince Charles (later Charles II) would reign in the millennium and restore the Jews to their own land.[19] When James II and his queen Mary of Modena had a son, John Dryden, an ardent supporter of the Stuart monarchy, responded with apocalyptic language to celebrate the occasion. He described James II as a new Constantine and likened the opponents of the Stuarts to the dragon of Revelation 12.

> For see the Dragon winged on his way,
> To watch the travail, and devour the prey.[20]

Dryden's predictions of prosperity under the newly born prince were short-lived. A few months later, James II and his family fled from Britain, and the son, who came to be known as the Old Pretender, spent his long life in exile.

During the Napoleonic wars, many British writers regarded their country as a chosen instrument in the accomplishment of the divine purpose. In 1812, at the time of Napoleon's invasion of Russia, Frederic Thruston expressed his confidence that England would survive.[21] The 1,260 years of papal power would end in 1866 and be followed by the millennium, "a world for ever happy, and a Christianity for ever pure."[22] The rider on the white horse (Rev. 19:11-16) symbolized England and its established church.[23] England was to be "the river of life which, for ages almost without end, beautifies, and gladdens, and supports, the Holy Catholic Church of the New Jerusalem."[24]

The sense of national destiny did not die out with the end of the Napoleonic Wars. "There is the strongest reason to believe," wrote George Croly some twenty years after the conflict, "that as Judaea was chosen for the especial guardianship of the original Revelation, England has been chosen for the especial guardianship of Christianity."[25] Nevertheless, a nation with a special destiny could be corrupted. Henry Drummond (1786–1860), a founder of the Catholic Apostolic Church, was deeply concerned about his country's condition. Although Britain had been "selected by Jehovah to be his witness against the Popish Apostasy," it had fallen from God's favor. Drummond regarded the emancipation of Catholics in Britain as a concession to the forces of Antichrist. The millennium he envisaged was decidedly undemocratic. Drummond believed in the divine right of monarchs and lamented the breakdown of the old social order. Things would be set right when the New Jerusalem was established on earth. Christ would be its absolute monarch, and people would know and keep their places in the hierarchy.[26]

Apocalyptic hopes flourished in North America. In the early years of the American colonies there was talk of a millennial New England, and Grindall Rawson described the inhabitants of Boston as "citizens of the New Jerusalem."[27] America was a place congenial to dreamers of a millennial new earth. Americans regarded their country as a champion of God's cause against the powers of evil. In the first part of the eighteenth century, France, which posed a recurring threat to the colonies, was the Antichrist figure. The fall of Quebec prompted John Mellen and Samuel Langdon to describe France as Babylon.[28] During the American Revolution, however, Britain became the Antichrist. Samuel West described the British army as "the horrible wild beast" of the Apocalypse.[29] David Austin (1760–1831) proclaimed that the man-child of Revelation

12, though in one sense born at the Reformation, was also "the hero of civil and religious liberty," born on July 4, 1776, in America. The man-child continues to fight against tyranny. "See him, with his spear already in the heart of the beast!"[30] But the identification of Britain with Antichrist was short-lived. At the close of the century, Americans directed their theological anger once more against France, and Timothy Dwight and others branded revolutionary France as the beast.[31]

One of the most remarkable schools of apocalyptic thought was British and American Israelism, which associated the British and American peoples with the lost tribes of Israel. Britain, said Edward Hine, one of the first representatives of the school, is Ephraim, and the United States of America is Manasseh. The British monarch is descended from David, and Britain fulfills the biblical prophecies of an everlasting kingdom. The coronation stone in Westminster Abbey is the stone on which Jacob slept when he saw a ladder stretching between heaven and earth.[32]

Some of Hine's predictions were extremely wide of the mark. Germany, he affirmed, was never likely to become Britain's enemy, and the British and American nations would always preserve a strict observance of Sunday.[33] Although his prophetic capacity was flawed, Hine's patriotism was impeccable and reached its pinnacle of pride in his account of Queen Victoria's role in the divine plan.

> Her Personage becomes surrounded by a Glory never before seen; there becomes attached to Her an importance, yea, may I say, almost a Sacred importance, never before recognized.[34]

It was her destiny to accomplish the restoration of Israel. The dispersed Jews, Hine predicted, would gather together in England and return to Israel. From 1873 the missionary work of the church would greatly expand, and in 2240, six thousand years after the creation, the millennium would begin.[35]

Other Israelists took up the theme. While Hine expected a time of great prosperity before the millennium, American C. A. L. Totten predicted that the millennium would follow immediately after Antichrist's "Reign of Horror," which would last from 1892 until

1899. Russia, symbolized in the Bible by Gog, would enter into conflict with Britain over India, but when the millennium came, there would be a life of bliss on earth with an abundance of material and spiritual blessings.[36]

The emphasis of British and American Israelism on the chosen status of the Anglo-Saxon people exposed this movement to the temptation of racism. W. H. Poole totally surrendered to the temptation in his explanation of the words "I will make a full end of all the nations where I send thee" (Jer. 46:28AV). He regarded them as a prophecy of the extinction of North American Indians, Australian aborigines, and New Zealand Maoris in lands colonized by the Anglo-Saxons.[37] Poole's interpretation of the prophecy provided a convenient justification for genocide.

Israelism continued in the twentieth century, and received publicity through the television ministry of the American Herbert Armstrong. The Jewish people, said Armstrong, are the house of Judah. The United States and the nations of the British Commonwealth are the house of Israel. At the beginning of the eighteenth century Britain and America entered into their birthright as Ephraim and Manasseh and became the wealthiest nations on earth, but because of their pride and disobedience God has subjected them to punishment. Britain has lost its empire, and the power of the United States is diminished. In past times the whore of Babylon was the Roman Catholic Church, ruling over its Holy Roman Empire. Babylon was revived by the Italian dictator Mussolini and will finally reemerge in the European Economic Community. These events will lead to the Third World War, but genuine Christians will escape to "a place of safety" during the great tribulation (Rev. 3:10-11).[38]

In the nineteenth century, as the movement for the unification of Germany grew in strength, Germans used the Apocalypse in support of patriotic themes. Sometimes it was a muted celebration of past triumphs. There was nostalgia in Hengstenberg's identification of the millennium with the period of the Germanic Empire, which began in 800 with Charlemagne and collapsed in the age of Napoleon. He recalled Germany's past with a mixture of sadness and pride. "This glory is now certainly gone, though only at the close of the thousand years, and we may well lament with the poet,

'German people, once in glory so transcendent, your oaks remain, you are yourselves fallen.' "[39] Hengstenberg's sadness gives a clue to the pent-up frustration of many Germans. The Apocalypse gave them the language with which to express both their disappointments and their hopes. They regarded the Napoleonic wars as a period of tribulation and the French armies as the locusts of Revelation 9. Paris was the whore of Babylon. Napoleon was the beast, the dragon, and the devil, and his defeat fulfilled the prophecy that death, suffering, and weeping would be no more (Rev. 21:4).[40] Many years later, when Prussia overwhelmed France in the war of 1870–71, German Protestant preachers were quick to detect the hand of God in history. In the words of Revelation 14:7, "the hour of his judgment has come."[41]

The use of apocalyptic language in support of Germany became more strident in the twentieth century. Biblical critics made their loyal contribution to the exaltation of their nation. During the First World War, Adolf Deissmann, professor of New Testament at the University of Berlin and a leading historical critic, was an eloquent advocate of his country's cause. The books of the New Testament, he said, were not written for a particular war but for the perpetual struggle against "the world, sin, and darkness." But in World War I, Germany was God's agent,[42] whose function was to be the "salt of the earth," enriching the world with the German spirit. German soldiers were martyrs whose blood was fertilizing the earth, and the exhortation, "Be faithful until death" (Rev. 2:10), spoke to their needs.[43] The four horsemen of the Apocalypse were active in the conflict, but their function was no longer the same as in the early church. In John's day the horses stood for forces opposed to Christ. In World War I they represented Germany's fulfillment of its divine destiny. The white horse stood for conquest, which Germany was successfully undertaking. The red horse stood for war, an activity in which Germany showed its mastery. The black horse stood for famine, and by its system of rationing Germany had overcome the problem of food shortage. The pale horse stood for death, and the death of German soldiers was an inspiration to the nation.[44]

Deissmann was only one among many theologians and preachers who championed the German cause in the First World War. They made extensive use of the Bible to support their position, and although the Apocalypse was not the most frequently mentioned book in their assortment of proof texts, it played its part. They believed their nation to be passing through a period of tribulation, oppressed and hemmed in by its enemies. Germany's early victories in the war were evidence of its destiny to establish a new humanity, and the German people were the vehicle of divine revelation and salvation. "German spirit," said the theologian Friedrich Gogarten, "is the revelation of eternity."[45] Apocalyptic ideas had an impact on German Nazi leaders during the events that led to World War II. The Nazi movement had both an Antichrist and a millennium. "The Jew," wrote Hitler's associate Joseph Goebbels, "is probably the Antichrist."[46] At the 1934 Nuremberg rally, Hitler gave the movement its millennium. He announced that the Third Reich would last a thousand years.[47]

African religious and political leaders have turned to the Apocalypse in their struggle for justice and independence. In the 1930s Filipo Tse, a Ghanaian prophet, claimed to be the second Adam who would reestablish Paradise on earth. He tried to reconstruct the conditions of the Garden of Eden and instructed his followers to practice community ownership of property, wear no clothes, and be celibates and vegetarians. Tse prophesied that the British, who then ruled Ghana, would fight against both the Germans and the French. He also predicted the return of Napoleon, who was the wounded head of the beast.[48]

Zulu churches in South Africa used the Apocalypse to express their beliefs. One of their prophets said that, in addition to the twelve gates mentioned in Revelation 21:2, 12, a thirteenth gate in heaven was specially reserved for Africans to pass through. A hymn of the Zulu Nazirite Church, founded by the prophet Isaiah Shembe, speaks of that church's headquarters in terms of a New Jerusalem, where believers may drink freely from the springs of living water.[49] The notion of a holy city has been common among black South African churches, some of whom have made a reality of their dream. The Church of New Salem built its own special Salem, and the Zion Christian Church erected its Zion City Moriah.[50]

Apocalyptic language is used by the Ras Tafarian movement, which arose in Jamaica. Its members proclaim that Haile Selassie, the emperor of Ethiopia, was a sign of deliverance for the black race, and some of them expect Africans in the Americas to return to Africa. Ras Tafarians draw their biblical teaching mainly from Isaiah, Jeremiah, and Proverbs, but they explain Haile Selassie as a fulfillment of prophecy in the Apocalypse. They hail him as king of kings and lord of lords, and as the Lion of Judah.[51]

Members of different nations, states, and races in Europe, America, and Africa have turned to the Apocalypse to vindicate their preference for their own particular group. Many of these interpretations of apocalyptic prophecies were the expression of national ambitions and of the thirst for power and wealth. Some of them were the product of a desire to be liberated from foreign overlords and to attain political independence. Whatever the motives behind them, they could easily lapse into idolatry of the kind that the Apocalypse vehemently opposed. The British Israelists' veneration of Victoria and the Nazis' devotion to Hitler were forms of emperor worship. In practice, if not in theory, nations, empires, cities, and their rulers became the supreme objects of adoration.

It was not only pride and ambition that encouraged these interpretations. Fear and a sense of oppression were also powerful influences. In the seventeenth and eighteenth centuries, the conviction that England was a special agent of God was fueled by fear of the papacy and France. Many Germans in the early nineteenth century regarded France as the incarnation of evil because it had put Germany to shame. And in the first part of the twentieth century Germans believed that their nation was hemmed in and victimized by other great powers of Europe. Modern Africans see themselves as the objects of exploitation by members of the white race. This sense of oppression has forged a bond between later generations and the churches for which the Apocalypse was written.

Apocalyptic language was often used to denounce a particular enemy without explicitly exalting the interpreter's own nation. Indeed, Joseph Priestley and James Bicheno used the Apocalypse to pass severe criticism on their own nation. Priestley, who regarded the French Revolution as the earthquake of Revelation 11:13, thought that it heralded the dawn of a new era. The battle of Armageddon was the clash between the monarchs of Europe and the French Republic, a battle in which France was likely to be victorious.[52] Bicheno (d. 1831), a Dissenting minister and schoolteacher in Newbury, Berkshire, had similar views to Priestley's. He did not deny that the leaders of the French Revolution had committed atrocities. But he argued that God used unworthy people to bring about worthy ends. He was critical of Britain's readiness to go to war with revolutionary France. He also attacked Britain's participation in the slave trade, its attitude toward church patronage, and its commercial greed. The spirit of Antichrist, he said, was active not only in the papacy but also in all forms of religious intolerance. It was specially active, however, in Catholic France; and Louis XIV, the persecutor of Protestants, was the beast who put the witnesses to death (Rev. 11:7).[53]

During the First World War, British writers and preachers concentrated their thoughts on the iniquity of their enemy. The Bishop of London, Arthur Foley Winnington-Ingram, declared that Britain was engaged in a Holy War against the forces of Antichrist.[54] James Plowden-Wardlaw accused the German Kaiser Wilhelm II of worshiping "Satan under the alias of the Prussian tribal god."[55] When it came to the interpretation of the Apocalypse, the way was clear. In a sermon at the end of the war, J. A. Carnegie announced that Babylon had fallen.[56] Writing soon after the war, the biblical scholar Beckwith described the conflict as "the most gigantic struggle between righteousness and governmental iniquity known to history." He likened the beast from the sea to an emperor (presumably Wilhelm II) "seeking to make himself a world-ruler."[57] In his discussion of the apocalyptic beasts, R. H. Charles was equally specific. "In regard to the present war," he wrote, "it is difficult to determine whether the Kaiser or his people can advance the best claims to the title of a modern Antichrist." The victory of the Allies was "the overthrow of the greatest conspiracy of might against right that has occurred in the history of the world, and at the same time the greatest fulfillment of the prophecy of the Apocalypse." Charles published his commentary two years after the end of World War I and was still ready to voice the hostility that conflict had aroused in him.[58]

Americans made similar statements. Lynn Harold Hough, in defense of Christian participation in war, pointed out that the Christ of the Apocalypse has a two-edged sword in his mouth (Rev. 1:16).[59] And James R. Day, chancellor of Syracuse University, described Wilhelm II as "the beast of Berlin."[60] In the light of subsequent history, these remarks about the war and the Kaiser seem outdated, and although they are not explicitly nationalistic, they owe more to patriotic fervor than to a calm evaluation of events.

During World War II it was not difficult for the opponents of Nazism to select an individual to fulfill the role of the beast. Hitler was understandably identified with the forces of evil, not only in Allied countries but also in Germany. According to a theory that had German supporters, if A = 100, B = 101, C = 102, and so forth, the letters of the name "Hitler" add up to 666.[61] But the Apocalypse also inspired more sober reflections. Comments by British theologians were more restrained than they had been during World War I. Nathaniel Micklem, although he did not claim that the final manifestation of evil had appeared, argued that the term *Antichrist* could legitimately be applied to Nazi Germany, because it asked the church to bow down and worship it.[62] H. H. Rowley, however, pointed out that there have been many Antichrists, and uttered a word of caution to people who assumed that Hitler was the ultimate fulfillment of the expectation of the Beast.[63]

The agonies of the Second World War were acutely felt in Nazi-occupied countries; and the Apocalypse was a vehicle for the French priest H.-M. Féret's reaction to the conflict. In a series of Bible studies given in Paris during the German occupation he refrained from explicit allusions to contemporary events. The beast and the false prophet, he explained, stand for political powers that demand adoration and impose false doctrines.[64] Féret delivered his studies in 1942 and published them a year later, when the Germans still occupied France. He did not mention the Germans by name, but his audience would have no difficulty in decoding his message.

After the Second World War, during the period of the "Cold War," the Soviet Union and Communist China became the apocalyptic foes for many people in the West. They were the dreaded enemies from the North and the East. Although Hal Lindsey did not specifically identify them with the beast, he gave them a prominent part in the final apocalyptic drama. When American president Ronald Reagan branded the Soviet Union as the "evil empire," he was expressing an attitude that was not confined to biblical interpreters but was widely current in society.

The imagery of the Apocalypse is easily adaptable to most situations of conflict. Victims of injustice, participants in war, and men and women who live in fear of other nations have instinctively used the Apocalypse to express their hostilities and grievances and give utterance to their hopes. In its original setting, the Apocalypse served that very purpose, giving voice to John's feelings about Rome and his dreams for the future. But when interpreters use the Apocalypse to foster the view that one nation is superior to all others, they are at variance with the purpose for which it was written. According to interpreters like Morgan, Baur, and Renan, the Apocalypse gives a privileged place to the Jews. But, even if that doubtful hypothesis is true, the book balances its references to Judaism with allusions to God's purpose for the Gentile world. If the 144,000 whose names are sealed in heaven are literally Jews—a debatable proposition—the Apocalypse also contains a vision of an innumerable crowd of redeemed persons "from every nation, from all tribes and peoples and languages" (Rev. 7:9). In the New Jerusalem the leaves of the tree are for the healing of the nations (Rev. 22:2). The Apocalypse was written when Rome was forcing people to worship the emperor, and it opposed any attempt to deify nations, empires, or their rulers.

In spite of the pitfalls that surround the interpretation of the Apocalypse in relation to political events, the book is relevant in the great crises of history. When people are victims of war and injustice, the book can clothe their thoughts and feelings in memorable words and pictures and help them to come to terms with the reality of their fearful experiences. Yet, it is an easy step from such a treatment of the book to treating it as a tract in support of national or racial pride. Interpreters who use the Apocalypse to exalt their own nation or state above others are in fundamental disagreement with John's intention. They set the book into reverse motion, sending it back to a narrow vision that it has rejected.[65]

CHAPTER ELEVEN

THE TRANSFORMATION OF SOCIETY

Many interpreters of the Apocalypse have understood its prophecies of the millennium and the New Jerusalem as predictions of a just society on earth. The early Chiliasts expected an earthly reign of Christ in a realm of justice and peace, and with the renewal of millennial hopes such dreams were revived. Postmillennialism was especially congenial to this kind of hope. Samuel Hopkins, the eighteenth-century postmillennialist, gave the impression that the world of the millennium would be a sanctified welfare state.[1] Its people will practice "piety" and "benevolence," and obtain "a great increase of light and knowledge."[2] They will live in an era of universal peace with a united church and probably one language.[3] They will be free from natural disasters, war, crime, and lawsuits. As a result of temperance in the use of the earth's resources and "by the smiles of heaven" they will enjoy general health, "by which much expense of time and money will be prevented."[4] They will improve their skill in the cultivation of land and make advances in the "mechanic arts" and the building of houses, bridges, and roads. They will need to work only two or three days a week and will spend the rest of their time in reading, conversation, and making progress in knowledge, "especially in the knowledge of divinity." The needy will obtain relief and assistance.[5] Death will not "be brought on by long or painful sickness, or be accompanied with any great distress of body or mind." Men and women will be ready for death and "welcome it with the greatest comfort and joy."[6] Hopkins, in accordance with Lowman's calculations, expected this era of happiness to begin in 2016. Had he been alive in the late twentieth century, Hopkins would have found that the world was still falling miserably short of his ideal.

Hopkins found a place for the Apocalypse's expectation of a conflict in the future days. Armageddon is yet to come. It will not be one swift battle but a conflict that lasts for many years, "probably for more than a century and a half."[7] Hopkins did not deny that setbacks will occur in the future. But Joseph Emerson was more optimistic when he wrote, "It is my decided opinion that every step of the way to the very pinnacle of science, may be strewed with flowers."[8]

Many interpreters, especially since the seventeenth century, have used the millennium and the New Jerusalem as symbols of a just society on earth. The poet Samuel Taylor Coleridge (1772–1834) explained the French Revolution as the opening of the fifth seal vision in which the martyrs cry for vengeance.[9] But he did not use the Apocalypse to exalt the role of Britain. Coleridge dreamed of a millennium of individual freedom and social justice, in which everyone would "enjoy the equal produce."[10]

The Christian Socialist Charles Kingsley (1819–75) looked forward to "the end of this system of society, of these present ways of religion, and money-making."[11] The signs of the coming millennium, he thought, were already present. When medical science prolonged the span of human life, Christ was performing a greater miracle than raising a few people from the dead.[12] Kingsley's dream is expressed in one of his hymns, written for the laying of the foundation stone of a workingmen's block of the Queen's Hospital, Birmingham:

> And hasten, Lord, that perfect day,
>   When pain and death shall cease,
> And thy just rule shall fill the earth
>   With health and light and peace.[13]

The poet Tennyson used the images of the Apocalypse to express his hopes for a better world. He dreamed of a millennium of peace and justice and a "Christ that is to be."

Ring out old shapes of foul disease;
   Ring out the narrowing lust of gold;
   Ring out the thousand wars of old,
Ring in the thousand years of peace.

Ring in the valiant man and free,
   The larger heart, the kindlier hand;
   Ring out the darkness of the land,
Ring in the Christ that is to be.
("In Memoriam")

Tennyson expected the ideal society to appear as a result of divinely guided human initiative. Although he did not pronounce himself a postmillennialist, he was in that tradition.

Biblical scholars were ready to enlist the support of the Apocalypse for their dreams of a better world. A. S. Peake explained the New Jerusalem in terms of a new social order as well as the transformation of individuals. The New Jerusalem, said Peake, is "to be slowly built by men from earthly foundations." It comes down from heaven in the sense that God "grants the ideal which is the inspiration of the builders."[14] R. H. Charles and Beckwith, as well as using the Apocalypse in support of the Allied cause in the World War I, connected the book with social issues. "John the Seer" wrote Charles, "insists not only that the individual follower of Christ should fashion his principles and conduct by the teaching of Christ, but that all governments should model their policies by the same Christian norm."[15] Beckwith was equally explicit: "Great problems of social, industrial, and humanitarian right may arise, very likely bringing righteousness into bitter conflict with tyranny and iniquity, calling for our Prophet's exhortation to courage and self-sacrifice and for his proclamation of divine wrath and doom."[16] As biblical scholars, Peake, Charles, and Beckwith devoted a great deal of attention to the meaning of the Apocalypse in the first century, but they also recognized its relevance for social and economic problems of the world that emerged from World War I.

Some advocates of reform stressed the function of their own nation in bringing about the millennium. Kingsley regarded England as a privileged country, chosen by God for special tasks. He lamented its failure to carry out its mission. Christ had already come to judge the nations of the European Continent in the revolutions of 1848, and if England continued in its present state, its punishment would be seven times as harsh as that of France, Germany, and Austria, because it had received seven times as many divine blessings.[17]

Americans have often linked their dreams of a millennium with the view that the American continent or the United States in particular has a special function in the divine plan. In colonial times Edward Johnson, foreshadowing the American work ethic, expected the colonists to bring about the millennium through the transformation of the land and the building of roads and bridges.[18] In the eighteenth century, Joel Barlow expected an era of peace and happiness to begin in North and South America without a spectacular divine act.[19] Timothy Dwight, who regarded America as the new Canaan, did not expect the millennium until about the year 2000 but thought that the founding of the United States was a preparation for the event and that from America the blessings of freedom, truth, and virtue would spread over the whole earth.[20] The poet Philip Freneau (1752–1832) envisaged an American New Jerusalem, where the saints were "to live and reign on earth a thousand years," the lion would lie down with the lamb, and human beings would cease from war.[21]

The concept of "manifest destiny" received even more forceful expression than before in the nineteenth century. Orators and writers proclaimed the mission of the United States to establish a millennial kingdom on earth. Alexander Campbell (1788–1866) believed that America would share that mission with Britain. He aimed at "the development and introduction of that political and religious order of society called the Millennium, which will be the consummation of that ultimate amelioration of society proposed in the Christian Scriptures."[22] To Britain and America God had granted a special part in the divine plan. "Because the sun never sets upon our religion, our language and our arts, he has vouchsafed to us, through these sciences and arts the power that annihilates time and annuls the inconveniences of space. Doubtless these are but preparations for a work which God has in store for us."[23]

Walt Whitman reflected the apocalyptic hope in his portrayal of America as a "Beautiful world of new superber birth" (from "Thou Mother with thy equal brood"). Washington Gladden affirmed that "here, if anywhere, is to rise that city of God, the New Jerusalem, whose glories are to fill the earth."[24] The Shaker Frederick W. Evans expected a "Shaker Reconstruction of the American Government," in which poverty would disappear. The Shaker societies would be the kingdom of heaven, and male and female would share the highest offices of government.[25]

American champions of social justice saw their own land as the stage on which the conflict between good and evil was being enacted. Julia Ward Howe (1819–1910) understood the American Civil War in an apocalyptic sense. In "The Battle Hymn of the Republic" (February, 1862), written for the 12th Massachusetts Infantry Regiment of the Army of the Potomac, she portrayed the struggle between North and South in terms of the advent of Christ, who would tread "the winepress of the fury of the wrath of God the Almighty" (Rev. 19:15; see also 14:19).

> Mine eyes have seen the glory of the coming of the Lord:
> He is trampling out the vintage where the grapes of wrath are stored;
> He hath loosed the fateful lightning of his terrible swift sword:
> His truth is marching on.

She held up Christ's death on the cross as an example for the soldiers of the North to follow.

> As he died to make men holy, let us die to make men free.

Howe was not a biblical literalist. She belonged to a circle with a liberal outlook on religion. But the Apocalypse had a powerful appeal for her, and she used it to interpret the cataclysmic event of the American Civil War. She did not deny the hope of eternity and gave full recognition to God's activity in history, but the electrifying feature of her poem is its exhortation to join the fight for the liberation of slaves.

The Apocalypse has been used to describe the situation in Latin America during the second half of the twentieth century. It has been surprisingly absent from the writings of Latin American liberation theologians. They frequently refer to the story of the Exodus and Jesus' teaching in the Gospels, but less often to the Apocalypse. In the late 1980s, however, a commentary on the Apocalypse by Ricardo Foulkes examined it from a Latin American perspective. Foulkes approached the book from the viewpoint of historical criticism. But he was also concerned to show its relevance for Latin America in the late twentieth century. In its original setting, he recognized, the Apocalypse dealt with Roman emperor worship. Foulkes also emphasized its relevance for later situations. Movements that set themselves in God's place function as the beast from the sea. When the church supports them, it fulfills the role of the false prophet. Examples are the Lutheran Church in Germany under Hitler and the Catholic Church and the Baptist communion in Nicaragua, on those occasions when they supported the Somoza regime.[26] The warning about oil and wine (Rev. 6:6) leads Foulkes to reflect on the way in which the United States persuaded the Dominican Republic, pre-Castro Cuba, and Costa Rica to devote their agricultural produce to the needs of the United States while they impoverished themselves.[27]

In discussing the prophecies of the beast and the fall of Babylon in Revelation 13 and 18, another Latin American, Dagoberto Ramírez Fernández, expresses similar concerns to those of Foulkes. He draws a parallel between the twentieth and the first centuries. He compares the power exercised by Rome to the economic power of the transnational corporations that have their origins in "the countries of the North." Ramírez implies that the function of the beast is performed by governments that maintained economic systems imposed "from the North." Clearly Ramírez regards "the North" as the Western industrialized countries and especially the United States. He blames them for the poverty, ill health, lack of education, and sharp distinctions between rich and poor in Third World countries.[28] When John described the mournful reaction of kings, merchants, and shipmasters to the fall of Babylon (Rev. 18:9-20), he was denouncing the oppressive economic system of the Roman Empire. Like other early Christians, he endured persecution for refusing to worship the emperor, who symbolized that system. In a similar manner, Ramírez argues, critics of the oppressive regimes of Latin American countries have suffered imprisonment and martyrdom. It is the function of the community of faith to carry out active resistance to these regimes. Ramírez does not regard it as a violent resistance. It includes three elements: withdrawal from the oppressive system, denunciation of its injustice, and announcement of the judgment of God, which will finally destroy the system.[29] But, nonviolent though it is, it provokes the wrath of the entrenched powers of government, finance, and industry. In fact, the Apocalypse does not lay as much emphasis on economic injustice as does Ramírez. It is more concerned to object to the enforcement of emperor worship. But Ramírez is justified in appealing to Revelation 18, because that chapter contains an implied criticism of the economic system of the Roman Empire.

In the 1980s the Apocalypse found an eloquent interpreter in Allan Boesak, the black South African church leader. Boesak, who suffered imprisonment for his beliefs and preaching, is conscious of experiences shared with John and recognizes that John's message speaks to the twentieth century.[30] The Apocalypse is not "a practical guide to heaven and hell." It is protest literature, which challenges people to choose between God and Caesar.[31] Although its author understood the Roman emperor as the beast from the sea, later generations have witnessed new fulfillments of these prophecies.

This book was written before either the Dutch Reformed Church or the South African government rejected the policy of apartheid. Because of their support for that policy, Boesak identified the beast from the sea with the government and the beast from the land with the church.[32] Boesak uttered a warning that the regime would suffer a fate like Rome's.[33] He is fully in sympathy with the martyrs' cry for vengeance. God is "the God of the poor and the oppressed."[34] Boesak does not rule out the possibility of violence, though he cannot find clear support for it in the Apocalypse. It is not for financially prosperous Christians to criticize victims of oppression for demanding the overthrow of their oppressors.[35]

Boesak does not confine his denunciations to the South African regime. His condemnation extends to polluters of the atmosphere, perpetrators of nuclear warfare, Nazis who massacre Jews, Israelis who destroy Palestinian camps in Lebanon, and, worst of all, "those powerful and mighty men in top hats, sashes, and uniforms who threaten and maim, kill and destroy, and then go to prayer breakfast and call upon the name of God."[36] Boesak is confident about the future, and he focuses his hopes on a transformation of human relationships in this present life. The world as a whole, not just the church, is the bride who will marry the Lamb; and the New Jerusalem is a city where people will enjoy their work and their homes in freedom from fear of racial oppression.[37]

Although Foulkes, Ramírez, and Boesak concentrate on the Apocalypse's implications for the present, they accept the validity of modern biblical criticism. They seek to establish the book's meaning in the first century, and then they consider its relevance for their own day. While writers like Charles and Beckwith alluded in passing to the book's relevance for the twentieth century, Boesak and the Latin Americans understand their task to be to demonstrate that relevance in greater detail.

Some of the most vigorous protests against authority in the second half of the twentieth century have been organized by the movement for nuclear disarmament. In 1977 the American Jesuit priest Daniel Berrigan was confined in prison after an anti-nuclear demonstration outside the Pentagon. In that situation, he turned to the Apocalypse. His book on the subject is a free-flowing rhapsody on the song of Moses and the Lamb (Rev. 15:2-4). The beast, the nuclear bomb, the imperial state, says Berrigan, are all one.[38] The beast works through the military and the government establishment. It seduces the people, and they follow it and worship it. Yet Berrigan conveys a message of hope. He does not clearly envisage how his ideals will be achieved, but he affirms that all the nations will worship God, who is their king.[39]

In another work on the Apocalypse, published in 1973, the Episcopalian William Stringfellow makes a similar protest to Berrigan's against the established structure of power in his world. He describes the Babylon of the Apocalypse as an archetype or parable of all nations. It depicts their fallen state. In former times, he explains, Babylon was incarnate in the Roman Empire and Nazi

Germany. Now it is incarnate in the United States of America. Babylon sets itself up as God. It is characterized by denial of truth, deception, violence, and death; and the power and presence of death are demonstrated by the event of the Vietnam War.[40] By contrast, the Jerusalem of the Apocalypse is a parable of the church. By "church" Stringfellow does not mean America's religious denominations, which are "American cultural productions or Babylonian shrines." He means an "emerging confessing movement" that is active where men and women have the courage to say no to Babylon and where they seek to "act humanly now."[41]

A late twentieth-century movement with vastly different standards of values from those that have been mentioned looks for a far different kind of social change. It is Reconstructionism, which is opposed to any form of socialism and resents government interference except in enforcing a severe code of punishment. It seeks to set up a kingdom that observes the Law of Moses together with the biblically prescribed punishments. One of its advocates, David Chilton, argues that the millennium is the period between Christ's first and second advents. It is a period of progress that will reach its climax with the establishment of the legal system depicted in the Law of Moses.[42] Chilton's theory is a reminder that interpretations of the Apocalypse can move in diametrically opposite political directions.

Some writers have given purely secular interpretations of the Apocalypse. The social reformer Robert Owen, who had renounced Christianity, was a secular prophet, claiming a messianic role for himself. He lived under the shadow of the Industrial Revolution and believed that his mission was to deliver people from the harsh conditions of their lives and provide them with adequate education. "On this day," he wrote in 1817, "the most glorious the world has seen, the religion of charity, unconnected with faith, is established for ever. Mental liberty for man is secured: and hereafter he will become a reasonable, and consequently a superior being."[43] Many years later Owen affirmed that his life's task was "to prepare the population of the world to understand the vast importance of the second creation of humanity." He predicted that "the earth will gradually be made a fit abode for superior men and women, under a New Dispensation, which will make the earth a paradise and its inhabitants angels."[44]

Even before Owen made these pronouncements he had won fame for his enlightened reforms at his mills in New Lanark, Scotland, and his endeavors contributed to the passing of Britain's 1817 Factory Act. In 1825 he purchased the town of Harmonie, Indiana, from the Rappists and founded there the community of New Harmony. He intended to establish a secular Utopia with equal rights for all people, freedom of speech and action, and community property. Dissension led to the dissolution of the community in 1827, and Owen returned to Britain. But New Harmony continued as a cultural and scientific center.[45]

Equally secular was the view of James Smith (1801–57), an advocate of trade unionism. The true Messiah, he said, was "the spirit of God manifested in the adoption of a beneficent ruling principle by human society." This principle included "social love and equality." The millennium would be an earthly paradise in which everyone would be a Christ, and the mainstream churches, which were the Antichrist, would be destroyed.[46] These writers did not advocate violence but expected to achieve their goal by peaceful reform.

Marxism, which was also an apocalyptic movement, had a different attitude. In the *Communist Manifesto,* Engels and Marx attacked the "conservative, or bourgeois socialism," which sought a peaceful redressing of social grievances. While bourgeois socialism promised a New Jerusalem, they complained, it really desired the welfare of the bourgeois. Marx and Engels dismissed the Utopian communities founded by these idealists as "duodecimo editions of the New Jerusalem."[47] The two communist leaders produced a secular version of apocalyptic literature. They agreed with the Apocalypse's conviction that conflict would precede the millennium, but their willingness to initiate violence was not in accord with the book's spirit.

In an essay on the Apocalypse, Engels recognized the similarities between socialism and the attitudes expressed in the Apocalypse, a book that he believed to be the earliest surviving document of the Christian church, written in either 67 or 68. Both were mass movements and both included groups at variance with each other. Both were aware of the need to struggle against opposition from inside and outside the movement. Engels quoted with approval Renan's comparison of early Christian communities with the International Workingmen's Association. In spite of the hostility of Marxism to religion, Engels respected first-century Christianity as depicted in the Apocalypse. It was, he recognized, a movement that faced conflict and looked for salvation; and in the circumstances in which they lived, the early Christians had little alternative but to seek salvation beyond this world.[48]

Marx and Engels were not even attempting to use the Apocalypse in explaining their ideas. But most of the other writers mentioned in this chapter readily employed its imagery. The Apocalypse's visions of the millennium and the New Jerusalem have an obvious appeal to social activists. But it expects both the millennium and the New Jerusalem to come through divine action, not as the result of human endeavor. In this respect it differs from many of these interpretations. It is arguable, however, that the different circumstances of later ages require a more activist protest against injustice and idolatry than the Apocalypse advocates. In any case, the book's diagnosis of the ills of society and its dreams of the future have stirred the imaginations of social reformers. They have been inspired by its affirmation of God's control of history, its confidence in God's ultimate victory, and its readiness to take a stand against the injustice of the ruling power.

CHAPTER TWELVE

THE CULTURAL HERITAGE

The Apocalypse has become so much a part of the West's cultural heritage that its words and images have entered into the common tradition. It functions like the stories of the gods and heroes of ancient Greece, in which the Greeks gave expression to their thoughts about the meaning of life. Even writers who rejected the traditional religion were attracted by the stories of the heroes and heroines of Greek mythology. The myths are still alive, having outlasted the beliefs with which they were associated. Modern thinkers readily speak of Oedipus, Orestes, and Electra without having any commitment to the religion of Greece and Rome. Because these stories express deep-seated conflicts in human relationships, they have a universal appeal. In Western civilization the visions of the Apocalypse have an appeal that rivals that of the Greeks and extends far beyond the church that accepts it as scripture. Not everyone who uses the book is a professing Christian. Men and women who reject or doubt the Christian gospel have employed the Apocalypse as an evocative means of communicating their ideas.

The cultural influence of the Apocalypse is clearly visible in the spheres of art and literature. It has made its mark outside the community of professing Christians. Artists and writers with no commitment to the Christian faith have gladly availed themselves of the language and ideas of the book. But although its impact has extended beyond the church, its strongest influence has been within the Christian community.

THE APOCALYPSE IN ART

From the end of the fourth century until the present, the Apocalypse has attracted the attention of artists. Its portraits of heaven and the New Jerusalem occupy a prominent position in places of worship, both ancient and modern. Apses in early churches contain mosaics of these visions. Typical of them is an early fifth-century mosaic in the church of Santa Pudenziana in Rome that portrays Christ on the heavenly throne. Above him is the cross, surrounded by the four living creatures of Revelation 4, and beneath him are the twelve apostles and Paul.[1]

Representations of heavenly worship are to be seen in medieval cathedrals, churches, and abbeys. The stained glass and sculpture of the cathedral at Chartres are fine examples. The theme of worship dominates the "Adoration of the Lamb," painted by Jan van Eyck (c.1390–1441) for St. Bavo's Cathedral, Ghent. The blood of the Lamb flows into a eucharistic cup, while a large number of the faithful stand or kneel in adoration.[2]

Moreover, the Apocalypse's visions of heaven were reflected in the general impression conveyed by medieval churches and cathedrals. With their windows, paintings, sculptures, columns, and their soaring arches, spires, and towers, they symbolized the New Jerusalem and provided a glimpse of the glory of eternity. A pledge of the heavenly city, they rose above the meanness of the world around them.

Artists did not limit themselves to visions of heavenly bliss. Pictures in Cappadocian churches (9th–11th cent.) portray the lake of fire, the sea giving up its dead, and the books that record the deeds of men and women (Rev. 4:4; 20:11-15).[3] Frescoes by Giotto (c.1266–c.1337) in the church of Santa Croce, Florence, depict John on Patmos, the woman with the child, and the "one like the Son of Man" ready with a scythe to gather in the harvest (Rev. 14:14).[4] *The Apocalyptic Woman* by Rubens (1577–1640) portrays the woman of Revelation 12 with her child, the dragon, and the victorious Michael.[5] A window at Bourges depicts Christ holding the sealed book with a sword coming out of his mouth (Rev. 1:16; 5:7; 19:15).[6] In *The Opening of the Fifth Seal* by El Greco (c.1541–1614) the souls of the martyrs stand naked as they wait for the last day, while John lifts his hands to heaven.[7] One of the best-known paintings in the English-speaking world in the nineteenth century was the *Light of the World* by the Pre-Raphaelite Holman Hunt (1827–1910). It derives its title from John's Gospel (John 8:12; 9:5) but is also based on the words, "Behold, I stand at the door, and knock" (Rev. 3:20 AV).

The four horsemen were a popular subject. The woodcut by Albrecht Dürer (1471–1528) has won enduring fame. William Blake (1757–1827) created a vivid portrait of the pale horse. A painting of the same vision by the American artist Benjamin West (1738–1820) was probably rejected by George III, who indicated that he did not want "a Bedlamite scene from the Revelations." But the work won the approval of viewers as diverse as Napoleon and the Prince Regent.[8]

The Apocalypse has also left its mark on traditional pictures of the Virgin Mary. From early times commentators identified her with the woman in Revelation 12. Paintings and sculptures that depict her with a crown of twelve stars are dependent on the Apocalypse's description of the woman "clothed with the sun, with the moon under her feet, and on her head a crown of twelve stars" (Rev. 12:1-2).

Many works, such as the thirteenth-century sculptures in Reims Cathedral and John Thornton's fifteenth-century stained-glass window in York Minster, depict a series of scenes from the Apocalypse.[9] The tapestry at Angers in France (1373) and the Brussels tapestry (1540–53), now housed in Spain, cover a comprehensive selection of episodes.[10] In the altar piece at St. John's Hospital, Bruges, Hans Memling (c.1430–94) showed John on Patmos looking at a selection of scenes that give a panoramic view of the whole book.[11] And a sixteenth-century work in the Kremlin's Cathedral of the Dormition depicts the heavenly throne, the Lamb, the elders, and the four horsemen.[12]

Illuminated medieval manuscripts contain some of the most vivid representations of the visions.[13] Prominent examples are texts of Beatus's commentary, produced in Spain during the tenth and eleventh centuries.[14] These and other illuminated manuscripts of the Apocalypse and its commentaries are important contributions to medieval art.[15] The lively illustrations in these works depict all the main episodes of the book, including John on Patmos, the seal, trumpet, and bowl visions, the beasts, the witnesses, the fall of Babylon, and the marriage of the Lamb, as well as the millennium and the New Jerusalem. Their pictures of horror are as memorable as their scenes of glory. The monstrous dragon-like beasts and the gaping mouth of hell are favorite themes.

Much of this art was clearly relevant for its own times. The thirteenth-century Cambridge Apocalypse depicts monks and friars as defenders of the faith against the forces of evil. The prominence given to a noblewoman in this manuscript's illustrations supports the theory that it was produced for Queen Eleanor, wife of Henry III of England. The woman brandishes a sword before the seven-headed beast, and at the last judgment she stands with Peter, Dominic, Francis, and Benedict at Christ's right hand.[16]

Some of this art takes sides in religious controversy. A West Flemish Apocalypse, composed after 1400, probably reflects both the conflict in the Franciscan movement and the persecution inflicted on Hus. In this work's portrait of Revelation 13, a bishop and a king worship the beast, and the false prophet wears the robe of a Franciscan; the king may represent the emperor Sigismund, who was responsible for the burning of Hus.[17]

Albrecht Dürer's woodcuts imply sharp criticism of the world as he knew it. Although he later joined the Protestant cause, he did not identify the papacy with the beast or the whore but made pointed allusions to persons of power and esteem. He portrayed the Roman emperor Domitian in a turban, dressed like a Turk. The fourth horseman, death, rides over an emperor who is falling into hell. One of the four angels from the Euphrates is striking a pope. A cleric, a merchant, a Turk, an emperor, and a queen are among the worshipers of the beast. Even though his woodcuts do not attack specific individuals, Dürer made it plain that he had a low opinion of the state of church and society in his day.[18]

In the sixteenth century the polemic became sharper. Woodcuts by Lucas Cranach and his workshop in Luther's *September Testament* portray the beast and the whore as the pope and dress the two witnesses in the garb of Germans of that time. At the end of the eighteenth century Blake depicted the seven heads of the beast as leaders of church and state: a judge, a warrior, a warlord, a pope, a king, a bishop, and a

The Judgment (Rev. 20:11-15). Cambridge Apocalypse (13th cent.). Trinity College, R 16 2, f. 28. By permission of the Master and Fellows of Trinity College, Cambridge.

The Fifth Seal Vision: The Souls of the Martyrs under the Altar (Rev. 6:9-11). The Douce Apocalypse (13th cent.) © Bodleian Library, Oxford. MS. Douce 180, p. 17.

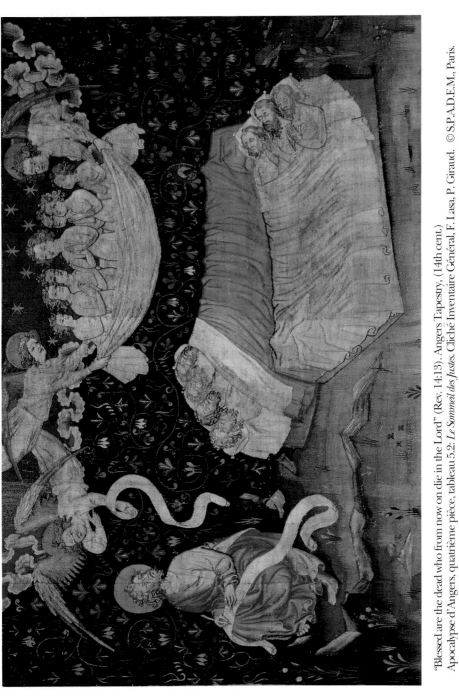

"Blessed are the dead who from now on die in the Lord" (Rev. 14:13). Angers Tapestry, (14th cent.)
Apocalypse d'Angers, quatrième pièce, tableau 5.2: *Le Sommeil des Justes*. Cliché Inventaire Général, F. Lasa, P. Giraud. © S.P.A.D.E.M., Paris.

The River of the Water of Life. The angel rebukes John (Rev. 22:1-2, 8-9). Flemish Apocalypse (c. 1400), Paris, Bibliothèque Nationale. BN Neerl 3. fol. 23. Photo. Bibl. Nat. Paris.

The Whore of Babylon (Rev. 17:1-18). Woodcut from Luther's *Das neue Testament Deutzsch* (Wittenberg: Melchior Lotter the Younger for Christian Doring and Lucas Cranach the Elder, September 1522), in the Richard C. Kessler Reformation Collection, Pitts Theology Library, Emory University. Used with permission.

Death on a Pale Horse (Rev. 6:7-8) by William Blake (c. 1800). Reproduction by permission of the Fitzwilliam Museum, Cambridge.

W. Kandinsky, *The Apocalyptic Riders, II* (Rev. 6:1-8), 1914 © 1993 ARS, New York/ADAGP, Paris. Städtische Galerie im Lenbachhaus, Munich, Germany.

"We have no territorial demands; we want the world!" Anti-nazi cartoon, based on the visions of the horsemen, Rev. 6:1-8, by "Bert," in *Never Vorwärts* Karlsbad, Czechoslovakia, 15 März, 1936, Nr. 144 (Beilage). Source: Die Deutsche Bibliothek, Deutsches Exilarchiv 1933-1945, Frankfurt am Main.

priest.[19] Francis Danby's *The Opening of the Sixth Seal* (1828) may allude to the French Revolution.[20] Twentieth-century artists made attacks on Nazism. Johannes Wüsten, a German who took the pseudonym Niki and died in prison in 1943, depicted the four horsemen riding to the League of Nations at Geneva, a satire on the hypocrisy of Nazi pretensions for peace. In 1936 an unknown artist with the pseudonym Bert portrayed three of the apocalyptic horsemen as Goebbels, Goering, and Hitler. Beneath Bert's sketch is the slogan, "We have no territorial claims. We want the world!"[21]

Even works that do not indulge in precise polemic give expression to the mood of their times. The portrait of John and the beast by the black South African Azaria Mbatha (b. 1941) comes from a background of racial oppression.[22] Kandinsky's *Apocalyptic Horsemen* reflects the turbulence of the years that culminated in the outbreak of World War I.[23] Throughout the twentieth century, the visions of the horsemen were a favorite topic, suggesting the threat of a catastrophic conflict.[24] They were appropriate expressions of the disastrous events and cultural confusion of the age.

Paintings, sculptures, woodcuts, and drawings have rivaled all other forms of expression in the vividness with which they convey both visions of heaven and predictions of catastrophe. Many of these works were products of a religious environment, intended for the church and inspired by Christian faith. But when art is not designed for use in worship or devotion, it is not always clear that it belongs to the sphere of faith. This ambiguity is especially true of works that depict confusion and despair or comment on the political events of the day. Yet a painting or sculpture in a church or an illustration in a Bible is set in a context where men and women profess Christianity. It gives expression to faith in the midst of religious controversy and above all in the sphere of worship.

THE APOCALYPSE IN LITERATURE AND DRAMA

Besides attracting the attention of artists, the aesthetic qualities of the Apocalypse have appealed to writers. Hymns and liturgies, which will be discussed in the next chapter, belong to the category of literature, and they are of the utmost importance for under-standing the function of the Apocalypse in a religious context. The book's influence on literature, however, extends far beyond wor-ship. It is the most poetical in spirit of the books of the New Testa-ment, and poets have made plentiful use of its images. Dante employed them to attack the papacy.[25] Spenser incorporated them into his *Faerie Queen*. His Red Cross Knight is like the man on the white horse in Revelation 19:11. Duessa, one of the monstrous crea-tures who defy the knight, is similar to the whore of Babylon, and the other creature, Archimago, resembles the false prophet. The Red Cross Knight's combat with a dragon, his nourishment by the well and by the tree of life, and his betrothal recall passages from the Apocalypse (Rev. 12:7-9; 19:6-10; 21:6; 22:2).[26] Milton shows the influence of the Apocalypse in his writings. He describes the battle between Michael and Satan, although he places it in the distant past.[27] At the last judgment, he says, the Son of God will bring "New Heav'ns, new Earth, ages of endless date."[28] He echoes the Apoca-lypse in his poem "At a Solemn Musick." He tells of "the sapphire-colour'd throne" and the "solemn jubilee":

> Where the bright seraphim in burning row
> Their loud up-lifted angel-trumpets blow,
> And the cherubic host in thousand choirs
> Touch their immortal harps of golden wires,
> With those just spirits that wear victorious palms,
> Hymns devout and holy psalms
> Singing everlastingly.
> (lines 10-16; see Rev. 4:8; 5:8; 7:9; 8:6; Ezek. 1:26)

Poets have made the book's language a vehicle to describe partic-ular people or events. Marvell used it to exalt Cromwell, and Dry-den to praise the Stuart monarchy.[29] Blake, who mixed apocalyptic imagery from the Bible with a mythology all his own, turned to the Apocalypse to express his hostility to reason. He treated Newton, Bacon, and Locke, whom he regarded as champions of reason, as Antichrist figures,[30] and he described Whitefield and Wesley as the two witnesses.[31] Because of its support for war, he identified con-ventional religion as the dragon and the harlot that John saw on

Patmos.[32] Blake also used the Apocalypse to express his hopes for the future. Jerusalem, he said, had once been built in England, and men and women could build it there again.

> Nor shall my sword sleep in my hand
> Till we have built Jerusalem
> In England's green and pleasant land.[33]

Yet Blake was not constricted by national interests, and his vision transcended nationalism.

> In my Exchanges every Land
> Shall walk, and mine in every Land,
> Mutual shall build Jerusalem,
> Both heart in heart & hand in hand.[34]

The Apocalypse is reflected in the titles and the contents of works of literature. In his novel *The Four Horsemen of the Apocalypse,* Vicente Blasco Ibañez (1867–1928) wrote in a foreboding tone of the opening months of the First World War. "God is asleep," says one of the novel's characters, "forgetting the world. It will be a long time before he awakes, and while he sleeps the four feudal horsemen of the Beast will course through the land as its only lords."[35] The beast, Ibañez contended, is a monster that resurfaces every thousand years and is manifested in the Kaiser's Germany.[36]

While Ibañez focused on the beginning of World War I, the American Katherine Anne Porter (1890–1980) wrote about its conclusion. The title of her short novel *Pale Horse, Pale Rider* is based on the Apocalypse, though it is directly derived from an African American spiritual, "Pale horse, pale rider, done take my lover away!" The novel tells of a young woman and a young man during the influenza epidemic at the end of the war. Porter's is a sad apocalypse. At its end there is "only the dazed silence that follows the ceasing of the heavy guns."[37] All she looks forward to is the "dead cold light of tomorrow." Unlike the Apocalypse, her novel ends in pessimism.

During World War II, Robert Sherwood's play about life in Finland under attack by the Soviet Union took its title, *There Shall Be*

No Night, from the Apocalypse's description of the New Jerusalem (Rev. 22:5).[38] Sherwood was more optimistic than either Porter or Ibañez in his reaction to events.[39] The sound of the guns is "the long deferred death rattle of the primordial beast," and the victory over human bestiality does not have to wait for a spectacular divine intervention. Sherwood's line of thought has echoes of postmillennialism. The glories of the new world will come after a period of human struggle and achievement. "We have within ourselves the power to conquer bestiality, not with our muscles and our swords, but with the power of the light that is in our minds."[40]

In the twentieth century a new art form, the film, made vivid use of themes from the Apocalypse. *Apocalypse Now* depicts the Vietnam War as an apocalyptic event. The *Omen* trilogy, *The Seventh Sign,* and *The Rapture* are focused on the book's prophecies. Both the title and some of the evocative symbolism of Ingmar Bergman's *The Seventh Seal* are drawn from the Apocalypse. The twentieth century's horrific wars and the fear of nuclear disaster disposed filmmakers and their audiences to respond to this kind of drama.

The Apocalypse has appealed to writers who have explicitly rejected Christianity. George Eliot (1819–80), a professed agnostic, couched some of her works in apocalyptic terms,[41] and the German poet Hölderlin wrote of John on Patmos. The book made its mark on the thought of secularists like Robert Owen. The presence of allusions to the Apocalypse in writings is not a guarantee of their authors' theological views; the book's imagery has a power that is independent of religious beliefs, and indeed can be used in such a way as to question what appears to be its original intention. The Irish poet William Butler Yeats (1865–1939) turned the traditional expectations on their head with his allusion to the beast that "Slouches towards Bethlehem to be born."[42]

Moreover, the attitude of Shakespeare to the book of Revelation is highly ambiguous. It has been suggested that he questioned the validity of apocalyptic ideas. His tragedy *King Lear* speaks of thunder, earthquakes, the dragon, and monsters of the deep, but instead of treating them as signs of an approaching millennium it uses them as a prelude to tragedy. Critics have argued that *King Lear* is a "broken apocalypse" that expresses disillusionment with the expectation of a millennium.[43] Opponents of the theory, however, contend that the play culminates in the assurance that the younger generation still has its life to live.[44] But Shakespeare's use of apocalyptic ideas is sufficiently ambiguous to raise the possibility that he challenged traditional views.

Other authors were positive about the Apocalypse. The Russian Vasily Rozanov, writing in 1917 and 1918, when his country was in the throes of revolution, combined an optimistic view of the book with a critical attitude to traditional Christianity. The Christian gospel, he said, promised suffering and distress. But the Apocalypse's New Jerusalem, in which tears will be wiped from the eyes, belongs to the post-Christian world.[45]

The book has often provided inspiration for traditional Christians. It lies beneath the surface of C. S. Lewis's *The Last Battle,* the last of his seven chronicles of the imaginary land of Narnia. The lion is the Christ figure, and his enemies are the forces of evil. The battle itself is reminiscent of Armageddon. Lewis describes the falling of the stars, the coming of night to the land, the disappearance of islands, the transformation of valleys into lakes, the reddening of the sun and the moon, all of which are apocalyptic themes. And his new Narnia is reminiscent of the New Jerusalem.[46]

The poet Christina Rossetti (1830–94) wrote many poems based on the Apocalypse at different stages of her life. And she wrote them from the standpoint of Christian faith. "Paradise: In a Dream," written in her early twenties, conveys the intensity of her hopes for the New Jerusalem. She tells of the songs of Paradise, the fourfold river, and the tree of life. And she reveals her hope to see these sights in reality.

> I saw the gate called Beautiful;
>> And looked, but scarce could look, within;
>> I saw the golden streets begin,
> And outskirts of the glassy pool,
> Oh harps, oh crowns of plenteous stars,
>> Oh green palm-branches many-leaved—
> Eye hath not seen, nor ear hath heard,
>> Nor heart conceived.

> I hope to see these things again,
> But not as once in dreams by night;
> To see them with my very sight,
> And touch, and handle, and attain:
> To have all Heaven beneath my feet
> For narrow way that once they trod;
> To have my part with all the Saints,
> And with my God.
> ("Paradise: In a Dream")

Few of these writers gave detailed interpretations of the Apocalypse, but Rossetti was one of the exceptions. Toward the end of her life she wrote a devotional commentary on the book, which gives an insight into her inner life, and which will be discussed later.

Two other writers with well-established reputations in literature have made detailed comments on the Apocalypse, and their interpretations are diametrically opposite to each other.

One of them, the French poet and dramatist Paul Claudel (1868–1955), was a devout Catholic who was attracted to the Apocalypse not just because he was a poet but also because he was a believing Christian. Claudel was a prolific writer of plays and poems, many of them on religious themes. He was the author of several works on the Apocalypse, one of which he completed during the Nazi occupation of France, although he did not publish it until 1952.[47] Claudel, who accepted Augustine's view of the millennium,[48] recognized that the Apocalypse had a message for its own day but also believed that it spoke to all generations. He was a Catholic of the more exclusive kind and did not hesitate to include Protestantism among the powers of evil. The beast from the sea is materialism, paganism, and idolatry. It has been active in individual rulers and religious leaders: Mohammed, Luther, Henry VIII, Louis XIV, Napoleon, Stalin, and Hitler.[49] It is also active in religious and political movements: Islam, Protestantism, the French Revolution, and Bolshevism. The beast from the land is present in Islam and in Christian heresies, especially in Calvinism.[50] And it is to be found in "the gentle Antichrists," Buddha, Socrates, Voltaire, and Renan, who seek the general good of humanity but do not give God an essential place in their thought.

Claudel attacked modern biblical critics, with the exception of Allo, whom he held in high esteem. The seven thousand persons slain at the destruction of the city (Rev. 11:13) reminded him of biblical scholars, especially the contributors to the journal *Revue Biblique*.[51] He identified Babylon with many cities, both past and present: Jerusalem, Rome, Constantinople, Paris under the commune of 1870, and both London and the cities of Germany in the aerial attacks of World War II.[52]

The prejudices of Claudel are obvious. He never hesitated to take sides. But his explanations of the Apocalypse are always relevant. His assumption that a prophecy has several fulfillments leaves the door open for fresh interpretations in every generation.

The other man of letters who commented in detail on the Apocalypse was D. H. Lawrence (1885–1930). His perspective was far removed from Claudel's. Lawrence categorically rejected Christianity and was unashamedly hostile to the Apocalypse. "The Apocalypse of John," he asserted, "is, as it stands, the work of a second-rate mind. It appeals intensely to second-rate minds in every country and every century."[53] Lawrence did not regard himself as the owner of a second-rate mind, but he devoted a large portion of the final years of his life to the study of the book. The Apocalypse fascinated him because it reminded him of the cultic myths of the ancient world. In its present form it repelled him, but its images captured his imagination. He could not resist their magnetism. John, he was convinced, had adapted an existing Jewish apocalypse, and after John's death others mangled the text. It was the climax of a process of deterioration. The Apocalypse we read today is much worse than what John actually wrote, and what John wrote was worse than the Jewish source he inherited. Even that source was a distortion and devitalization of the universal myth behind it.

Lawrence thought that the first eleven chapters of the Apocalypse were based on pagan accounts of the death and resurrection of both the individual and the world. But in the twelfth chapter, with the introduction of Michael, it changes its tone. It moves from the world of paganism to the world of Judaism. The exception is the vision of the whore of Babylon. "She is the Magna Mater in malefic aspect, clothed in the colours of the angry sun, and throned upon the great red dragon of the angry cosmic power. Splendid she sits, and splendid is her Babylon."[54]

Although Lawrence had praise for parts of the book, his overall verdict was strongly negative. The Apocalypse, he said, represents the Christianity of "the middling masses." It is the "Judas" among New Testament books,[55] that speaks for people who fail to attain their inward desires and seek satisfaction by wishing destruction on the life they cannot attain.

Lawrence's account is a blend of scholarship, psychology, and theosophy.[56] Above all, it breathes the spirit of his paganism: the love of life, the transcendence of morals, and the rejection of Christianity. That writers of the stature of Lawrence and Claudel should give this detailed attention to the Apocalypse is evidence of its appeal to the poetic imagination. It is especially remarkable that it exercised a fascination on Lawrence, the renouncer of Christianity. In spite of his hostility, the book cast its spell on him.

The Apocalypse's cultural impact is not limited to art and literature. Its use in psychology and sociology demonstrates the breadth of its influence. It has also had a strong impact because its phrases have entered into common usage. The words *apocalypse, millennium, four horsemen, New Jerusalem,* and *new earth* are used to express human hopes and fears and human triumphs and tragedies. In an age of upheaval and transformation, they evoke a vibrant response in people's minds.

In one sense the Christian religion is a part of Western culture. Its stories, its terminology, and many of its ideas belong to the shared tradition. In another sense, the Christian religion is larger than Western culture. It had its origins in a Near Eastern country, became the traditional religion of Western civilization, and now extends to many non-Western societies. Non-Christians as well as Christians speak of the four horsemen, the beasts, the millennium, and the New Jerusalem.

When artists, writers, playwrights, filmmakers, politicians, and political commentators allude to the Apocalypse, they are making use of a tradition that belongs to their civilization. Whether they are Christian or not, and whether their audience is Christian or not, the language and poetry of the book function as a means through which they communicate their ideas and emotions.

Nevertheless, the Apocalypse is primarily a part of the Christian scriptures. It was written by a member of the church for the benefit of the church. It is concerned with Christian faith and obedience. Although its use extends far beyond the church, believing Christians have been and continue to be its chief interpreters. And they, too, as much as anyone else, are heirs of the cultural heritage.

CHAPTER THIRTEEN

THE INNER LIFE AND WORSHIP

Although much of the Apocalypse seems to be concerned with struggles against outward forces, interpreters have also explained it in terms of the inner conflicts of individuals. The battle between good and evil takes place not only in the arena of history but also in human hearts. The four living creatures, said Andreas, as well as symbolizing the four Gospels, stand for the four cardinal virtues: the lion for courage, the calf for justice, the eagle for temperance, and the human being for wisdom. The dragon's seven heads may represent wicked spiritual powers or vices; and its ten horns are the sins that break the Ten Commandments.[1]

This kind of interpretation has a strong appeal for mystical writers. The seven heads of the beast, according to John of the Cross (1542–91), make war against the soul as it climbs the seven steps of love, freeing itself from "sensual things" and entering into "purity of spirit."[2] The waters from the fountain of life (Rev. 21:6) are "the inmost love of God,"[3] and the supper that Christ brings when he knocks on the door of the soul (Rev. 3:20) is "his own sweetness." It is the occasion of the union between God and the "Bride-Soul."[4]

The Flemish mystic John Ruusbroec (or Ruysbroeck) (1293–1381) gave prominence to Revelation 2:17: "To everyone who conquers I will give some of the hidden manna, and I will give a white stone, and on the white stone is written a new name that no one knows except the one who receives it." The person who overcomes, explained Ruusbroec, is the one who transcends self and all other things. The hidden manna is "an interior, hidden savor and heavenly joy." The stone is Christ himself.[5] The words "They will rest from their labors, for their deeds follow them" (Rev. 14:13) describe the condition of those who have left themselves and their works behind them and eternally die to themselves.[6]

Some writers blended an emphasis on inward change with a concern for change in church or society. They often combined this emphasis with hostility to conventional religion. The Quaker leader George Fox (1624–91) made a contrast between the true church, which emphasizes inner life, and false churches, which concentrate on outward rites.[7] The false churches, said Fox's colleague, Isaac Penington, were those of Rome, Scotland, and England. Even the independent churches, which declared their freedom from state control, were guilty of preoccupation with external things. The true church does not rely on outward ceremonies or traditional orders of ministry. Its only temple is inward. It has the marks of the New Jerusalem, whose temple is "God and the Lamb."[8] The power of Antichrist is present in the worldliness of false churches with their intellectual and spiritual pride. But in spite of the prevalence of evil, the true church survives. "There hath been," wrote Penington, "a simplicity and sincerity of heart stirring in some people towards God, in all ages." And the change that has already begun in human hearts will extend to society as a whole.

> The battle is begun; the territories of antichrist are assaulted; the Lamb hath appeared on his white horse, and hath gathered many of his called, faithful, and chosen about him; the ensign is lifted up; the light (which searcheth the inwards of the enemy's dominions) hath appeared.[9]

The French mystic Antoinette Bourignon (1616–80) shared some of the characteristics of the early Quakers. She combined an emphasis on the inward and outward fulfillment of the prophecies with antagonism to the established churches. Antichrist was active in those churches and in their rites of baptism and the eucharist. But he was also at work in the sinful passions and actions of individuals. Bourignon understood the millennium in a twofold sense. It would soon arrive physically on earth, but it was already taking place spiritually in individuals, when they were inwardly renewed.[10]

The English prophet Jane Lead (1624–1704), a founder of the Philadelphian Society, named after the most faithful of the seven churches in the Apocalypse (Rev. 3:7-13), emphasized the inwardness of the religious life. She expected her small group of followers to prepare the way for Christ's second coming. She regarded herself and her society as the first fruits of the 144,000.[11] The kingdom of the beast, she said, "consists in sensual pleasures, and worldly advantages."[12] The last days were approaching. Between 1697 and 1700 the beast and the dragon would be overthrown, the millennium would begin on earth, and everything would be restored to its original purity. Victory over evil in the hearts of individuals is an indication of the nearness of those days. "There is no surer sign of the approaching Personal Reign of Christ, than to see the Beast wounded in the Heart."[13]

A characteristic of these writers was hostility to the growing emphasis on reason in intellectual circles. According to Bourignon, the Antichrist was at work in the developments of science, and the falling stars of Revelation 12:4 were the souls of scientists who denied the divine mystery. And Lead explained the beheading of the saints (Rev. 20:4) not as a physical decapitation but as their loss of the life of reason.[14]

Lead was in the theosophical tradition derived from Jacob Boehme, and one of its most famous representatives was Emanuel Swedenborg (1688–1772). Born in Stockholm, the son of a Lutheran theologian and bishop, Swedenborg was an adviser on mines and the author of works on biology, atomic theory, and astronomy. In 1744, at the age of fifty-six, he claimed to have received revelations about the spiritual world. From then on he devoted his time to spiritual matters and wrote voluminously about them. Swedenborg believed that the millennium had already begun. He proclaimed himself the agent through whom the second coming of Christ had taken place.[15] On January 9, 1757, he said, he witnessed the last judgment and the beginning of the era of the New Jerusalem. He claimed to have seen thousands of people cast out of the spiritual world into a fiery gulf and a dark cavern.[16]

Swedenborg was hostile to the mainstream churches. He accused traditional Christianity of distorting the truth. The fault lay with Lutherans and Calvinists as well as Catholics. He found the doctrines of predestination and justification by faith alone to be especially repulsive. In contrast with these corrupt churches was the New Church, symbolized by the woman of Revelation 12. Her crown of stars signified wisdom and intelligence. Her child was the New Church's doctrine, and the dragon stood for the Reformed churches.[17] The beast from the sea represented laity who accepted the doctrine of justification by faith, and the beast from the earth represented the Reformed clergy.[18]

While Swedenborg believed that the Apocalypse prophesied events of a corporate nature, he taught that it was also concerned with the condition of individual souls. Its seven churches represent people with varying attitudes to the relationship between doctrine and works. Its four living creatures stand for different aspects of divine truth: the lion for power, the calf for affection, the human being for wisdom, and the eagle for knowledge.[19] In the visions of the horsemen, the white horse signifies understanding of truth, and the other three horses symbolize the destruction of that understanding.[20] The 200 million cavalry stand for reasonings about the doctrine of justification by faith alone.[21] The two witnesses are either love and intelligence or charity and faith,[22] and Armageddon signifies "the love of honor, of dominion, and of supereminence."[23]

Although Swedenborg's teaching provoked vehement opposition and many people thought that he was mad, his emphasis on good works and his belief in a spiritual world had a powerful appeal. He won the admiration, though not the wholehearted agreement, of writers as diverse as Blake, Coleridge, and Emerson. One of his best-known twentieth-century adherents was the author and lecturer Helen Keller. Robbed at an early age of sight and hearing, she welcomed his assurance of the existence of a vibrant spiritual world. Impatient with traditional theology, she was attracted by his emphasis on love and his rejection of orthodox doctrine.[24]

The theosophical tradition, of which Swedenborg was a representative, was esoteric, claiming to provide a secret, higher knowledge to its initiates. Helena Petrovna Blavatsky (1831–93), founder of the Theosophical Society, preserved the characteristic emphases of the tradition. She expressed hostility to the existing churches and identified the beast with ritualistic religions that stifled true knowledge.[25] Her follower, James Pryse, described Christianity as a mystery religion that preserves "a secret traditional lore, an arcane science, handed down from times immemorial." The early church lost the knowledge of this lore because of the selfishness of its priesthood, but the secrets remain hidden in the pages of the Apocalypse.[26]

Pryse argued that the Apocalypse was designed for the initiation of people into the esoteric mysteries. Its subject matter is the "process of transcendental self-conquest, the giving birth to oneself as a spiritual being." John the Apostle, its author, has provided "an almost complete outline of the psycho-psychological process of regeneration."[27] The book is a drama with one performer, the person who is being initiated. All its other characters are personifications of forces and principles.[28]

Rudolf Steiner (1861–1925), the leader of the anthroposophists, another branch of the esoteric movement, agreed with Pryse that the Apocalypse describes an initiation. He praised it as "the most profound document of Christianity." It develops "powers and capacities slumbering in every soul." John goes though the experience of the initiate.[29] He is terrified by the flashing sword and falls at the feet of the Son of Man as though dead. But then he enters the new life: "And I was dead; and behold, I am alive for evermore" (Rev. 1:18 AV), and he is taken up into heaven to "the spiritual fountain-head of things." But this fountainhead will not be forever confined to heaven. It will soon be realized on earth through the process of physical evolution.[30]

Pryse and Steiner had detailed beliefs about the nature of heaven and human souls, but there are other ways of linking the Apocalypse with the inner life. It is possible to make the connection without accepting the esoteric teaching of theosophists and anthroposophists. Writers have understood the Apocalypse in terms of inward struggles and growth without being enmeshed in speculations about human consciousness.

One such writer, Jeanne-Marie Bouvier de la Motte Guyon (1648–1717), won a controversial reputation as a spiritual guide. Guyon was a visionary, and some of her actions departed from the accepted norms. The idea of spiritual marriage has played a leading part in mystical thought, and the Apocalypse's account of the marriage of the Lamb (Rev. 19:6-10) is one of the biblical supports for the idea. The metaphor gives powerful expression to the idea of close personal union with Christ. It was in Jeanne-Marie Guyon's mind when, even during her husband's lifetime, she signed a marriage contract with the child Jesus and claimed to be marked with the sign of the cross, which she likened to the name received by the saints (Rev. 7:3).[31]

Guyon created a stir when she asserted that she was the woman of Revelation 12 and that her child was a divine gift that she wished to communicate to her followers.[32] But when Bossuet, the well-known preacher and bishop, questioned her, she gave a less provocative explanation. The woman, she said, referred primarily to the church and Mary, and only in a secondary sense to people like herself.[33]

Although these actions may suggest that she was on a par with the fanatical prophets of her age, in fact she made an important contribution to the life of devotion. She attracted followers, the best known of whom was the archbishop Fénelon. She wrote a lengthy commentary on the Bible that emphasized the inner life, an emphasis that is clearly evident in her volume on the Apocalypse. She treated the visions of the four horsemen as stages of spiritual development. The first vision, with the white horse, stands for the repentance with which the new life begins. The second, with the red horse, depicts the inner conflict that follows that beginning. The third, with the black horse, expresses the sense of deprivation and despair that comes in the midst of the spiritual life. The fourth, with the pale horse, represents the terrors of death. In Revelation 7 the 144,000 are "interior persons," the true Israelites; and the countless multitude that stand before the throne wear the white robes of innocence, although they have not attained the spiritual heights of the 144,000.

Guyon gave a spiritual explanation of the Apocalypse's demonic figures. The army of 200 million cavalry stands for evils that overwhelm the soul. The two witnesses are faith and pure love. The beast from the sea is pride, the beast from the land is self-love, and the whore of Babylon is self-will. When individuals overcome these sinful passions, the millennium begins within them.[34]

The poet Christina Rossetti (1830–94), another author of a devotional commentary on the Apocalypse, regarded its account of the struggle against the dragon and the beasts as a confrontation between good and evil within the individual heart.

> Whatever this Apocalyptic beast may prove in fullness of time, it exhibits some likeness to that world, flesh, devil, which are my daily antagonists; of which I must daily, hourly, momentarily beware.[35]

The seven heads of the beast, said Rossetti, stand for the seven deadly sins.[36] Although the angel may chain the devil and throw him into the pit at some unknown time in the future, each of us can overthrow him today by means of prayer. "Prayer is a chain apt presently to bind him, and which he cannot snap."[37]

It is debatable whether John intended to devote a large proportion of his book to the inner life. Yet his language about the beast and the whore is sufficiently ambiguous for it to be an appropriate description of conflicts in the individual soul. Furthermore, parts of the Apocalypse speak directly to the condition of the individual. The letters to the churches talk of faithfulness and unfaithfulness, of obedience and disobedience. The message to the church at Laodicea, "Behold, I stand at the door, and knock" (Rev. 3:20 AV), is a famous example of an exhortation that concerns the inner life. Although these words may allude to a personal communion with Christ at the last day, they are also likely to refer to a present-day communion with him in the eucharist or in private devotion. That is how many people have understood the words. Andreas, Primasius, and Bede explained them as an allusion to Christ knocking at the door of the heart,[38] and Bridget of Sweden (c.1303–73) said that Christ was like a stranger on earth, who went from place to place and, like a traveler, knocked at many people's doors.[39]

As well as referring to the inner life, the Apocalypse is a catalyst for inward change. John Wesley prized its visions of heaven as a means of conveying religious experience. "It is scarce possible," he wrote, "for any that either love or fear God not to feel their hearts extremely affected in seriously reading either the beginning or the latter part of the revelation."[40] Paul Claudel said that our primary concern should not be to understand the Apocalypse but to walk inside it as we walk inside a cathedral and look with admiration at its windows, choir, and columns. When we move through the book, we ought to fall on our knees and worship God, who is present in every page of the Bible.[41] The Apocalypse is a place for encounter with God.

Spiritual interpretations produce spiritual experience. Jeanne-Marie Guyon found the very act of interpreting to be an occasion for inward illumination. In her study of the scriptures, she claimed to rely not on information obtained from others but on direct divine guidance.

> Before writing I did not know what I was going to write; while writing I saw that I was writing things I had never known, and during the time of manifestation light was given me that I had in me treasures of knowledge and understanding that I did not know myself to possess.[42]

Nowhere did she discover these treasures more than in the Apocalypse. Her explanation of the conflict with evil powers as an account of the inner struggles of human souls reflects the course of her own religious life.

Christina Rossetti also found the study of the Apocalypse to be an occasion for religious experience. In her commentary, she did not attempt a detailed explanation of its meaning. She treated it as a call to prayer.

> Much of this awful Apocalypse opens to my apprehension rather a series of aspects than any one defined and certified object. It summons me to watch and pray and give thanks; it urges me to climb heavenward. Its thread doubtless consists unbroken: but my clue is at the best woven of broken lights and shadows, here a little and there a little.[43]

Rossetti's commentary is a record of her interaction with the Apocalypse. Although she never questioned the book's authority and inspiration, she was uncomfortable with its message of judgment and stressed the theme of love, which has little place in the Apocalypse itself. Christ the slain and exalted Lamb (Rev. 5:6) is a formidable figure with seven eyes and seven horns, but he awakened in Rossetti a sense of love and devotion.

> None other Lamb, none other Name,
>> None other Hope in heaven or earth or sea,
>> None other Hiding-place from guilt and shame,
>> None beside Thee.[44]

Rossetti treated even the prophecies of disaster and judgment as occasions for devotion; she responded to the vision of the rider on a red horse with a hymn to love.[45] In reflecting on the bowl visions, she did not dwell on the horrors of the plagues but prayed only for deliverance. When the Apocalypse predicted the scorching of men and women by the sun (Rev. 16:8-9), her response was: "Though the sun smite us by day and the moon by night, yet to us let the Sun of Righteousness arise with healing in His wings. Though Thou destroy our flesh, save our spirit."[46] When the Apocalypse declared, "And every island fled away, and the mountains were not found" (Rev. 16:20 AV), Rossetti prayed, "When all faileth, save Thou, fail us not Thou; Thou Who never failest them that seek Thee. Lord, Lord, give us grace to seek and find Thee."[47] Rossetti used prayer to respond to scripture and answered the savage forebodings of the Apocalypse with petitions of gentler tone. Her commentary is full of prayers, hymns, and litanies, giving a glimpse of her own devotional life.

THE APOCALYPSE IN WORSHIP

Private meditation and public worship are not far removed from each other. Even when prayers and hymns have been designed for public worship, they can function as a means of private devotion.

And when the Apocalypse is used in public liturgies, it affects both individual and corporate lives.

In its original setting, the Apocalypse was probably read aloud to assembled congregations, since it speaks of "the one who reads" and "those who hear" (Rev. 1:3). It is filled with the atmosphere of worship. It contains numerous hymns and dwells on the theme of adoration more than any other book of the New Testament.

Besides having a powerful impact on worship through the medium of art, the Apocalypse has an important role in Christian lectionaries, liturgies, and hymns. While sculpture, paintings, stained glass, and other forms of art depict the beasts and the horsemen as well as the scenes of heavenly adoration, the words from the book most frequently spoken in worship are from its descriptions of heaven and the exalted Christ.

When the Apocalypse is read in worship, these passages, rather than the prophecies of disaster, are usually selected. In the East, the Apocalypse is absent from the main lectionaries, but the practice has been different in the West. In Spain, the Fourth Council of Toledo (633) prescribed the sentence of excommunication for any priest who failed to read from the Apocalypse during the season between Easter and Pentecost. The Lateran Cathedral in Rome required it to be used in worship during the same season, and there is evidence of a similar practice in France.[48] None of the prescribed readings, however, included the visions of disaster, and none of them mentioned the beast or the last judgment. Nor did they contain the passage about the millennium. Their themes were the heavenly throne, the exalted Christ, the martyrs, the 144,000, and the New Jerusalem.

Later lectionaries reveal similar preferences. For many years the Church of England's *Book of Common Prayer* made very little provision for the reading of the Apocalypse, but the table of lessons authorized in 1871 prescribes the whole of the Apocalypse except chapters 9, 13, and 17 in its daily readings for the year. The prayer book is much more selective in its use of the Apocalypse for Sundays and holy days, concentrating on those chapters that describe worship. An exception is its use of the middle part of Revelation 12 and the latter part of Revelation 14 for the holy day connected with the angel Michael. The triennial lectionary adopted in American churches in the late twentieth century narrows the field in a similar way. Its selections from the Apocalypse, which are few in number, come from chapters that deal with worship. The compilers of lectionaries have consistently shown a preference for those parts of the book.

The extent to which the Apocalypse has influenced communion liturgies is doubtful. Most of the material that may be derived from it may just as easily have been taken from the Old Testament. The eucharist's "Holy, holy, holy" is dependent on Isaiah 6:1-3, and its allusion to worship by angels may go back to Daniel 7:10. But the emphasis on the perpetual nature of the angels' praise may be derived from Revelation 4:8 ("Day and night without ceasing they sing").[49] And in the ancient liturgy of St. James the introduction of martyrs into the heavenly choir recalls Revelation 7:9-17.[50] The passages where there is a possible dependence on the Apocalypse are accounts of worship in heaven.

Hymns that are reminiscent of the Apocalypse reflect the same themes as do the lectionaries. In the Te Deum Laudamus, one of the earliest Christian hymns, the words "The white-robed army of martyrs praise you" echo Revelation 7:9-17.[51] Martyrs were a favorite topic of early and medieval hymns. Aurelius Prudentius (348–c.413) had the same verses in mind when he wrote:

> Now consort of the angels bright
> Thou shinest clothed in robes of white;
> Robes thou hast washed in streams of blood,
> A dauntless martyr for thy God.[52]

The heavenly city was a popular theme. John of Damascus (8th cent.) wrote of the New Jerusalem and the martyrs.[53] And numerous Western hymns sang of the celestial city. "Blessed City, Heavenly Salem" (7th or 8th cent.) tells of its pearly gates, its precious stones, and its descent from heaven.[54] Fulbert, bishop of Chartres (c.960–1028), wrote of the praises uttered by the "choirs of New Jerusalem."[55] Bernard of Cluny's poem "De Contemptu Mundi" (c.1140) reflects Augustine's contrast between the city of God and the city of the world.

> And now we watch and struggle,
>   And now we live in hope,
> And Zion in her anguish
>   With Babylon must cope.

But Bernard also speaks of the glories of the heavenly Jerusalem.

> They stand, those halls of Zion,
>   All jubilant with song,
> And bright with many an angel
>   And all the martyr throng.[56]

A hymn ascribed to Thomas à Kempis focuses on the absence of night in the heavenly city:

> Light's abode, celestial Salem,
> Vision dear whence peace doth spring.
> . . . .
> Endless noonday, glorious noonday,
> From the Sun of suns is there.[57]

After the Reformation, the Lutheran Philipp Nicolai (1556–1608) wrote a hymn about the second advent that focused mainly on the parable of the wise and foolish virgins but also echoed the Apocalypse with:

> the choir immortal
> Of angels round thy dazzling throne.[58]

Heinrich Theobald Schenck (1656–1727) blended several passages from the Apocalypse in his picture of the heavenly choir:

> Who are these, like stars appearing,
>   These before God's throne who stand?
> Each a golden crown is wearing;
>   Who are all this glorious band?
>   "Alleluya!" hark they sing,
>   Praising loud their heavenly king.[59]

In sixteenth- and seventeenth-century Britain, under Calvinist influence, the churches were reluctant to use any hymns but metrical versions of psalms, but people began to break the mold. Toward the end of the sixteenth century, two hymns about the heavenly Jerusalem became popular in England and Scotland. In modified forms, they were sung for many centuries, and parts of them were used as carols. One of them was by W. Prid:

> O mother dear Hierusalem,
> Jehovah's throne on high,
> O sacred city, queen and wife
> Of Christ eternally.[60]

The other was by the anonymous F.B.P., who may have been an English Catholic priest:

> Jerusalem, my happy home,
> When shall I come to thee?
> When shall my sorrows have an end?
> Thy joys when shall I see?

F.B.P.'s description of the city suggests the ideal of an English castle. He praised its walls, turrets, and pinnacles. His description of the landscape with its vineyards and crops of cinnamon, sugar, nard, and balm suggest an Eastern setting, but some of his words would readily apply to his own country:

> Thy gardens and thy gallant walks
> Continually are green;
> There grow such sweet and pleasant flowers
> As nowhere else are seen.

David with harp in hand is "master of the choir"; Mary sings the Magnificat; Ambrose and Augustine chant the Te Deum; Zechariah sings the Benedictus; and Simeon sings the Nunc Dimittis, as they do in Luke's Gospel.[61]

From the earliest times to the present day hymns have described the New Jerusalem as a state of existence that awaits people after this life is over. Such was the intent of the American Robert Lowry (1826–99) during an epidemic in New York, when he wrote:

> Shall we gather at the river,
> Where bright angel feet have trod,
> With its crystal tide for ever
> Flowing by the throne of God?

Some writers, however, have explained the New Jerusalem in terms of this present world. Francis Turner Palgrave (1824–97) rejected the otherworldly interpretation, although his outlook remained intensely spiritual. Heaven is present in the Christian community:

> Not throned above the skies,
> Nor golden-walled afar,
> But where Christ's two or three
> In his name gathered are,
>   Be in the midst of them,
>   God's own Jerusalem!

The New Jerusalem, says Palgrave, is to be found in individuals, when Christ is spiritually present in them.

> Where in life's common ways
> With cheerful feet we go;
> Where in his steps we tread
> Who trod the way of woe;
>   Where he is in the heart,
>   City of God, thou art.[62]

Walter Russell Bowie (1882–1969), rector of Grace Episcopal Church in New York, dreamed of the New Jerusalem as a just order of society and used the Apocalypse to champion the cause of social justice. He was thinking of the transformation of his country's urban areas when in his hymn "O Holy City, Seen of John" he prayed for "strength to build" the New Jerusalem.[63]

The stanzas from Tennyson's "In Memoriam" that speak of the "thousand years of peace" and "the Christ that is to be" convey the same kind of hope.[64] Although Tennyson did not write them as a hymn, later generations used them for that purpose. During World War I, Blake's poem "And did those feet in ancient time," written over a century earlier, was set to a stirring tune by Parry and from that time onward was used to give expression both to patriotism and to the desire for a more just society. It was once sung at a service of thanksgiving for the passage of a bill in Parliament to give votes to women, but it also spoke to the needs of a beleaguered Britain in wartime. Its vow to build Jerusalem "in England's green and pleasant land" gave men and women a vision of a new world that would follow the tribulation of war. The song became part of the national repertoire, learned in school at an early age. It gave voice to hope in peacetime as well as war. Among the victims of economic hardship, it awakened dreams of a transformed society, free from poverty and unemployment.[65]

It was not just the description of the New Jerusalem that attracted hymn writers. They concentrated on other passages from the Apocalypse as well. John Mason (c.1645–94), who was a strong advocate of millenarianism, sang of the angels' worship depicted in Revelation 5:11:

> How shall I sing that majesty
>   Which angels do admire?
> Let dust in dust and silence lie;
>   Sing, sing, ye heavenly choir.
> Thousands of angels stand around
>   Thy throne, O God most high;
> Ten thousand times ten thousand sound
>   Thy praise; but who am I?[66]

Isaac Watts had the same vision in mind when he wrote an invitation to worship:

> Come let us join our cheerful songs
>   With angels round the throne;
> Ten thousand thousand are their tongues,
>   But all their joys are one.[67]

217

Watts also turned his thoughts to Revelation 7:13-14:

> I ask them whence their victory came;
>   They, with united breath,
> Ascribe their conquest to the Lamb,
>   Their triumph to his death.[68]

Charles Wesley's "Ye Servants of God" is inspired by the same passage:

> The praises of Jesus the angels proclaim.
> Fall down on their faces and worship the Lamb.[69]

And from a Lutheran perspective, Paul Gerhardt (1607–76) said that the multitude before the throne (Rev. 7:9-17) made their clothes bright in "the bath of faith."[70]

Writers in later generations maintained the emphasis on heaven. One of the most famous examples is Reginald Heber's "Holy, Holy, Holy! Lord God Almighty" with its description of the saints, "Casting down their golden crowns around the glassy sea." William Walsham Howe's "For All the Saints" is in the same tradition. Its opening words recall the reference to "the dead which die in the Lord" who are to "rest from their labours" (Rev. 14:13 AV); and it alludes to the "gates of pearl" and "the victor's crown of gold" (Rev. 2:10; 4:4; 21:21). Other hymns that present this picture of heaven are Henry Alford's "Ten Thousand Times Ten Thousand" and Christopher Wordsworth's "Hark! The Sound of Holy Voices, Chanting at the Crystal Sea." These were popular hymns, and their writers were leaders of the English church establishment. The Apocalypse played a part in African American spirituals, many of which had their origin in the days of slavery. These songs give voice to more than one kind of hope. They express a desire both for political freedom and for the heavenly liberty that death will bring. They make vivid use of biblical images to express these aspirations: crossing the Jordan, entering the promised land, riding to heaven in a chariot, the falling stars, and the sound of a trumpet. Some of the songs have the Apocalypse specifically in mind:

> King Jesus rides on a milk-white horse,
> No man can a-hinder me.[71]

Spirituals about the New Jerusalem have a double meaning, expressing a yearning for both justice on earth and bliss in heaven. They look forward to life in the heavenly city:

> I want to be ready,
> To walk in Jerusalem just like John.

They tell of the new song that people will sing there (Rev. 5:9; 14:3):

> When I go to heaven, gonna sing a new song,
> Gonna sing all over God's heaven.

Walking and singing in heaven refer not only to life beyond the grave but to life in a society where slavery is abolished. But another spiritual affirms that people can enjoy an inward freedom even when they are slaves. A privilege of the New Jerusalem is to drink "of the fountain of water of life freely" (Rev. 21:6 AV); and the author of a spiritual claims to have received that blessing:

> I've just come from the fountain. . . .
> My soul's set free at the fountain.[72]

The vision of the marriage supper of the Lamb (Rev. 19:6-10) was a basis for allusions in eucharistic hymns. Horatius Bonar (1808–89) put the point very clearly:

> Feast after feast thus comes and passes by;
> Yet, passing, points to the glad feast above,
> Giving sweet foretaste of the festal joy,
> The Lamb's great bridal feast of bliss and love.
> ("Here, O My Lord, I See Thee")

And the idea is found much earlier in a eucharistic hymn by Thomas Aquinas that prays that Jesus who feeds us here on earth will make us his table guests in heaven.[73]

The promise to the church at Laodicea, "Behold, I stand at the door, and knock" (Rev. 3:20 AV) had a special appeal to evangelistic writers. It is the basis for Charles Wesley's words:

> He now stands knocking at the door
> Of every sinner's heart.[74]

Fanny Crosby (1820–1915) meditated on the passage:

> Behold Me standing at door,
> And hear Me pleading evermore,
> Say, weary heart, oppressed with sin,
> May I come in? May I come in?[75]

Hymns have elaborated on the Apocalypse's promises of victory. When Robert Lowry wrote "My soul will overcome by the blood of the Lamb" (see Rev. 12:11 AV),[76] he was thinking of victory over evil in the individual. But the language of victory does not refer only to the triumph over evil in the individual soul. It also signifies victory over injustice. The song "We Shall Overcome Someday," used in the American civil rights movement, may not depend on any particular biblical text, but the Apocalypse is one of its possible sources.[77] And the song has established itself as an expression of hope for a society free from poverty and prejudice.

While hymn writers have valued the Apocalypse chiefly for its visions of heaven, they have also used other themes from the book. The second advent and the last judgment are among them. Revelation 1:6-7 was the source for Charles Wesley's "Lo! he comes with clouds descending":

> Those who set at naught and sold him,
> Pierced and nailed him to the tree,
> Deeply wailing,
> Shall the true Messiah see.

The "Dies Irae" by Thomas of Celano (d. 1250) echoes the Apocalypse when it speaks of the summons before the throne and the book in which people's names are recorded.[78] An African American spiritual repeats the book's warnings about the catastrophes of the last days (Rev. 6:14; 16:20) but blends them with the psalmist's affirmation, "Thou art my hiding place" (Pss. 32:7; 119:114 AV).

> Oh, the rocks and the mountains shall all flee away,
> And you shall have a new hiding-place that day.
> Seeker, seeker, give up your heart to God,
> And you shall have a new hiding-place that day.[79]

The Apocalypse has provided inspiration for hymns on other themes. Writers in the Middle Ages depicted the Virgin Mary as the woman clothed with the sun (Rev. 12).[80] Luther described the woman as the church under God's protection.[81] A hymn by Pope Gregory IX (d. 1241) gives credit to Francis of Assisi for overthrowing the seventh head of the dragon.[82] Watts depicts the conflict between Michael and the dragon.[83] And Allendorf's verses about the death of a girl echo the Apocalypse's final chapters (Rev. 19:6-10; 22:3).

> In golden robes, a queen, a bride,
> She standeth at her Sovereign's side,
> She sees His face, unveil'd and bright.[84]

But most of the hymns that have won popularity are invitations to communion with Christ, promises of victory, and portrayals of heaven and the New Jerusalem. Sometimes, especially in the nineteenth and twentieth centuries, it was a heaven achieved on earth through human effort. More often it was heaven regarded as a transcendent realm of being. When people are conscious of the imminence of death and the precariousness of their life, they are strongly attracted by the Apocalypse's promise of heavenly bliss.

Musicians have not used the Apocalypse as much as the Old Testament psalms or New Testament canticles like the Magnificat and the Nunc Dimittis. But anthems and choruses have drawn inspiration from the Apocalypse's visions of heaven and its ascriptions of glory.[85] Tchaikovsky (1840–1892) composed an anthem, "I am the Alpha and the Omega" (Rev. 21:6). Vaughan Williams (1872–1958) wrote a work based on the doxology of Revelation 1:5-6. The words "I heard a voice from heaven," often repeated by John, have attracted composers.[86] It was to an utterance of the heavenly voice, "Now have come the salvation and the power" (Rev. 12:10), that Johann Sebastian Bach (1685–1750) set a cantata, "Nun is das Heil und die Kraft" for the feast of St. Michael. The theme of conflict occurs in Bach's cantata "Es erhub sich ein Streit" ("There arose a strife"), which, though it does not quote the words of the Apocalypse, describes Michael's victory over the dragon.[87] But the book's visions of worship have provided the chief attraction for composers.

In the English-speaking world, the most famous musical settings of the Apocalypse are choruses by Handel (1685–1759). In his oratorio *Messiah*, Handel blended "Hallelujah: for the Lord God omnipotent reigneth" (Rev. 19:6 AV) with "The kingdom of this world has become the kingdom of our Lord and of his Christ; and he shall reign for ever and ever" (based on Rev. 11:15 AV), to which he added the acclamation "King of Kings and Lord of Lords" (Rev. 19:16 AV). The chorus "Worthy is the Lamb" uses a selection of texts from the vision of heaven in the book's fifth chapter.[88] Even the final "Amen" is inspired by John's vision (Rev. 5:14). For two centuries these choruses have been among the best-known works of music in the English-speaking world. Although Handel did not specifically compose the oratorio for use in churches, even in the secular surroundings of a concert hall it brings with it the spirit of devotion. Many people who are unacquainted with the Apocalypse have found its words to be a source of spiritual strength through the medium of Handel's music.

In words, music, and visual arts the Apocalypse has made an enduring contribution to public and private devotion. Its influence is pervasive, and its images remain an integral part of Christian worship. Artists use its accounts of conflict and judgment as readily as they use its visions of heaven. But the musical settings to the book, the lectionary readings, and the hymns most frequently used in worship are those that speak of heaven, the New Jerusalem, and the promise of eternal bliss. In every age and in most branches of the Christian church the Apocalypse has made its impact through worship, bringing comfort in times of sorrow, giving expression to dreams and hopes, and providing the language and images of adoration and praise.

CHAPTER FOURTEEN

CONCLUSION

No simple explanation can be given of the Apocalypse's fascination for its readers and its audiences. It has strengthened their faith during persecution, war, church division, and times of social and political unrest. Natural disasters, like the Black Death and the Lisbon earthquake, have had an impact on interpretation, though not as great as the impact of human conflict. The Apocalypse appeals to people who believe themselves to be in a crisis. Even when their fears are unjustified, they may experience real distress. Few men and women, if any, are free from the fear of war, persecution, injustice, or personal tragedy. Many of them feel themselves to be threatened even when their lives outwardly appear to be untroubled. In this frame of mind, they turn to the Apocalypse.

All of these factors that attract people to the book were present when it was written. The church was either suffering persecution or living in fear of it. War was a real danger. Some of the congregations that John addressed were torn by ecclesiastical controversy. Poverty, slavery, and class distinction caused social unrest. The world had a full quota of natural disasters: famines, earthquakes, and volcanic eruptions. People believed themselves to be in a situation of crisis. These conditions have been present in the first century and have been present ever since. Not everyone who has undergone such experiences is interested in the Apocalypse, but in these situations many people have found it to be a source of consolation and strength.

Two other factors are present when men and women give attention to the book. First, it is part of their religious and cultural world. One of the main reasons for its influence is its status as Christian scripture. For many of its readers, its presence in the Bible guarantees the accuracy of its statements. Even if they are not victims of injustice and their lot in society has many advantages, they believe that the Apocalypse has a direct message from God.

Its status as scripture also enhances its claim on the attention of Christians who are not biblical literalists. They regard the Bible as neither inerrant nor infallible, but they take the Apocalypse seriously because it is part of their spiritual heritage. It is included in their Bible and has influenced their liturgy, their art, their literature, and their lives. They expect to find important truth there. They may criticize its theological perspectives and believe it to have the mistaken expectation that the second advent would occur long ago, but they value it as a document that raises relevant issues for the present day and attests to the faith and courage of early Christians.

The book's attraction extends to non-Christians, because they share the cultural heritage. Engels took the Apocalypse seriously. D. H. Lawrence found himself impelled to write about it. Writers' choice of its language and imagery no more proves that they give assent to Christianity than does their use of Greek mythology guarantee that they are devotees of Greek gods and goddesses. The Apocalypse, like the Greek myths, is their inheritance. Its imagery has a powerful appeal and is a means by which non-Christians as well as Christians express their thoughts and emotions. Although it is not formally a work of poetry, it is poetic in spirit and charged with dramatic power. It is an integral part of Western culture.

The other additional factor that influences interpretation of the Apocalypse is the person of the interpreter. The difference between Justin and Origen is not just the outcome of their environment or education. Both men were acquainted with Greek philosophy, and both were persecuted. Both of them accepted the Apocalypse as divinely inspired. But Justin was a Chiliast, and Origen rejected Chiliasm. Bolingbroke, Newton, Whiston, and Whitby were reared in similar environments and lived in the same country at the same time in history, but their reactions to the Apocalypse ranged from scornful rejection to trusting acceptance. One of the main reasons for their differences was that they were different individuals, who held different views of Christianity and the scriptures. The special appeal of the Apocalypse is grounded in its status as scripture, which has ensured its place in the religious and cultural heritage. But the interpretation it receives depends on the choice and inclination of the interpreters, which cannot be wholly explained by the circumstances in which they live.

The Apocalypse has appealed to people in every age since it was written and has attracted them from many areas of society. The poor, the persecuted, and the oppressed find a message for themselves in its pages. The rich and powerful have claimed it as support for the causes they embrace. It has appealed to both the educated and the uneducated. Its interpreters include not only biblical scholars and members of the church hierarchy but also artists, poets, and experts in the natural and social sciences.

Women have had an important role in the interpretation of the Apocalypse. Churches that would not ordain them as clergy or accept them as theologians have been ready to recognize them as prophets, and in that capacity they have contributed to the interpretation of the book. Outside the mainstream churches, in prophetic groups, they have often participated freely in interpretation. And in the twentieth century, having obtained entry into the academic world, they have played a prominent part in scholarly research.

The diversity of interpretations is even more remarkable than the diversity of its interpreters. For nineteen centuries, men and women have attempted to probe the book's mystery. They have emerged with a bewildering assortment of answers. So numerous and conflicting are its interpretations that many people despair of making sense of it. A tempting solution to the problem is to seize on one particular account of the book and dismiss all others as worthless. Such a procedure fails to do justice to the seriousness of interpreters. It also neglects the essential character of the book, which is written in such a way as to be capable of a variety of meanings.

In recent years, critics have questioned the value of inquiring into an author's intention. But the writer of the Apocalypse clearly has an intention, which is to effect changes in the audience and readers, to strengthen their faith, and to keep them loyal in time of persecution. He did not write his book primarily as a work of art; he wrote it to convey a message. The question of his intention is inescapable.

One of the virtues of historical criticism is that it tries to ascertain the meaning of a book in the mind of its author and its first readers. In this quest, critics of the Apocalypse have failed to reach agreement. They disagree about its date and authorship. They dispute whether it was written during persecution. They debate about its literary genre, and about the sources, if any, the author used. And when they try to uncover its meaning for its author and its first audiences, they fail to attain unanimity.

Their disagreement does not mean that they have squandered their energies on wasted labor. Their very failure to achieve unanimity is instructive. The divided voice of scholarship testifies to the book's ambiguity and is evidence that the Apocalypse resists attempts to find agreed answers to the questions that are asked. The disagreement of scholars gives weight to the supposition that the meaning was ambiguous even for John.

In the midst of this ambiguity, some probabilities emerge. The Apocalypse gives strong clues to its author's attitude to the Roman Empire. His identification of the seven heads of the beast with seven hills is likely to be an allusion to the city of Rome. The vision of the mortally wounded head of the beast that returns to life suggests the idea of a resurrected Nero. John regarded Rome as an agent of the devil and in his prophecy about the fall of Babylon predicted the collapse of the Roman Empire. Although John had Rome especially in mind, he may have entertained the possibility of wider meanings. The visions are sufficiently ambiguous to leave themselves open for further interpretation. John may have understood them to refer both to specific events that he expected to happen in his own time and to events of a less definite nature in an undetermined future. Because of this open-ended quality, his visions are capable of many interpretations.

Human beings and institutions who share characteristics of the beasts or the whore have emerged on many occasions in history. States, nations, and their rulers have behaved like God and claimed from their citizens and subjects the honor and devotion that are appropriately given to God alone. When institutions and people in power behave in this manner, they are partial fulfillments of the prophecies about the beasts. And it is conceivable that a supremely evil power will arise before history reaches its conclusion.

The account of the millennium is another good example of the book's ambiguity. John does not make it clear whether the thousand years have already begun or lie entirely in the future, and we are not in a position to probe fully into John's mind. Many commentators have assumed that he must have intended one interpretation to the exclusion of the other. But if he was reporting real visions, he may have recognized that they could be understood in more ways than one.

The vision of the New Jerusalem is also open to different interpretations. It is not clear whether John expected the New Jerusalem to coincide with the millennium or to come after it. Nor is it clear whether he expected it to be a visible reign of God on earth or a spiritual presence of God in human hearts or life in a transcendent heavenly realm. And if he regarded it as a visible reign, he has not specified whether it refers to the life of the church or to the establishment of a new form of government.

The book's openness makes it relevant for every generation. It is legitimate to understand the teaching about the millennium in different ways. The past, the present, and the future all have millennial qualities. The New Jerusalem is also capable of several meanings. It can be understood as the church, as an ideal society on earth, as an inner spiritual renewal, or as a heavenly mode of existence. Moreover, the beasts can be explained in several ways. Beast figures emerge in every age. Institutions or individuals claim the ultimate allegiance of men and women and behave as if they were gods.

Nevertheless, some interpretations are contrary to the spirit of the Apocalypse. To suggest that the millennium or the New Jerusalem is brought about by human achievement without God's initiative is not in accordance with the message of the book. To claim that the Apocalypse teaches the superiority of one nation over another is also contrary to its message. Like other New Testament writings, it may give a special place in the divine plan to the Jewish nation, although it is debatable how far it does so. But it also indicates that the leaves of the tree in the New Jerusalem are for the healing of nations. It has a vision that transcends nationalism.

Some explanations are obviously wrong. Events have disproved predictions of the visible return of Christ in 1666 and 1844. History has pronounced its indisputable verdict on prophecies of the collapse of the papacy in 1836 and the rapture of believers in 1988. If these conjectures correctly represent John's intention, then John was wrong. But if, as seems likely, he never had this intention, the mistake is the interpreter's.

Because it is part of the cultural heritage, the Apocalypse gives expression to the hopes and fears of many people who do not profess the Christian religion. Its influence extends across nations and continents. It has appealed to men and women in many ages and countries, with varied cultural and religious backgrounds. The experience of persecution and the possession of a poetic imagination establish bonds with the author that do not depend on Christian faith. The Apocalypse, however, is a Christian book. It is widely known because it is part of the Christian Bible; and Christian interpreters share with the author the bond of faith in Christ.

Interpreters of the Apocalypse approach it with standards of judgment. They derive those standards from many sources, from their own reason, tradition, and sense of what is right and fitting. If they are professing Christians, the Apocalypse is part of the tradition to which they are indebted. As they study the Apocalypse, their standards may be modified. But inevitably they have to exercise judgment about the appropriate way to make use of the book's prophecies and visions. And, since Christianity is a religion of the Spirit, they pray that the Spirit may guide them in their decisions.

The Apocalypse has always been a mysterious work. With the passage of time scholars have acquired additional knowledge about its symbolism and the world in which its author lived. Yet these researchers have not clarified all its uncertainties, and the mystery still remains.

Mystery involves ambiguity, and ambiguity has its dangers. It is easy to use the book as a storehouse of ammunition to be used against political, religious, or personal enemies. In violent hands the Apocalypse is a dangerous document that can lead to tragedy. But underlying the book's lack of clarity is a challenge. Since there are many possible fulfillments of the prophecies of beasts, the Apocalypse invites us to consider which individuals or institutions function as the beast for us and claim from us the devotion and allegiance that is fittingly given only to God. A purely polemical use of the Apocalypse is destructive. A use of it for self-examination is creative.

The Apocalypse is ambiguous in its presentation of good news. We can understand a millennium and a New Jerusalem in many ways. The possibility of more than one meaning challenges us to consider whether an ideal state of affairs can be realized now or must await us in the future. If it is even in a small measure present now, it is evidence of God's grace in action. If it can be a reality in the future, the promise is nurture for hope.

In the setting of worship, the mysteriousness of the Apocalypse is entirely appropriate. The book evokes a sense of the transcendence of God. The strangeness of its symbols conveys the notion of a realm that is beyond human understanding. For centuries its pictures of heaven have provided material for praise and adoration. Protestants and Catholics, revivalists and visionaries, adherents of both high and low church traditions, slaves and free men and women, social activists and mystics have chosen the same passages from the Apocalypse for use in worship. At this level the book has a unifying effect.

Christianity does not stand or fall by the interpretation of the Apocalypse, for the essence of the Christian message is contained in the Gospels, the Acts, and the Epistles. But the Apocalypse occupies a fitting place at the end of the Bible. It affirms God's sovereignty and the ultimate fulfillment of God's purpose. It offers strong support to individuals in maintaining their faith. In poetical power, it exceeds all other New Testament writings. It is a book for the Christian, the church, and the world. To all men and women, whether they profess or reject its author's faith, it offers its treasure of poetical images and mythical pictures. And to those who share that faith, though they do not hold it in precisely the same form as its author, it gives assurance of the victory of God and the triumph of the Lamb.

NOTES

2. MILLENARIANISM IN THE EARLY CHURCH

1. The Epistle of Barnabas 15 (late 1st or early 2nd cent.) says that God will bring everything to an end 6,000 years after the creation, and that the subsequent condition will correspond to the seventh day, when God rested from the creation. But it is not clear that Barnabas expects an earthly millennium. See Pierre Prigent, *L'Épître de Barnabé* SC 172: 185.

2. Eusebius *Historia Ecclesiastica* 3.39.

3. According to Jerome *De viris illustribus* 61 (PL 23:707), and Andreas, *Preface* (J. Schmid, *Studien zur Geschichte des griechischen Apokalypsetextes,* 1 Teil, *Der Apokalypse-Kommentar des Andreas von Kaisareia,* [Münchener theologische Studien. Munich: Karl Zink Verlag, 1955], 10), Hippolytus wrote on the Apocalypse. The fragments of his writing on the subject, however, need not be from a commentary on the book. See Pierre Prigent and Ralph Stehly, "Les fragments du De Apocalypsi d'Hippolyte," *TZ* 29.5 (1973): 313-33; 30.2 (1974): 82-85.

4. Some scholars date Commodianus in the mid fourth or sixth century, but his allusion to the Goths and his implication that Christianity was practiced in secret fit the earlier date. See Joseph Martin in Commodianus, *Carmina,* CCL 128:xi-xiii.

5. Eusebius *HE* 5.1.29-31.

6. Justin *Dialogus* 81. According to Justin 1 *Apologia* 51-52, Christ at his second coming will raise everyone from the dead. But in his Dialogue the millennium separates the resurrection of the righteous from that of the unrighteous.

7. Irenaeus *Adversus Haereses* 5.30.4; 5.33.1—35.2.

8. Lactantius *Divinae Institutiones* 7.24.

9. Irenaeus *Adv. Haer.* 5.35.2; Tertullian *Adversus Marcionem* 3.24.3-6; Victorinus *Commentarius in Apocalypsin* 21.1 (CSEL 49:146); Commodianus *Instructiones* 1.43-45 (CCL 128:37-39).

10. See Georg Kretschmar, *Die Offenbarung des Johannes: die Geschichte ihrer Auslegung im 1. Jahrtausend* (Stuttgart: Calwer Verlag, 1985), 70. W. M. Calder, "Philadelphia and Montanism," *BJRL* 7 (1922-23): 309-54, argued that Montanism had its origins in Philadelphia, one of the churches to which the Apocalypse was written. See also Colin J. Hemer, *The Letters to the Seven Churches of Asia in Their Local Setting* (Sheffield: JSOT Press, Department of Biblical Studies, University of Sheffield, 1986), 170-74.

11. Justin *Dial.* 28.

12. Tertullian *Adv. Marc.* 3.24.4.

13. Hippolytus *In Dan.* 4.; Lactantius *Inst.* 7.25.

14. Irenaeus *Adv. Haer.* 5.28.2-3; 5.29.2; 5.30.1-4; 5.26.1.

15. Hippolytus *De Christo et Antichristo* 15, 25, 49-50; Tertullian *De Resurrectione Mortuorum* 24.18; *Apologeticum* 32.1; *Scorpiace* 12.11.

16. Victorinus *In Apocalypsin* 13; 17 (CSEL 49:118, 120).

17. Lactantius *Inst.* 7.15-17; Commodianus *Instr.* 1.41; *Carmen* 805-998 (CCL 128:33-34, 102-10).

18. Justin *Dial.* 80.

19. Victorinus *In Apocalypsin* 4.4; 5.1 (CSEL 49:50, 60).

20. Irenaeus *Adv. Haer.* 11.8. Victorinus *In Apocalypsin* 4.4 (CSEL 49:50, 52, 54) gives the same interpretation.

21. Victorinus *In Apocalypsin* 1.7 (CSEL 49:26, 28).

22. Ibid., 12.1-2 (CSEL 49:104, 106); see also Methodius *Symposium* 8.4.

23. Hippolytus, "Kapiteln gegen Gaius," fragment 6 (GCS, Hippolytus 2:245); *De Chr. et Antichr.* 43; Tertullian *De Anima* 50.5; Victorinus *In Apocalypsin* 11:3 (CSEL 49:98).

24. Tertullian *De Res. Mort.* 27.1; Victorinus *In Apocalypsin* 7; 12:4; 20:1 (CSEL 49:82, 112, 140); Methodius *Symp.* 1.5.

25. In his homily on Exodus 1, Origen identifies the 144,000 with the whole church, but in his commentary on John 1 he describes them as the first fruits of Jewish and Gentile converts. Scholia written by Origen or his school identify them with the whole church. See Constantin Diobouniotis and Adolf Harnack, eds., *Der Scholien-Kommentar des Origenes zur Apokalypse Johannis* (TU 38.3 [1911]: 38), Scholion 32.

26. Victorinus *In Apocalypsin* 6.1-3 (CSEL 49:68, 70, 72).

27. Ibid., 8.2; 21.1 (CSEL 49:84, 86, 146).

28. Ibid., 8.2 (CSEL 49:86).

29. Lactantius *Inst.* 7.16, 18-24.

30. Eusebius, *HE* 3.28.2; Gerhard Maier, *Die Johannesoffenbarung und die Kirche* (Tübingen: J. C. B. Mohr [Paul Siebeck], 1981), 82-83. Fragments of Hippolytus, cited by Dionysius bar Salibi, *In Apocalypsim Ioannis,* CSCO 60, give evidence of the views of Gaius. The Alogoi (or Alogi) were said to deny the doctrine of the Word (Logos) in John's Gospel. See Epiphanius *Adversus Haereses* 51.3 (PG 41:891).

31. Eusebius *HE* 7.25. Dionysius was answering the Chiliast Nepos, a bishop in Egypt.

32. Ibid., 7.25.5.

33. Origen *De Principiis* 2.11.2-3.

34. Origen *In Matt.* PG 13:1673-74.

35. The Gnostic *Apocalypse of Paul,* probably a second-century Valentinian work, may include a veiled criticism of the book of Revelation. Valentinians exalted Paul above the twelve apostles; and while in Revelation 21 the twelve are foundation stones for the New Jerusalem, in the *Apocalypse of Paul,* Paul inhabits a higher region of heaven than do the twelve. See James M. Robinson, ed., *The Nag Hammadi Library* (San Francisco: Harper & Row, 1981), 241.

3. THE MILLENNIUM AS THE PERIOD OF THE CHURCH

1. Eusebius *HE* 1.28; 7.25; 3.25.

2. Wilhelm Bousset, *Die Offenbarung Johannis,* 2nd ed. (Göttingen: Vandenhoeck & Ruprecht, 1906), 26.

3. Cyril of Jerusalem *Catechesis* 4.36 (PG 33:500-1).

4. Bousset, *Offenbarung*, 30.

5. Epiphanius *Adv. Haer.* 77:36 (PG 42:696).

6. Quintus Julius Hilarianus *Chronologia, sive Libellus de Mundi Duratione* 16-19 (PL 13:1104-6).

7. Eusebius *Demonstratio Evangelica* 15, fr.

8. Eusebius *HE* 10.2,4; *De Vita Constantini* 3:33.

9. The name is spelled Ticonius, Tichonius, Tychonius as well as Tyconius. According to Gennadius *De Scriptoribus Ecclesiasticis* 3.18 (PL 58:1072), he lived during the reign of Theodosius in the latter half of the fourth century.

10. Tyconius, *Liber Regularum* 6 (F. C. Burkitt, *The Rules of Tyconius* [Texts and Studies 3.1 (Cambridge: University Press, 1894)]: 66-70), describes the rule of recapitulation as a principle whereby words of the Old Testament can have two fulfillments, one under the Jewish and the other under the Christian dispensation. According to Augustine's statement of the principle (*De Doctrina Christiana* 3:122-23), however, events need not be narrated in the order in which they occur.

11. Maier, *Johannesoffenbarung*, 108-29, discusses recent literature on Tyconius.

12. Tyconius *Liber* 5 (Burkitt, 61). Beatus, *In Apocalipsin Libri Duodecim* 5.12.6 (ed. Henry A. Sanders [Rome: American Academy in Rome, 1930], 450), who may be reproducing Tyconius's views, says that there are 350 years between the passion and the time of the Antichrist. Paula Fredriksen Landes, however, in "Tyconius and the End of the World," *REAug* 18.1-2 (1982): 59-75, argues that Tyconius did not understand the 350 years literally.

13. Gennadius *De Script. Eccl.* 18 (PL 58:1071-72).

14. Beatus *In Apocalipsin* 9.3 (Sanders, 574). Donatists regarded themselves as a martyr church, and Tyconius probably had them in mind when he referred to persecution in Africa (ibid., 2.6.82; 4.1.41; Sanders, 243, 341-42).

15. According to Bede, *Explanatio Apocalypsis* 1.1 (PL 93:132-34), Tyconius explained the Apocalypse correctly, except in his defense of the Donatists and his condemnation of their persecution by Rome. Primasius (*Commentarius in Apocalypsin*, Prologue, CCL 92:1-2) was more severe than Bede and accused Tyconius of mocking the church.

16. Augustine *Sermones* 259. Cf. *De Civitate Dei* 20.7.

17. Augustine *Civ. Dei* 20.6.

18. Ibid., 20.7-8.

19. Ibid., 18.53.

20. Ibid., 20.17, 19.

21. Ibid., 14.28–18.46.

22. Ibid., 8.24; 13.16; 15.1, 7; 20.9.

23. Ibid., 18.2-26; 20.8, 13.

24. Ibid., 20.11.

25. Ibid., 20:11, 30; 21:2, 10, 26.

26. Ibid., 20.16-17; 22.30.

27. Victorinus *In Apocalypsin* 20:2 (CSEL 49:145-47).

28. Jerome *In Dan.* 2 (on 7:4-8) (CCL 8:38-44).

29. See Kretschmar, *Offenbarung*, 112-13. Caesarius is listed under Augustine, *Expositio in Apocalypsim*, PL 35:2415-52.

30. Bede's divisions are: (1) 1–3; (2) 4:1–8:1; (3) 8:2–11:19; (4) 12–14; (5) 15–16; (6) 17:1–19:5; (7) 19:6–22:21 (*Explanatio*, Epistola ad Eusebium [PL 93:129-31]).

31. Alcuin *Commentarii in Apocalypsin* PL 100:1085-1156.

32. Haimo *Expositio in Apocalypsin* PL 117:937-1220.

33. *Glossa Ordinaria* PL 114:709-52. For a long time assumed to be the work of Walafrid Strabo (c.808–49), abbot of Reichenau, the *Glossa* may be based on the commentary by Anselm of Laon (d.1117).

34. Bruno of Segni *Expositio in Apocalypsim* PL 165:603-736; Martin of Leon *Expositio Libri Apocalypsis* PL 209:299-420.

35. See, for example, Cassiodorus *Complexiones* 3 (PL 70:1405); Bede *Explanatio* 1.1 (PL 93:135).

36. Apringius de Béja, *Son commentaire de l'Apocalypse*, ed. Marius Férotin (Paris: Bibliothèque patriologique, 1900), 7; Epiphanius *Adv. Haer.* 51 (PG 41:909).

37. Primasius *In Apocalypsin* 3:9; 4:13, 17 (CCL 92:152-56, 193-94, 197-98, 237-39). Cassiodorus, *Complexiones* 25 (PL 70:1414), however, points out that some interpreters identify the seven heads of the beast in Rev. 17 with Rome, but does not commit himself to that viewpoint.

38. Primasius *In Apocalypsin* 4:14 (CCL 92:209-14); Bede *Explanatio* 2.14 (PL 93:173-74). See also Augustine *De Virginitate* 12, 14, 26-29.

39. Primasius *In Apocalypsin* 1:1, 4; 2:7; 3.12 (CCL 92:9, 48, 108-9, 179); cf. Bede *Explanatio* 1.1; 2.12 (PL 93:134, 165). Bede, *Explanatio* 1.7 (PL 93:152), says that the countless multitude are those who will overcome the final persecution.

40. Primasius *In Apocalypsin* 3:11 (CCL 92:166); see also Bede *Explanatio* 2:11 (PL 93:162).

41. Primasius *In Apocalypsin* 2:6 (CCL 92:94); Bede *Explanatio* 1.6 (PL 93:146).

42. Primasius, *In Apocalypsin* 2:7 (CCL 92:105), lists them as Assyrians, Medes, Persians, and Romans; Bede *Explanatio* 1.7 (PL 93:149), says they are Assyrians, Persians, Greeks, and Romans.

43. Primasius *In Apocalypsin* 3:9 (CCL 92:145); Bede *Explanatio* 2:9 (PL 93:157-58).

44. Anselm of Havelberg *Dialogi* 1.7-13 (PL 188:1149-60); Richard of St. Victor *In Apocalypsim Joannis* 7.10 (PL 196:887). In Richard's opinion, the seal visions refer to the early church's preaching; persecution from Nero's time to the accession of Constantine; preaching against heretics from Constantine's time onward; hypocrites; the cry of the martyrs under the altar; persecution in the time of Antichrist; and the end of the world. He divides the periods of the trumpet and bowl visions in a slightly different way: Richard *In Apocalypsim* 2.2, 5; 3.2, 4; 5.3-9 (PL 196: 760-63, 778-81; 823-38). See Walter Kamlah, *Apokalypse und Geschichtstheologie* (Berlin: Verlag Dr. Emil Ebering, 1935), 41-53.

45. Primasius *In Apocalypsin* 3.9 (CCL 92:145, 150, 154-56); Ambrosius Autpertus *Expositio* CCM 28:350-51); Bede, *Explanatio*, 1.6 (PL 93:147).

46. Quodvultdeus *Liber Promissionum*, "Dimidium Temporis," 13 (22) (CCL 60:207).

47. Kamlah, *Apokalypse*, 15; Kretschmar, *Offenbarung*, 137.

48. The periods are the times of: (1) the elect from the beginning until the flood; (2) patriarchs and other righteous people until the giving of the law; (3) the people under the law; (4) prophets; (5) apostles and believing Jews; (6) believing Gentiles; and (7) the elect in the last days. Christ's face suggests an eighth group: the church after the future resurrection. Berengaud, *Expositio super Septem Visiones Libri Apocalypsis*, PL 17:850-52.

49. According to Berengaud, the first four seal visions correspond to the first four divisions already mentioned, but the last three visions depart from his previous scheme. The fifth depicts martyrs under the new covenant, and the sixth refers to the rejection of the Jews and the call of the Gentiles. The seventh vision does not follow in chronological sequence but alludes to the nativity of Christ. The trumpet visions signify the periods of (1) the patriarchs, (2) the giving of the law, (3) the prophets, (4) Christ and his apostles, (5) the defenders of

the faith against heresy, (6) the martyrs, and (7) holy preachers in the last days. Ibid., PL 17:895, 905, 915, 920-21, 923, 930, 934-37, 943, 956.

50. Ibid., PL 17:985-95. Berengaud suggests that the vision of the woman, the dragon, and the child (Rev. 12) may refer to Herod's attempt to kill the infant Jesus (ibid., 960), but he admits that it may refer to the church, the devil, and baptized Christians. He explains Revelation 17 and 18 as a prediction of the destruction of Rome by Goths, Vandals, and others (ibid., 995-1001) but recognizes that the harlot may also refer to the city of the devil in a general sense.

51. Rupert of Deutz (Rupers Abbas Tuitensis) *Commentaria in Apocalypsin* 5, 6 (PL 169:969-1004, 1035-40).

52. Primasius *In Apocalypsin* 3.8, 11; 4.16 (CCL 92:100-103, 138-41, 174, 234).

53. See Henri Stierlin, *Le livre de feu; l'Apocalypse et l'art mozarabe* (Geneva: La bibliothèque des arts, Paris, 1978), 83-102, argues that Beatus wanted to encourage Spanish Christians in their resistance to Muslim enemies.

54. Andreas *Apokalypse*, 216-21; Arethas *Commentarius in Apocalypsin* PG 106:749.

55. Oecumenius *The Complete Commentary of Oecumenius on the Apocalypse Now Printed for the First Time from Manuscripts at Messina, Rome, Salonika and Athos*, ed. with notes by H. C. Hoskier (Ann Arbor: University of Michigan, 1928), 215-21. Oecumenius's commentary disappeared from view for many centuries and did not appear in print until Hoskier's edition.

56. Dionysius Bar Salibi *In Apocalypsim Ioannis*, CSCO 60:19-22.

57. Shawqi N. Talia, "Bûlus al-Bûsi's Arabic Commentary on the Apocalypse of St. John: An English Translation and Commentary," Ph.D. dissertation, The Catholic University of America (Ann Arbor: University Microfilms International, 1987), 224-25.

58. Oecumenius *Apocalypse*, 93, 132, 181; Andreas, *Apokalypse*, 65.

59. Oecumenius *Apocalypse*, 82-103, 135-48.

60. Ibid., 183-89. Presumably Oecumenius assumed that the vision was seen from the perspective of Valerian's reign, two centuries after the Apocalypse was written.

61. They are the times of the apostles; martyrs; famine; persecution, especially under the emperor Maximin; Christian martyrs (who may also include Hebrew prophets); Antichrist; and the end of the earthly city. See Andreas, *Apokalypse*, 59-73, 86.

62. Ibid., 180-89. The kings are Ninus of Assyria, Arbacus of Media, Nebuchadnezzar of Babylonia, Cyrus of Persia, Alexander of Greece and Macedon, Romulus of old Rome, and Constantine of New Rome. Andreas agrees with Oecumenius that the beast of Revelation 17 is the devil.

63. Andreas *Apokalypse*, 223; Arethas *In Apocalypsin*, PG 106:672.

64. *Apocalypse of Daniel*, ed. and trans. G. T. Zervos, in *The Old Testament Pseudepigrapha*, ed. James H. Charlesworth, 2 vols. (Garden City, N.Y.: Doubleday, 1983), 1:757-58, 764-66 (3:13; 6:2, 10).

65. Quintus Julius Hilarianus *Chronologia* 16-19 (PL 13:1104-6).

66. Quodvultdeus *Liber Promissionum*, "Dimidium" 4 (6) (CCL 60:193), compares the time between Christ's first advent and the loosing of the devil with the 490 years of Daniel 12. He may therefore have expected the millennium to end in 490.

67. Beatus *In Apocalipsin* 4.5.16 (Sanders, 368).

68. Abbo *Apologeticus*, PL 139:471-72.

69. Sulpicius Severus *Dialogi* 1 (2.14) (CSEL 1:147); Victorinus *In Apocalypsin* 13 and 17.1-2 (CSEL 39:116, 118, 120).

70. Primasius *In Apocalypsin* 3:11 (CCL 92:169); Bernard McGinn, *Visions of the End: Apocalyptic Traditions in the Middle Ages* (New York: Columbia University Press, 1979), 84-85; Adso Dervensis *De Ortu et Tempore Antichristi* CCM 45:22-23.

71. Paul J. Alexander, *The Byzantine Apocalyptic Tradition* (Berkeley: University of California Press, 1985), 185-92.

72. See Richard of St. Victor *In Apocalypsin* 7:10 (PL 196:885).

73. Primasius *In Apocalypsin* 1:4 (CCL 92:48); Beatus *In Apocalipsin* 3:2.19-20 (Sanders, 270). Andreas *Apokalypse*, 49, recognized this explanation as a possibility.

74. Andreas *Apokalypse*, 51-52.

75. Primasius *In Apocalypsin* 1.4 (CCL 92:53). Primasius says that on this point he is in agreement with Augustine.

76. Jerome's revision of Victorinus *In Apocalypsin* 4.4 (CSEL 49:51, 53); Ambrosius Autpertus *Expositio* 4.6b (CCM 27:220-22); Beatus *In Apocalipsin* 3.3.1-16 (Sanders, 278-81).

77. Oecumenius, *Apocalypse*, 73.

78. See, for example, Quodvultdeus *Liber Promissionum*, "Dimidium" 13-16 (22-25) (CCL 60:206-209); Andreas *Apokalypse*, 113-18; Arethas *In Apocalypsin* PG 106:648-49; Berengaud, *Expositio*, PL 17:868.

79. See Francesco Lo Bue, ed., *The Turin Fragments of Tyconius' Commentary on Revelation* (Cambridge, Eng.: Cambridge University Press, 1963), 143.

80. Primasius *In Apocalypsin* 3.11 (CCL 92:167-68); Bede *Explanatio* 2.11 (PL 93:162-64). Bede also recognizes the possibility that the witnesses are Elijah and Enoch.

81. Rupert of Deutz *In Apocalypsim* 6:11 (PL 169:1022). Primasius *In Apocalypsin* 3.11 (CCL 92:166), explained them as martyrs by disposition and martyrs in practice.

4. THE APOCALYPSE AS A CHART OF HISTORY

1. See Bernard McGinn, *The Calabrian Abbot: Joachim of Fiore in the History of Western Thought* (New York: Macmillan, 1985), 26-29.

2. Joachim of Fiore, *Expositio in Apocalypsim* (Venice, 1527: reprinted Frankfurt am Main: Minerva, 1964), f. 39v.

3. Rupert of Deutz, *De Trinitate*, Prologus (PL 167:198-99), gave a different account of three ages: (1) that of the Father, from the creation to the fall of Adam; (2) that of the Son, from the fall to Christ's death; (3) that of the Spirit, from Christ's resurrection to the general resurrection.

4. Joachim, *Expositio*, ff. 5r-v.

5. Ibid., f. 211r.

6. Joachim, *Liber Concordiae Novi ac Veteris Testamenti* (Venice, 1519; reprinted Frankfurt am Main: Minerva, 1964), f. 56r; Marjorie Reeves, *The Influence of Prophecy in the Later Middle Ages: A Study in Joachimism* (Oxford: Clarendon Press, 1969), 48-49.

7. Joachim, *Expositio*, ff. 6r-9v. The periods in the first age were: (1) from Jacob to Moses and Joshua; (2) from Moses and Joshua to Samuel and David; (3) from Samuel and David to Elijah and Elisha; (4) from Elijah and Elisha to Isaiah and Hezekiah; (5) from Isaiah and Hezekiah to the exile; (6) from the end of the exile to Esther and Malachi; and (7) from Malachi to Zechariah, the father of John the Baptist. The periods of the second age are: (1) from Zechariah, the Baptist's father, or from Christ's resurrection to the death of John, the son of Zebedee; (2) from the death of John to Constantine; (3) from Constantine to Justinian; (4) from Justinian to Charlemagne; (5) from Charlemagne to Joachim's own day; (6) beginning in Joachim's day and including the destruction of the Holy Roman Empire, described as New Babylon; (7) the sabbath rest, which leads into the third age.

8. Ibid., f. 10r. See also f. 196v.

9. Ibid., f. 168r.

10. Ibid., f. 120v.

11. Ibid, ff. 106r, 146r, 148v.

12. Alexander Minorita, *Expositio in Apocalypsim,* ed. Alois Wachtel, Monumenta Germaniae Historica. Quellen zur Geistesgeschichte des Mittelalters, 1 (Weimar: Hermann Böhlaus Nachfolger, 1955,) 22-49.

13. The four horsemen were the emperors Caligula, Nero, Titus, and Domitian. The fifth seal vision depicts martyrs under Trajan's reign, and the sixth alludes to persecutions from Hadrian's time until Constantine became emperor (ibid., 89-110). Revelation 7 describes the reign of Constantine, who is "the angel ascending from the rising of the sun," and Revelation 8–9 takes the story to 500 (ibid., 110-53).

14. Ibid., 153-320. The two witnesses are Pope Silverius and Patriarch Menas of Constantinople (ibid. 230).

15. Ibid., 366-510.

16. Ibid., 234, 273-92, 407, 427-28.

17. Ibid., 112, 153, 157, 162, 197, 299, 310, 384-85, 408-09.

18. Ibid., 411-13, 430-33, 450-54, 509.

19. Ibid., 454, 469.

20. Henri de Lubac, *Exégèse médiévale, les quatre sens de l'Écriture,* 2 parts in 4 vols. (Paris: Aubier, 1959–64), 2.2: 344-58; Alois Wachtel, "Einleitung," in Alexander, *Expositio,* xli-xliv; Gordon Leff, *Heresy in the Later Middle Ages,* 2 vols. (Manchester: Manchester University Press, 1967), 2:538; Gustav Adolf Benrath, *Wyclifs Bibelkommentar* (Berlin: Walter de Gruyter, 1966), 300-309.

21. Lubac, *Exégèse,* 2.2:363-67.

22. Martin Luther, *Works,* 35 (Philadelphia: Muhlenberg Press, 1960): 300, 409.

23. Heinrich Bullinger, *A Hundred Sermons upon the Apocalypse* (London: Iohn Day, 1561), 593-94, 605-6; Arthur Dent, *The Ruin of Rome, or An Exposition upon the Whole Revelation* (London: Printed for T. Kelly, 1850), 274. For Junius see *Geneva Bible,* 1602 edition.

24. John Foxe, *Actes and Monuments* (1583), 86. The title of Foxe's 1563 edition gives the earlier date. See Katharine R. Firth, *The Apocalyptic Tradition in Reformation Britain 1530–1645* (Oxford: Oxford University Press, 1979) 82, 92.

25. John Napier (Napeir), *A Plaine Discovery, of the Whole Revelation of S. Iohn* (Edinburgh: Printed by Andrew Hart, 1611), 6-8, 46-65, 294.

26. Thomas Brightman, *Apocalypsis Apocalypseos: A Revelation of the Revelation* (Amsterdam, 1615).

27. Alexander, *Expositio,* 95-100, 103, 241.

28. Luther, *Works,* 35:401-2.

29. Ubertino da Casali, *Arbor Vitae Crucifixae Jesus* (Venetiis: Andrea de Bonettis, 1485; reprint, Turin: Bottega d'Erasmo, 1961), 5.11, f. 2376v; Reeves, *Prophecy,* 234-38, 443; McGinn, *Visions,* 155-57.

30. Reeves, *Prophecy,* 60-62, 187-90.

31. Ibid., 194-201; Leff, *Heresy,* 2:100-39; J. J. Ignaz von Döllinger, *Beiträge zur Sektengeschichte des Mittelalters,* 2 vols. (Munich: Beck, 1890; reprint, New York: Burt Franklin, 1960), 2:559-60, 571-3; McGinn, *Visions,* 208-11.

32. Ubertino, *Arbor,* 5.1, ff. 204ab, 205r, 206v.

33. Ibid., 5,8, ff. 230rb-233ra; McGinn, *Visions,* 212-14; Reeves, *Prophecy,* 207-09.

34. Leff, *Heresy,* 1:197-99; Bernard Gui on Heresies, in *Heresies of the High Middle Ages,* Selected Sources translated and annotated by Walter L. Wakefield and Austin P. Evans (New York and London: Columbia University Press, 1969), 422-25.

35. McGinn, *Visions,* 169-70, 173-77.

36. Le Roy Edward Froom, *The Prophetic Faith of Our Fathers,* 4 vols. (Washington, D.C.: Review and Herald, 1948–50) 1:871-78.

37. Dante, *Paradiso* 12.139-41; *Inferno* 19.31-84, 106-11. For Jacopone da Todi, see McGinn, *Visions,* 206-7, 217-18.

38. Leff, *Heresy,* 2:610-19; Norman Cohn, *The Pursuit of the Millennium* (London: Granada, 1970), 206-7; John Hus, *The Letters of John Hus,* eds. Herbert B. Workman and R. Martin Pope (London: Hodder and Stoughton, 1904), 258, 270-71 (Letters 74, 80).

39. Leff, *Heresy,* 2:52-59, 578-89; Foxe, *Actes,* 86.

40. John Wycliffe, *Opera Minora* (London: C. K. Prad, 1903), 87, 227; *Opus evangelicum* (London: Trübner & Co., 1896), 3:106-8, 134-38, 181.

41. Leff, *Heresy,* 2:599-603; K. B. McFarlane, *John Wycliffe and the Beginnings of English Nonconformity* (New York: Macmillan, 1953), 160-82.

42. Leff, *Heresy,* 2:498.

43. Luther, *Works,* 36 (Philadelphia: Muhlenberg Press, 1959): 72.

44. Firth, *Apocalyptic Tradition,* 115-16. Junius's comments are in *The Geneva Bible: The Annotated New Testament 1602 Edition, with Introductory Essays,* ed. Gerald T. Sheppard, The Pilgrim Classic Commentaries (New York: The Pilgrim Press, 1989). Earlier editions contained notes on the Apocalypse by Bale and Bullinger.

45. James I of England (James VI of Scotland), *A Paraphrase Upon the Revelation of the Apostle S. Iohn,* in *The Workes of the Most High and Mighty Prince, Iames* (London: Printed by Robert Barker and Iohn Bill, 1616), 5, 39-43, 49-60, 66.

46. John Bale, *The Image of bothe churches* (1543?), n.p.

47. Reeves, *Prophecy,* 494-99; G. Brocardo, *The Revelation of St. John . . . Englished by J. Sanford* (London, 1582), ff. 7r, 40r, 92v, 133r.

48. Michael Servetus, *Christianismi Restitutio* (Vienna, 1553; reprint, Frankfurt am Main: Minerva, 1966), 398.

49. Ibid., 409-10; see also Roland H. Bainton, *Hunted Heretic* (Boston: The Beacon Press, 1953), 145-47.

50. Innocent III *Opera Omnia* PL 216:818.

51. Luther, "Preface to the Revelation of St. John [II]," *Works* 35:404-5, 409.

52. McGinn, *Visions,* 173-79; Luther, "Preface to the Revelation of St. John [II]," *Works,* 35:405-6.

53. Reeves, *Prophecy,* 276-78, 467-70.

54. Francisco Ribera, *In sacram Beati Ioannis Apostoli & Evangelistae Apocalypsin Commentarij* (Lugduni: Ex Officina Iuntarum, 1593), 35, 184-208, 284-301, 303, 374-78, 385.

55. Ibid., 498-548.

56. Robert Bellarmine, *Opera Omnia,* 12 vols. (Paris, 1870–74; reprint, Frankfurt: Minerva, 1965), 2:7-33.

57. See Blasius Viegas, *Commentarii Exegetici in Apocalypsim Ioannis Apostoli* (Eborae: Apud Emmanuelem de Lyra, 1601); Cornelius à Lapide, *Commentarius in Apocalypsin S. Ioannis* (Antwerpiae: Apud Henricum & Cornelium Verdussen, 1717); Thomas Malvenda, *De Antichristo* (Lugduni: A Sumptibus Societatis Bibliopolarum, 1647).

58. John Hentennius, in PG 106:485-94.

59. Luis de Alcazar, *Vestigatio Arcani Sensus in Apocalypsi* (Antwerpiae: Apud Ioannem Keerbegium, 1614), 12-15, 80, 85-120.

60. Hugo Grotius, *Opera Theologica* (Amsterdam: Heredes Joannis Blaev, 1679), 2.2:953,

201. Henry Hammond, *A Paraphrase and Annotations upon all the Books of the New Testament* (Oxford: The University Press, 1845), 2:292; 4:576, 503.

61. L'Abbé Guillaume, "Histoire de Bossuet" in Jacques Bénigne Bossuet, *Oeuvres complètes*, 11 vols. (Lyons: Librarie Ecclésiastique de Briday, 1877), 1: "Histoire de Bossuet" 188.

62. Ibid., 1: "Écriture" 305-26.

63. Ibid., 1: "Écriture" 326-70.

64. Ibid., 1: "Écriture" 305-70.

65. Ibid., 1: "Écriture" 276.

66. Thomas Brightman, *Apocalypsis Apocalypseos*; David Pareus, *A Commentary upon the Divine Revelation of the Apostle and Evangelist John*, trans. Elias Arnold (Amsterdam: C. P., 1644).

5. THE REVIVAL OF MILLENARIANISM

1. Theodor Bibliander, *Ad Omnium Ordinum Reip[ublicae] Christianae Principes Viros, Populumque Christianum, Relatio Fidelis* (Basileae: Ex Officina J. Oporini, 1545), 22.

2. John Bale, *Image of Bothe Churches*, n.p., offered two accounts of the millennium: (1) as thousand years after the ascension; (2) (in his comments on the breaking of the seventh seal) as a thousand years after the fall of the papacy.

3. Leif Crane, *The Augsburg Confession: A Commentary*, trans. John H. Rasmussen (Minneapolis: Augsburg, 1987), 178.

4. Calvin *Institutes* 3.25.5; Peter Toon, "Introduction," in Peter Toon, ed., *Puritans, the Millennium and the Future of Israel: Puritan Eschatology 1600 to 1660* (Cambridge, Eng.: James Clarke & Co., 1970), 19.

5. Johann Heinrich Alsted, *Diatribe de Mille Annis Apocalypticis*, 2nd ed. (Francofurti: Sumptibus Conradi Eifridi, 1630), 28-38. Excerpts from Alsted's book and its English translation, William Burton, *The Beloved City* (London, 1643), are included in Beate Griesing, Jürgen Klein, and Johannes Kramer, *J. H. Alsted, Herborns calvinistische Theologie und Wissenschaft* (Frankfurt am Main: Verlag Peter Lang, 1988), 20-71.

6. Charles Webster, *The Great Instauration* (New York: Holmes & Meier, 1975), 25-27.

7. Maier, *Johannesoffenbarung*, 319-20.

8. Joseph Mede, *Works*, 2 vols. (London: Printed by James Flesher, for Richard Royston, 1664), 2:747-51.

9. Ibid., 2:744-47, 813-14.

10. Ibid., 2:521-36.

11. Ibid., 2:546, 592-93, 722-23.

12. Robert Maton, *Israel's Redemption* (London: Printed for Daniel Frere, 1642); Henry More, *Opera Omnia* 1 (*Opera Theologica*) (Hildesheim: Georg Olms Verlagsbuchhandlung, 1960), ed. Serge Hutin (reprint of *Opera Theologica* [Londinii: Impensis Gualteri Kettilby, 1674]) 17-47, 176-203.

13. Pierre Jurieu, *The Accomplishment of the Scripture Prophecies* (London, 1687); Froom, *Prophetic Faith*, 2:636-39.

14. Frank Manuel, *The Religion of Isaac Newton* (Oxford: Clarendon Press, 1974), 90, 98-101.

15. Isaac Newton, *Observations upon the Prophecies of Daniel and the Apocalypse of St. John in Two Parts* (London: Printed by J. Darby and T. Browne, 1733), 251.

16. Edward Evanson, *Reflections upon the State of Religion in Christendom* (Exeter: Printed and Sold by S. Woolmer; London: Sold by Charles Law, 1802), 113-14, 138, 160-62.

17. Brightman, *Apocalypsis*, 87-123.

18. Ibid., 123-65.

19. Ibid., 137-38.

20. Christopher Hill, *Antichrist in Seventeenth-Century England* (London: Oxford University Press, 1971), 70.

21. Ibid., 53-54, 107, 110.

22. Andrew Marvell *Ode to OC* 311-12; cf. 296-98.

23. Thomas Burnet, *The Sacred Theory of the Earth* (London: Centaur Press, 1965), 82, 146-47.

24. Ibid., 270-76, 288-93.

25. Ibid., 276-77.

26. Ibid., 302-3, 373-74.

27. Ibid., 376.

28. Ibid., 264.

29. Ibid., 271.

30. William Whiston, *An Essay on the Revelation of Saint John, So Far as Concerns the Past and Present Times* (Cambridge, Eng.: University Press, 1706), 270-71; *The Literal Accomplishment of Scripture Prophecies* (London: Printed for J. Senex, 1724), 86; *An Essay on the Revelation of Saint John, So Far as Concerns the Past and Present Times*, 2nd ed. (Printed for the author; and sold by John Whiston, 1744), 275, 281, 282.

31. William Whiston, *A New Theory of the Earth*, 5th ed. (London: Printed for John Whiston, 1737), 182-83, 285-91, 372-75, 442-56.

32. John Locke, *Works*, 3rd ed. (London: Printed for Arthur Bettesworth et al.: 1727), 3:556.

33. John Wesley, *Works*, 13 vols. (London: Wesleyan Conference Office, 1872), 3:385.

34. Joseph Priestley, *Theological and Miscellaneous Works*, 25 vols. in 26 (London: Printed by G. Smallfield, 1817–32), 14:486-88; James Bicheno, *The Signs of the Times: in Three Parts. A New Edition, Corrected and Enlarged* (London: Printed by J. Adlard, 1808), iv, 64.

35. *The Gentleman's Magazine* (February 1756): 69.

36. John and Charles Wesley, *The Poetical Works*, 13 vols., ed. G. Osborn (London: Wesleyan-Methodist Conference Office, 1868–72), 6:46.

37. Froom, *Prophetic Faith*, 4:289-300.

38. Hal Lindsey, *The Late Great Planet Earth* (New York: Bantam Books, 1973), 52-53. For a critique of the Jehovah's Witnesses' views of the matter, see Carl Olof Jonsson and Wolfgang Herbst, *The Sign of the Last Days: When?* (Atlanta: Commentary Press, 1987), 46-87.

39. Alsted, *Diatribe*, 37; Mede, *Works*, 2:749.

40. John Cotton, *The Churches Resurrection* (London: Henry Overton, 1642), 20-21, in *The End of the World* (New York: AMS Press, 1982). Cotton predicted the end of the papacy in 1655, see ibid., 88-93.

41. *Annotations on all the Books of the Old and New Testaments*, vol. 2 (London: John Legatt, 1651); Thomas Goodwin, *Works*, 12 vols. (Edinburgh: James Nichol, 1866), 12:70, 74, 77, held similar views.

42. Philip Jacob Spener, *Pia Desideria*, trans. and ed. Theodore G. Tappert (Philadelphia: Fortress Press, 1964), 76-78; Maier, *Johannesoffenbarung*, 362-66.

43. Daniel Whitby, "A Treatise of the True Millennium," in *Paraphrase and Notes on the New Testament*, 2 vols. (London: Printed for Awnsham & John Churchill, 1703), 2:247-78.

44. Ibid., 2:268.

45. Ibid., 2:260.

46. Campegius Vitringa, *Anakrisis Apocalypseos* (Franeker: Franciscus Halma, 1705), 195, 218-21.

47. Moses Lowman, *A Paraphrase and Notes on the Revelation of St. John,* 2nd ed. (London: John Noon, 1745), xxxiii, 106-7, 20, 205-5. Lowman explained the prophecies as follows: seal visions, Domitian to Constantine; trumpet visions, Constantine to Charles Martel (732); the first five bowl visions, Martel to 1650. Lowman, contrary to Whitby, regards the New Jerusalem as a heavenly state that will follow the last judgment.

48. Ibid., xxvii.

49. John Guyse, *The Practical Expositor,* 2nd ed., 3 vols. (London: Printed for E. Dilly, 1761), vol. 3; Philip Doddridge, *The Family Expositor,* 6 vols. (London: Printed for C. Hitch and I. Hawes, etc., 1760-61), vol. 6; Thomas Scott, *The Holy Bible . . . with Explanatory Notes, practical Observations . . .* , 3 vols. (New York; Collins & Hannay, 1832), 3:964-66.

50. Jonathan Edwards, *Apocalyptic Writings,* ed. Stephen J. Stein, *The Works of Jonathan Edwards,* vol. 5 (New Haven and London: Yale University Press, 1977): 410. From *An Humble Attempt to Promote Explicit Agreement and Visible Union of God's People in Extraordinary Prayer,* first published in Boston in 1747.

51. Samuel Hopkins, *A Treatise on the Millennium* (Boston, 1793). See also 177-78.

52. See 178-81, 185-86.

53. Johann Albrecht Bengel, *Erklärte Offenbarung Johannis oder vielmehr Jesu Christi,* 2nd ed. (Stuttgart, 1773), 950-60; *Gnomon Novi Testamenti* (London: David Nutt, and Williams and Norgate, 1855), 810-11, 1123. Bengel argued that the seal visions refer to the years 97–98, the trumpet visions to the second to the tenth centuries, and the third woe (12:12) to the years 947–1836. The three and a half years are the years from 1058 until 1836, and Revelation 13–19 deals with that period (*Gnomon,* 1128-29).

54. John Wesley, *Explanatory Notes upon the New Testament* (London: Epworth Press, 1950), 932.

55. John Wesley, *Works,* 3:123.

56. Friedrich Lücke, *Versuch einer vollständigen Einleitung in die Offenbarung des Johannes,* 2nd ed. (Bonn: Eduard Weber, 1852), 1044; Maier, *Johannesoffenbarung,* 443-47; Klaus Vondung, *Die Apokalypse in Deutschland* (Munich: Deutscher Taschenbuch Verlag, 1988), 125-26.

57. See 67.

58. David Hartley, *Observations on Man, His Frame, His Duty, and His Expectations,* 2 vols. (London: J. Johnson, 1801), 2:380.

59. Ibid., 2:373-80.

60. Frederick Denison Maurice, *Lectures on the Apocalypse; or, Book of the Revelation of St. John the Divine* (Cambridge and London: Macmillan and Co., 1861), 384, 398, 390.

61. Ibid., 396.

62. Ibid., 391.

63. Ibid., 398.

64. S. R. Maitland, *An Enquiry into the Grounds on which the Prophetic Period of Daniel and St. John has been supposed to consist of 1260 Years* (London: Hatchard and Son, 1826). John Henry Newman (1801–1890), "The Antichrist," in *Essays Critical and Historical,* 4th ed., 2 vols. (London: Basil Montagu Pickering, 1877), 2:185, supported the refusal to identify the papacy with Antichrist.

65. John Nelson Darby, *The Collected Writings of J. N. Darby,* ed. William Kelly (Kingston on Thames: Stow Hill Bible and Tract Depot, 1962), 5 (prophetic vol. 2): 11-12, 21.

66. Ibid., 5:40-41; 11 (prophetic vol. 4): 595-97.

67. Ibid., 5:23-24, 36.

68. Ibid., 11:111-13.

69. Mede, *Works*, 2:949-51.

70. Froom, *Prophetic Faith*, 4:421-23.

71. *The Holy Bible Containing the Old and New Testaments: Authorized Version with a New System of Connected Topic References to all the Greater Themes of Scripture*, ed. C. I. Scofield (Oxford: Humphrey Milford, 1917), 1330. Scofield distinguished seven dispensations: (1) Innocency, from the creation until the fall; (2) Conscience, from the fall until the flood; (3) Human Government, from the flood, ending for the Jews with their exile and continuing for the Gentiles; (4) Promise, for the Jews only, beginning with Abraham; (5) Law, from the giving of the Law until Jesus' crucifixion; (6) Grace, when acceptance of Christ is the condition of salvation; (7) Kingdom, beginning with Christ's second advent, including the millennium and ending when he delivers the kingdom to the Father (notes on Gen. 1:28; 3:23; 8:20; 12:1; Exod. 19:8; John 1:17; Eph. 1:10).

72. Ibid., 1334, 1337, 1346-47 (notes on Rev. 4:1; 7:14; 18:2).

73. Ibid., 1348-52 (notes on 19:17, 20; 20:2, 5, 11, 12, 14).

74. John F. Walvoord, *The Revelation of Jesus Christ* (London: Marshall, Morgan & Scott, 1966).

75. John F. Walvoord and John E. Walvoord, *Armageddon: Oil and the Middle East Crisis* (Grand Rapids: Zondervan, 1974), 197.

76. Hal Lindsey, *There's a New World Coming: "A Prophetic Odyssey"* (New York: Bantam Books, 1973), 83-96.

77. Ibid., 111-33.

78. Ibid., 204-16.

79. Ibid., 167-83.

80. The first six letters allude to the periods of the apostles (33–100); persecutions (100–312); the church's compromise with the world (312–590); the church's corruption (590–1517); the reform of the church and its lapse into legalism (1517–1750); the church's missionary expansion (1750–1925). Ibid., 20-56.

81. Ibid., 64-65, 297-99. See also Lindsey, *Late Great Planet Earth*, 297-99.

82. Edgar C. Whisenant, *On Borrowed Time: The Bible Dates of the 70th Week of Daniel, Armageddon, the Millennium* (Nashville: World Bible Society, 1988), 4-25, 48-51. Whisenant predicted three raptures: (1) of all Christians, living and dead, between September 11 and 13, 1988 (Rev. 4:1-2); (2) of the two witnesses, Old Testament Jews, and Christian martyrs who died since the first rapture, on March 12, 1992 (Rev. 11:15-18); (3) of martyrs who become Christians during the tribulation, on September 25, 1995.

83. See Richard R. Reiter, Paul D. Feinberg, Gleason L. Archer, and Douglas J. Moo, *The Rapture: Pre-, Mid-, or Post-Tribulational?* (Grand Rapids: Zondervan, 1984). For post-tribulationism, see R. H. Gundry, *The Church and the Tribulation* (Grand Rapids: Zondervan, 1973) and George E. Ladd, *The Blessed Hope* (Grand Rapids: Eerdmans, 1956). For mid-tribulationism see J. Oliver Buswell, Jr., *A Systematic Theology of the Christian Religion*, 2 vols. (Grand Rapids: Zondervan, 1962), 2:389-90.

6. PROPHETS AND PROPHETIC MOVEMENTS

1. Reeves, *Prophecy*, 243-46; McGinn, *Visions*, 226-29.

2. William Harold May, "The Confession of Prous Boneta, Heretic and Heresiarch," in John H. Mundy, Richard W. Emery, and Benjamin N. Nelson, eds., *Essays in Medieval Life and*

Thought: Presented in Honor of Austin Patterson Evans (New York: Columbia University Press, 1955), 29-30; Reeves, *Prophecy,* 248.

3. Cohn, *Pursuit,* 142-44.

4. Reeves, *Prophecy,* 247; May, "Confession," 4.

5. Nelson H. Minnick, "Prophecy and the Fifth Lateran Council (1512–1517)," in Marjorie Reeves, ed., *Prophetic Rome in the High Renaissance Period* (Oxford: Clarendon Press, 1992), 74, 80.

6. Ibid., 85-86.

7. Cohn, *Pursuit,* 234-51.

8. Ibid., 254-55.

9. Reeves, *Prophecy,* 491-92; G. Williams, *The Radical Reformation* (Philadelphia: Westminster Press, 1962), 259-308.

10. Cohn, *Pursuit,* 256-61.

11. Ibid., 261-80.

12. Philadelphia was the church that demonstrated the greatest loyalty of the seven (Rev. 3:7-13).

13. Heinrich Corrodi, *Kritische Geschichte des Chiliasmus* (Frankfurt and Leipzig, 1781–83), 3.1:66-73.

14. Ibid., 3.2:50-52.

15. Ibid., 3.2:81-90.

16. Ibid., 3.2:70-71.

17. Christopher Hill, *Antichrist,* 115; *The World Turned Upside Down* (Harmondsworth: Penguin Books, 1975), 246; B. S. Capp, *The Fifth Monarchy Men: A Study in Seventeenth-century English Millenarianism* (Totowa, N.J.: Rowman and Littlefield, 1972), 43.

18. Hill, *World,* 316-17; *Antichrist,* 132-33; Cohn, *Pursuit,* 299-300.

19. Clarke Garrett, *Respectable Folly: Millenarians and the French Revolution in France and England* (Baltimore: The Johns Hopkins University Press, 1975), 21-23. These prophets may have been influenced by Jurieu's commentary on the Apocalypse.

20. Ibid., 25-26.

21. Ibid., 25, 77-96.

22. Ibid., 97-120.

23. J. F. C. Harrison, *The Second Coming: Popular Millenarianism, 1780-1850* (New Brunswick, N.J.: Rutgers University Press, 1979), 30-31, 33-38.

24. The usage was based on the Authorized Version of Genesis 49:10: "The sceptre shall not depart from Judah, nor a lawgiver from between his feet, until Shiloh come."

25. Garrett, *Respectable Folly,* 214.

26. Richard Brothers, *A Description of Jerusalem* (London: Printed for George Ribebau, Bookseller to the King of the Hebrews, 1801), 144.

27. Richard Brothers, *A Revealed Knowledge of the Prophecies and Times,* 2 vols. (London: 1794), 2:82.

28. Ibid., 1:39-45.

29. Richard Brothers, *Prophecy of All the Remarkable and Wonderful Events Which Will Come to Pass in the Present Year* (London, 1794), 2-7; Garrett, *Respectable Folly,* 195-96.

30. Ronald Matthews, *English Messiahs: Studies of English Religious Pretenders, 1656–1927* (London: Methuen & Co., 1936), 100; Garrett, *Respectable Folly,* 191-94.

31. Garrett, *Respectable Folly,* 195-96.

32. Richard Brothers, *A Letter to His Majesty . . .* (London, 1802), 21; Garrett, *Respectable Folly,* 213.

33. Clarke Garrett, *Spirit Possession and Popular Religion from the Camisards to the Shakers* (Baltimore and London: The Johns Hopkins University Press, 1987), 173.

34. *A Collection of Millennial Hymns, adapted to the Present Order of the Church* (Canterbury, N.H.: The United Society, 1847; reprint, New York: AMS Press, 1975), 72.

> From the eternal Father's throne,
> Our holy Mother Wisdom came,
> Her little ones to bless and own,
> And mark them with Jehovah's name.
> (No. 51)

35. *Testimony of Christ's Second Appearing Exemplified by the Principles and Practice of the True Church of Christ, . . .* 4th ed. (Albany, N.Y.: The United Society Called Shakers, 1856), 384, 400; Garrett, *Spirit Possession*, 215, 237-38.

36. *Millennial Hymns*, 36 (No. 22).

37. Garrett, *Respectable Folly*, 219; Matthews, *English Messiahs*, 49; Harrison, *Second Coming*, 86-92.

38. Harrison, *Second Coming*, 90-94.

39. Matthews, *English Messiahs*, 69.

40. Harrison, *Second Coming*, 96-99.

41. William Glover, *History of Ashton-under Lyne and the Surrounding District,* ed. John Andrew (Ashton-under-Lyne: J. Andrew and Co., 1884), 307, 314.

42. Matthews, *English Messiahs*, 129-59.

43. Ibid., 163-95.

44. Anne Taylor, *Visions of Harmony: A Study in Nineteenth-Century Millenarianism* (Oxford: Clarendon Press, 1987), 3-55; Don Blair, *The New Harmony Story* (New Harmony, Ind.: New Harmony Publications Committee, n.d.), 13-36.

45. See Richard O. Cowan, *Doctrine & Covenants: Our Modern Scripture,* rev. ed. (Provo, Utah: Brigham Young University Press, 1978), 92, 136-38, 154-55.

46. Froom, *Prophetic Faith*, 4:889-99.

47. Ibid., 4:956-63.

48. Ibid., 4:1098-1103.

49. *Seventh-day Adventists Believe . . . : A Biblical Exposition of 27 Fundamental Doctrines* (Washington, D.C.: Ministerial Association, General Conference of Seventh-day Adventists, 1988), 332-83.

50. See M. James Penton, *Apocalypse Delayed: The Story of Jehovah's Witnesses* (Toronto: University of Toronto Press, 1985), 71-72, 194-96.

51. Raymond Franz, *Crisis of Conscience* (Atlanta: Commentary Press, 1983), 172-222.

52. Elizabeth Clare Prophet, *The Great White Brotherhood in the Culture, History, and Religion of America: Teachings of the Ascended Masters Given to Elizabeth Clare Prophet* (Los Angeles: Summit University Press, 1978), 230, 236, 238, 246, 254-66, 344.

53. Ibid., 318.

54. Ibid., 295-99.

55. Ibid., 255.

56. See *Saint Germain on Prophecy: Coming World Changes, recorded by Elizabeth Clare Prophet* (Livingston, Mont.: Summit University Press, 1986), 2:57-68, 137-62, 179-84, 190; 4:92, 170.

57. This book goes to press soon after the devastating fire that killed nearly eighty people, including many children, in Koresh's compound. Evidence of Koresh's teaching has been

gleaned from newspaper and television reports. His full story remains to be told, and the circumstances of his encounter with federal agents are still under investigation. If, as seems likely, some of the deaths were suicides, the conduct of the Branch Davidians is reminiscent of the behavior of some fourth-century Donatists and seventeenth-century Russian Old Believers, as well as of the members of Jim Jones's community in Guyana in 1978. But neither the Apocalypse nor any other part of the Bible gives authorization for self-inflicted martyrdom.

58. See 'Abdu'l-Baha, *Some Unanswered Questions,* collected and translated by Laura Clifford Barnett, 4th ed. (Wilmette, Ill.: Bahá'i Publishing Trust, 1954), 53-71.

59. Ibid., 77-82. The Umayyad caliphs ruled over Damascus, Persia, Arabia, Egypt, Tunis, Morocco, Algeria, and Spain.

7. AUTHORITY, AUTHORSHIP, DATE, AND SOURCES

1. See 257, n. 17.

2. See 30.

3. Erasmus, *Opera Omnia,* 6 (Lugduni Batavorum: Petri Vabder, 1705; reprint, Hildesheim: Georg Olms, 1961): 1123-26.

4. Carlstadt (Andreas Bodenstein), *De canonicis scripturis libellus* (Wittenbergae: apud Ioannem Viridi Montanum, 1520), in Karl August Credner, *Zur Geschichte des Kanons* (Halle: Buchhandlung des Waisenhauses, 1847), 408. Henry H. Howorth, "The Origin and Authority of the Biblical Canon According to the Continental Reformers. I. Luther and Karlstadt," *JTS* 8 (1906-7): 349, thinks that Carlstadt's omission of Acts from his list was unintentional.

5. Ulrich Zwingli, *Sämmtliche Werke* 14 vols. (Zürich: Theologischer Verlag, 1982), 2 (*Corpus Reformatorum* 89):208-9.

6. Luther, *Works,* 35:399-408.

7. Matthew Tindal, *Christianity as Old as the Creation* (London, 1730; reprint, ed. Günter Gawlick, Stuttgart-Bad Cannstatt: Friedrich Frommann, 1967), 261-62.

8. Thomas Morgan, *The Moral Philosopher,* 3 vols. (London, 1738–40; reprint, ed. Günter Gawlick, Stuttgart-Bad Cannstatt: Friedrich Frommann, 1969), 1:361-79.

9. Henry St. John, Viscount Bolingbroke, *The Philosophical Works,* 5 vols. (London, 1754–1777; reprint, New York and London: Garland Publishing, 1977), 2:347-54.

10. Ibid., 3:35.

11. Ibid., 2:337.

12. Ibid., 3:100.

13. Ibid., 3:30.

14. F. M. de Voltaire, *Oeuvres complètes,* 52 vols. (Paris: Garnier Frères, 1878–85), 17:287, 289; 20:121.

15. Denis Diderot and Jean le Rond d'Alembert, *L'Encyclopédie ou dictionnaire raisonné des sciences, des arts, et des métiers* (Paris: Briasson et al., 1751), 1:527-28; compact edition (Elmsford, N.Y.: Pergamon Press), 1:156.

16. Thomas Paine, *The Age of Reason* (Worcester, Mass., 1794), 22.

17. Johann Salomo Semler, *Abhandlung von freier Untersuchung des Canon* (Halle: Hemmerde, 1771–75), 1:123.

18. Johann David Michaelis, *Introduction to the New Testament,* trans. Herbert Marsh, 2nd ed., 4 vols. in 6 (London: F. and C. Rivington, 1802), 4:511, 517-18, 528.

19. Ibid., 4:533, 534.

20. Corrodi, *Geschichte des Chiliasmus,* 1:vi.

21. Ibid., 2:320-21.

22. Ibid., 3:27.

23. Lücke, *Versuch*, 915-16, 922-23.

24. Friedrich Bleek, *Lectures on the Apocalypse*, ed. Th. Hossbach, ET, ed. Samuel Davidson (London and Edinburgh: Williams and Norgate), 140.

25. Ernest Renan, *Antichrist*, trans. and ed. Joseph Henry Allen (Boston: Roberts Brothers, 1897), 366.

26. Friedrich Schleiermacher, *The Christian Faith*, ET ed. H. R. Mackintosh and J. S. Stewart (Edinburgh: T. & T. Clark, 1928), 705, 722.

27. Albrecht Ritschl, *Justification and Reconciliation*, (New York: Scribners, 1900), 12.

28. Rudolf Bultmann, *Theology of the New Testament*, 2 vols. (New York: Charles Scribners, 1955), 1:4-6.

29. Ibid., 2:175.

30. Shirley Jackson Case, *The Millennial Hope: A Phase of War-Time Thinking* (Chicago: University of Chicago Press, 1918), 238.

31. Ibid., 231, 227.

32. Ibid., 227-28.

33. Harold Bloom, ed., *The Revelation of St. John the Divine* (New York: Chelsea House Publishers, 1988), 1-5.

34. Bossuet, *Oeuvres*, 1: "Écriture" 275.

35. Johann Gottfried von Herder, *Sämmtliche Werke*, ed. Bernhard Suphan, 9 (Berlin: Weidmannsche Buchhandlung, 1893): 241; Carl Gustav Auberlen, *The Prophecies of Daniel and the Revelations of St. John*, trans. Adolph Saphir (Edinburgh: T. & T. Clark, 1856), 396.

36. H. H. Rowley, *The Relevance of Apocalyptic*, 2nd. ed. (London: Lutterworth Press, 1947), 134.

37. R. H. Charles, *A Critical and Exegetical Commentary on the Revelation of St. John*, 2 vols. (Edinburgh: T. & T. Clark, 1920), 1:xiv.

38. G. B. Caird, *A Commentary on the Revelation of St. John the Divine* (New York: Harper & Row, 1966), 289.

39. William Barclay, *The Revelation of John*, 2nd ed., 2 vols. (Philadelphia: Westminster Press, 1976), 2:165.

40. Adela Yarbro Collins, *Crisis and Catharsis: The Power of the Apocalypse* (Philadelphia: Westminster Press, 1984), 172.

41. Charles, *Revelation*, 2:7-9.

42. Elisabeth Schüssler Fiorenza, *The Book of Revelation: Justice and Judgment* (Philadelphia: Fortress Press, 1985), 199.

43. Susan R. Garrett, "Revelation," in *The Women's Bible Commentary*, eds. Carol A. Newsom and Sharon H. Ringe (London: S.P.C.K.; Louisville: Westminster/John Knox Press, 1992), 377-82.

44. See 240, n. 30.

45. See Georg Heinrich August Ewald, *Commentarius in Apocalypsin Johannis Exegeticus et Criticus* (Lipsiae: Sumtibus Librariae Hahnianae, 1828), 78-81; Lücke, *Versuch*, 802; Charles, *Revelation*, 1:xxxviii-l; Bleek, *Lectures*, 64, 132-35; Friedrich Düsterdieck, *Critical and Exegetical Handbook to the Revelation of John*, trans. Henry E. Jacobs (New York: Funk & Wagnalls, 1887), 83; Bousset, *Offenbarung*, 38-49; Ferdinand Hitzig, *Über Johannes Marcus und seine Schriften* (Zürich: Orell, Füssli, 1843), 8; Josephine Massyngberde Ford, *Revelation*, Anchor Bible (Garden City, N.Y.: Doubleday, 1975).

46. B. W. Bacon, "The Authoress of Revelation: A Conjecture," *HTR* 23 (1930): 235-50.

47. Among those who accept traditional authorship are Friedrich Jakob Züllig, *Die Offenbarung Johannis*, 2 vols. (Stuttgart: E. Schweizerbart, 1834 and 1840), 1:134-39; Ferdinand Christian Baur, *The Church History of the First Three Centuries*, 3rd. ed., trans. Allan Menzies (London: Williams and Norgate, 1878), 86; E.-B. Allo, *Saint Jean, L'Apocalypse*, 4th ed. (Paris: Libraire LeCoffre, J. Gabalda et Cie, 1933), clxxxviii-ccxxii; Theodor Zahn, *Die Offenbarung des Johannes* (Leipzig and Erlangen: Deichert, 1924–1926; reprint, Wuppertal: Brockhaus, 1986.), 45-52; Karl Hartenstein, *Der wiederkommende Herr: eine Auslegung der Offenbarung des Johannes für die Gemeinde* (Stuttgart: Evangelische Verlag, 1953), 30-31; Henry Barclay Swete, *The Apocalypse of St John*, 3rd ed. (London: Macmillan, 1909; reprint, Grand Rapids: Eerdmans, 1951), cii, clxxxv; Isbon T. Beckwith, *The Apocalypse of John: Studies in Introduction* (New York: Macmillan Co., 1919), 206-7, 342-62. Though Baur and Züllig believed the apostle to be the author of the Apocalypse, Baur rejected the traditional authorship of John's Gospel and Epistles, and Züllig had his doubts about it.

48. C. K. Barrett, *The Gospel According to John* (London: S.P.C.K., 1955), 113-14.

49. Schüssler Fiorenza, *Revelation: Justice and Judgment*, 85-113. Aimo T. Nikolainen, "Über die theologische Eigenart der Offenbarung des Johannes," *TLZ* 93 (1968): 62, regards the author as a community prophet, but David Hill, "Prophecy and Prophets in the Revelation of St. John," *NTS* (1971–72): 412-13, disagrees with that suggestion.

50. Oscar Cullmann, *The Johannine Circle* (Philadelphia: Westminster Press, 1976).

51. Ernst Lohmeyer, *Die Offenbarung des Johannes* (Tübingen: J. C. B. Mohr [Paul Siebeck], 1953), 203.

52. Joseph Sickenberger, *Erklärung des Johannesapokalypse*, 2nd ed. (Bonn: Peter Hanstein, 1942), 33-34.

53. Herder, *Werke*, 9: 278.

54. Irenaeus *Adv. Haer.* 5.30.3; Epiphanius *Adv. Haer.* 51.12 (PG 41:909).

55. See Theodor Schermann, *Propheten-und Apostellegenden nebst Jüngerkatalogen des Dorotheus und verwandter Texte*, TU 31.3 (1907): 197, 257. Some scholars date the Pseudo-Dorotheus in the sixth century, but Schermann dates it in the ninth. Theophylact (11th cent.), *Enarratio in Evangelium Matthaei* 20.23 (PG 123:364), also thinks that the Apocalypse was written in Trajan's reign.

56. Firmin Abauzit, *Oeuvres diverses de M. Abauzit*, vol. 1 (London, 1770); Joannes Jacobus Wettstein, *Novum Testamentum Graecum*, 2 vols. (Amsterdam: Ex Officina Dommeriana, 1752), 2:746; Herder, *Werke*, 9:249-51.

57. Lücke (in his first edition) declared for the reign of Galba. Ewald opted for 69, toward the end of Galba's reign or soon after his death. Bleek, Lücke (in his second edition), Düsterdieck, and Renan dated it in 69 during the reign of Vespasian. Baur opted for the late sixties, and Renan chose 69. Lücke, *Versuch*, 848; Ewald, *Commentarius*, 50; Bleek, *Lectures*, 119; Düsterdieck, *Revelation*, 46-54; Renan, *Antichrist*, 16; Baur, *Church History*, 86.

58. Edward Evanson, *A Letter to Dr. Priestley's Young Man* (Ipswich, Eng.: Printed by G. Jermyn, Sold by B. Law and J. Johnson, 1794), 72; *Reflections upon the State of Religion*, 38-39.

59. Züllig, *Offenbarung*, 2:330-31; Bousset, *Offenbarung*, 134-35.

60. Hartenstein, *Der wiederkommende Herr*, 31; J. A. T. Robinson, *Redating the New Testament* (Philadelphia: Westminster Press, 1976); Kenneth L. Gentry, Jr., *Before Jerusalem Fell: Dating the Book of Revelation. An Exegetical and Historical Argument for a Pre-A.D. 70 Composition* (Tyler, Tex.: Institute for Christian Economics, 1989); Heinrich Kraft, *Die Offenbarung des Johannes* (Tübingen: J. C. B. Mohr [Paul Siebeck], 1974), 10-11; A. M. Farrer, *The Revelation of St. John the Divine* (Oxford: Clarendon Press, 1964), 37.

61. See, for example, Kraft, *Offenbarung*, 152.

62. Charles, *Revelation*, 1:274-76.

63. Grotius, *Opera*, 2.2. Preface to the Apocalypse.

64. Marie-Émile Boismard, "'L'Apocalypse' ou 'les Apocalypses' de S. Jean," *RB* 56 (1949): 507-41; "Notes sur l'Apocalypse," *RB* 59 (1952): 161-81.

65. Kraft, *Offenbarung*, 11-15.

66. Paul Joachim Sigismund Vogel, *Sacra Paschalia* (Erlangen: Kunstmann, 1813), 10-13.

67. Bleek, *Lectures*, 60.

68. Daniel Völter, *Die Entstehung der Apokalypse* (Freiburg im Bresgau: J. C. B. Mohr [Paul Siebeck], 1882); Eberhard Vischer, *Die Offenbarung Johannis*, TU 2.3 (1886); Gerard Johan Weyland, *Omwerkings- en Compilatie-Hypothesen toegepast op de Apocalypse van Johannes* (Groningen: J. B. Wolters, 1888).

69. Friedrich Spitta, *Die Offenbarung des Johannes* (Halle: Waisenhaus, 1889), argues that most of Revelation 1–8 and parts of 19 and 22 were written soon after 60. Subsequently this material was combined with two Jewish sources. One of them, which included the trumpet visions, came from the time of Caligula, and the other, which included the bowl visions, came from the time of Pompey, over half a century before Jesus' birth. A Christian redactor brought all this material together during the reign of Trajan.

70. Daniel Völter, *Die Offenbarung Johannis neu untersucht und erklärt* (Strassburg: J. H. Ed.Hertz, 1904).

71. Ford, *Revelation*, 3-4.

72. Carl Heinrich von Weizsäcker, *Das apostolische Zeitalter der christlichen Kirche* (Freiburg i. Br.: Mohr [Siebeck], 1886), claimed that Revelation 7:1-8 was written in 64–66, Revelation 11:1-13 about 66, Revelation 12:1-10 during the Jewish War, Revelation 13 in the reign of Vespasian, Revelation 17 in the reign of Domitian, and the letters of Revelation 2–3 at an even later date. Bousset, *Offenbarung Johannis*, 283-84, 324-30, 346-58, 374-79, 391-92, 410-18, 425-26, 453-55, argues that Revelation 7:1-8 is based on two fragments, one about winds and the other about sealing the servants of God. He claims that Revelation 11:1-13 is derived from two more fragments, the first dealing with the Temple and the second with the witnesses. Other examples of material that Bousset thinks may be based on earlier traditions are Revelation 12; 13:11-18; 14:14-20; 17-18, and possibly 21:9–22:5.

73. According to Charles, *Revelation*, 2:144-54, Revelation 21:9, 22:2, 14-15, 17 depict the heavenly Jerusalem during the millennium, and other parts of those chapters describe the New Jerusalem coming down from heaven after the last judgment.

74. John Oman, *Book of Revelation* (Cambridge, Eng.: University Press, 1923), 5-7.

75. Lohmeyer, *Offenbarung*, 39, 185-89, 202-3. Among other defenders of the book's unity are Swete, *Apocalypse*, xliv-liv. Beckwith, *Apocalypse*, 216-39, Allo, *L'Apocalypse*, clxxi-clxxx, Sickenberger, *Johannesapokalypse*, 30.

8. CONTEMPORARY-HISTORICAL CRITICISM AND MYTHOLOGY

1. Abauzit names the hills as Zion, Acra, Bezetha, Millo, Moriah, the Fortress Antonia, and Calvary. The high priests are Ishmael, Joseph son of Simon, Ananus, Jesus son of Damnus, Jesus son of Gamaliel, and Matthias, together with Phannias, the one who is yet to come. The beast's mortally wounded head is the high priest Ananus, who was put to death, and its eighth head is the soul of the Sanhedrin. Abauzit, *Oeuvres diverses*, 1:333.

2. Ibid., 1:329-42.

3. Herder, *Werke*, 9:167-84. In an earlier work, privately circulated, Herder had related the prophecies to both Jerusalem and Rome. Ibid., 9:1-100. Friedrich Gotthold Hartwig, *Apologie der Apokalypse wider falschen Tadel und falsches Lob*, 4 vols. (Chemnitz, 1780–83), also explained the Apocalypse in terms of Judaism, although he described the seven heads of the beast as emperors as well as high priests. See Bousset, *Offenbarung*, 34.

4. Züllig, *Offenbarung*, 2:320-24, 330-31. Züllig regarded the seven kings of Revelation 17:10 as Herod the Great, his three sons (Archelaus, Philip, and Antipas), Herod Agrippa I, Herod king of Chalcis, and Herod Agrippa II.

5. See Wettstein, *Novum Testamentum*, 2:746, 889-91.

6. Johann Gottfried Eichhorn, *Commentarius in Apocalypsin* (Gottingae: Typis Jo. Christ. Dieterich, 1791), 1:xix-xxiii; *Einleitung in das Neue Testament*, 2 (Leipzig: Weidmannische Buchhandlung, 1810): 331, 333.

7. Eichhorn, *Commentarius*, 2:32, 80-103, 198-254.

8. Ibid., 2:281-84.

9. Ewald, *Commentarius*, 28-31.

10. Bleek, *Lectures*, 106, 113, 248.

11. Lücke, *Versuch*, 366, 370-72.

12. Baur, *Church History*, 84-87, 155.

13. Renan, *Antichrist*, 16, 302-20.

14. Paul S. Minear, *I Saw a New Earth: An Introduction to the Visions of the Apocalypse* (Washington/Cleveland: Corpus Books, 1967).

15. Schüssler Fiorenza, *The Book of Revelation: Justice and Judgment*, 85-113.

16. Ewald, *Commentarius*, 235-38. See also Bleek, *Lectures*, 89, 284. See also note 17, below.

17. See Bleek, *Lectures*, 283-84. A fifth-century manuscript has the number 616, the numerical value of the Latin form "Nero Caesar," when it is transcribed in Hebrew letters. The existence of this variant reading is evidence that the number was associated with Nero in the early church.

18. Kraft, *Offenbarung*, 222.

19. Hermann Gunkel, *Schöpfung und Chaos in Urzeit und Endzeit:. Eine religionsgeschichtliche Untersuchung über Gen. 1 und Ap. Joh. 12* (Göttingen: Vandenhoeck & Ruprecht, 1895), 263-66.

20. G. R. Beasley-Murray, *The Book of Revelation*, New Century Bible Commentary, rev. ed. (Grand Rapids: Eerdmans; London: Marshall, Morgan, & Scott, 1978), 220, combines both these views.

21. Dieter Georgi, "Who Is the True Prophet?" *HTR* 79:100-26.

22. See, for example, G. B. Caird, *Revelation*, 218-19.

23. Renan, *Antichrist*, 303-8.

24. Charles, *Revelation*, 1:180-81, 291.

25. Ibid., 1:160, 163; Kraft, *Offenbarung*, 116; Bousset, *Offenbarung*, 266, 304, 397.

26. Beasley-Murray, *Revelation*, 132.

27. See, for example, Yarbro Collins, *Crisis and Catharsis*, 84-110.

28. William M. Ramsay, *The Letters to the Seven Churches of Asia* (New York: George H. Doran, n.d.), 294, 424-29.

29. Colin J. Hemer, *The Letters to the Seven Churches of Asia in Their Local Setting*, Journal for the Study of the New Testament Supplement Series 11 (Sheffield: Department of Biblical Studies, The University of Sheffield), 186-91. See also M. J. S. Rudwick and E. M. B. Green, "The Laodicean Lukewarmness," *ExpT* 69 (1957–58): 176-78, and P. Wood, "Local Knowledge in the Letters of the Apocalypse," *ExpT* 73 (1961–62): 263-64.

30. See 83-84.

31. Herder, *Werke*, 9:195-96; Bleek, *Lectures*, 306-7.

32. Hippolytus, *GCS* 1.2:236; Oecumenius, *Apocalypse*, 180; Andreas, *Apokalypse*, 175.

33. Grotius, *Opera*, 2:2, ad. loc. The meaning "mountain of assembly," was suggested by Hommel in the nineteenth century.

34. Gunkel, *Schöpfung und Chaos*, 263-66.

35. Bousset, *Offenbarung*, 399.

36. T. K. Cheyne, *Encyclopaedia Biblica*, 1:311.

37. See, for example, Charles, *Revelation*, 2:50-51; Pierre Prigent, *L'Apocalypse de Saint Jean*, 2nd ed. (Geneva: Labor et Fides, 1988), 249.

38. Wettstein, *Novum Testamentum*, 2:893.

39. Ibid., 2:875-79.

40. Ibid., 2:874-75.

41. Herder, *Werke*, 9:250-51.

42. Ibid., 9:191-97.

43. Ibid., 9:257-73.

44. Christopher Wordsworth, *Lectures on the Apocalypse* (Philadelphia: Herman Hooker, 1852; from 2nd London edition), 70, 73, 143-55, 159-79, 213, 216, 394.

45. Thomas Newton, *Dissertations on the Prophecies*, rev. W. S. Dobson (London: J. F. Dove; reprint, Philadelphia: J. J. Woodward, 1838), 529, 618-22; Priestley, *Works*, 14:442-43; Froom, *Prophetic Faith*, 3:303-24, 514-26. The passages from Priestley are in his *Notes on All the Books of Scripture*, first published in 1803–4 after his emigration to the United States.

46. Ernst Wilhelm Hengstenberg, *The Revelation of St John Expounded for Those Who Search the Scriptures*, trans. Patrick Fairbairn, 2 vols. (Edinburgh: T. & T. Clark, 1851), 1:451; J. C. K. Hofmann, *Weissagung und Erfüllung im alten und im neuen Testamente*, 2 vols. (Nördlingen: C.H. Beck, 1841, 1844), 2:370-72; Auberlen, *Prophecies*, 272, 415-23.

47. Moses Stuart, *A Commentary on the Apocalypse*, 2 vols. (New York: Van Nostrand and Terrett, 1851), 1:203; see also 1:378, 381-82.

48. Charles-François Dupuis, *Origine de tous les cultes, ou religion universelle* (Paris: H. Agasse, 1795), 3:187-323. For the link with the Passover, see 3:321. See also the English translation of Dupuis' abridgment of his work, *The Origin of All Religious Worship* (New Orleans, 1872: reprint, New York: Garland Publishing, 1984), 20-22, 63-66, 71-78, 255, 409-26.

49. R. H. Charles, *Studies in the Apocalypse*, 2nd ed. (Edinburgh: T. & T. Clark, 1915), 50, regards Dupuis' method as antiquated. Charles mentions that similar views had already been stated in an anonymous treatise, *Horus oder Astrognostiches Endurteil über die Offenbarung Johannis* (1783).

50. Albrecht Dieterich, *Abraxas: Studien zur Religionsgeschichte des späteren Altertums* (Leipzig: B. G. Teubner, 1891), 117-20.

51. Gunkel, *Schöpfung und Chaos*, 282.

52. Völter, *Offenbarung Johannis*, 86; Bousset, *Offenbarung*, 354-55.

53. Gunkel, *Verständnis*, 55. See Charles, *Revelation*, 1:310-14.

54. Franz Boll, *Aus der Offenbarung Johannis: Hellenistische Stücken zum Weltbild der Apokalypse* (Leipzig: Teubner, 1914), 122.

55. Nikolaus Morosow, *Die Offenbarung Johannis: Eine astronomisch-historische Untersuchung* (Stuttgart: W. Spemann, 1912), 60.

56. Ibid., 135.

57. Ibid., xviii, 140, 148.

58. Charles, *Revelation*, 1:305-14, argues that two myths lie behind chapter 12. One

describes the conflict between Michael and the dragon. The other tells of the woman, the child, and the dragon, and is a Jewish version of an ancient Babylonian myth.

59. Adela Yarbro Collins, *The Combat Myth in the Book of Revelation* (Missoula, Mont.: Scholars Press, 1976), 83-85.

60. Gunkel, *Schöpfung*, 233.

61. Lohmeyer, *Offenbarung*, 60.

62. Ibid., 194, 202.

63. Ibid., 191-92.

9. LITERARY CRITICISM, THE SOCIAL SCIENCES, AND THEOLOGY

1. See David Hellholm, ed., *Apocalypticism in the Mediterranean World and the Near East* (Tübingen: Mohr/Siebeck, 1983).

2. Frank Kermode, *The Sense of an Ending* (New York: Oxford University Press, 1967), 93.

3. Ibid., 27. Kermode claims that the plots of Elizabethan tragedies are closer to those of medieval apocalypses than to those of Greek tragedies. See ibid., 30.

4. Northrop Frye, *The Great Code: The Bible and Literature* (New York: Harcourt Brace Jovanovitch, 1983), 106, 135-38. Jacques Derrida, *D'un ton apocalyptique adopté naguère en philosophie* (Paris: Éditions Galilée, 1983). The philosopher of "deconstruction," Derrida has published reflections on the Apocalypse. He rejects the notion that it is a revelation about an actual divine being, breaks away from traditional modes of interpretation, and reflects on particular words, especially *revelation, send,* and *come.* (ET by John P. Leavey, Jr., "Of an Apocalyptic Tone Recently Adopted in Philosophy," *Derrida and Biblical Studies, Semeia 23* [Chico, Calif.: Scholars Press, 1982], 59-97).

5. *Geneva Bible,* 125-26, 135.

6. See 261, n. 49.

7. John W. Erwin, *Lyric Apocalypse: Reconstruction in Ancient and Modern Poetry* (Chico, Calif.: Scholars Press, 1984), 13-21.

8. Yarbro Collins, *Crisis and Catharsis,* 145-46.

9. Schüssler Fiorenza, *Revelation: Justice and Judgment,* 181-203.

10. Richard Bernard, *A Key of Knowledge* (London: Imprinted by Felix Kyngston, 1617).

11. Pareus, *Revelation,* 26-27.

12. Ibid., 19-20, 26-27. The visions are: (1) 1:9–3:22; (2) 4–7; (3) 8–11; (4) 12–14; (5) 15–16; (6) 17–19; (7) 20:1–22:5. All except (1) and (5) are divided into four acts, and all except (2), (4) and (7) have a preface. Each of them ends with the final judgment.

13. John Milton, *Complete Prose Works,* ed. D. M. Wolfe (Newhaven, Conn.: Yale University Press, 1953), 1:815; *Samson Agonistes,* preface.

14. According to Eichhorn, *Commentarius,* 1:xix-xxiii, and *Einleitung,* 2:334-65, the drama begins in the fourth chapter and has the following outline: Prelude: 4:1–8:5; Act One: 8:6–12:17, the siege and capture of Jerusalem and the persecution of the Jewish Church; Act Two: 12:18–20:10, the fall of Rome and the victory of Christianity; Act Three: 20:11–22:5, the New Jerusalem, the joy of the future life; Epilogue: 21:6-21.

15. Eichhorn, *Einleitung,* 2:340.

16. See, for example, Edward White Benson, *The Apocalypse* (London: Macmillan, 1900), 6, 37-41.

17. Frederic Palmer, *The Drama of the Apocalypse* (New York: Macmillan, 1903), 16, 21, 35-86. The acts are (1) 4:1–8:1; (2) 8:2-11; (3) 12–14; (4) 15–18; (5) 19:1–22:5.

18. Wikenhauser, *Offenbarung*, 6-8. The acts are (1) 5:1–11:14, the "beginning of sorrows"; (2) 11:15–20:15, the battle between God and Satan; (3) 21:1–22:5.

19. J. W. Bowman, *The Drama of the Book of Revelation* (Philadelphia: Westminster Press, 1955); s.v. "Revelation, Book of," *The Interpreter's Dictionary of the Bible* (New York: Abingdon Press, 1962), 4:58-65. Bowman divides each act into seven scenes. He makes a plausible case for treating the letters, and the seal, trumpet, and bowl visions in this way, but he is not as persuasive in his account of the other acts.

20. James L. Blevins, *Revelation as Drama* (Nashville: Broadman Press, 1984).

21. Stuart, *Apocalypse*, 1:190-91.

22. Samuel Davidson, *An Introduction to the New Testament*, 3 vols. (London: Samuel Bagster and Sons, n.d.), 3:616, described the Apocalypse as "a prophetic poem" that "nearly approaches *an epic.*"

23. Ewald, *Commentarius*, 7-15, described the Apocalypse as a mixture of two genres: (1) prophetic-symbolic, like Daniel, Enoch, and the Apocalypse of Ezra; and (2) epistolary.

24. Lücke took the term from the scholar Nietzsche. See *Versuch*, 14.

25. Lücke, ibid., 388, regarded Ezekiel, the Jewish writer of tragedies, as an exception. This Ezekiel, however, was of uncertain date. It is not agreed whether he lived before or after Christ.

26. Ibid., 379-92, 416-18. See Josephus *Antiquities* 15.8.1.

27. Lücke, *Versuch*, 932-34.

28. Ibid., 24-25.

29. Philipp Vielhauer, "Apocalypses and Related Subjects," in *New Testament Apocrypha* II, eds. E. Hennecke and W. Schneemelcher, trans. R. McL. Wilson (Philadelphia: Westminster Press, 1965), 583-94, enumerated the following features of apocalyptic literature: pseudo-nymity, account of the vision, surveys of history in future form, doctrine of the two ages, pessimism and hope of the beyond, universalism and individualism, determinism and imminent expectation, lack of uniformity in expression. Klaus Koch, *The Rediscovery of Apocalyptic* (London: S. C. M. Press, 1972), 24-33, gave a longer list: discourse cycles, spiritual turmoils, paraenetic discourses, pseudonymity, mythical images rich in symbolism, composite character, urgent expectation of the end, cosmic catastrophe, world history divided into segments, angels and demons, promise of salvation, the throne of God, a mediator with royal functions, the use of the catchword *glory*.

30. " 'Apocalypse' is a genre of revelatory literature with a narrative framework, in which a revelation is mediated by an otherworldly being to a human recipient, disclosing a transcendent reality which is both temporal, insofar as it envisages eschatological salvation, and spatial, insofar as it involves another, supernatural world." J. J. Collins, "Apocalypse: The Morphology of a Genre," in *Semeia* 14 (1979).

31. David Hellholm, "The Problem of Apocalyptic Genre," in *Early Christian Apocalypticism: Genre and Social Setting, Semeia* 36, ed. Adela Yarbro Collins (Decatur, Ga.: Scholars Press, 1986), 27.

32. Paul D. Hanson, *The Dawn of Apocalyptic* (Philadelphia: Fortress Press, 1979). Paul Hanson distinguishes "apocalypse" from "apocalyptic eschatology," which is a way of looking at life in relation to divine providence, and from "apocalypticism," which is a religious movement.

33. David Aune, "The Apocalypse of John and the Problem of Genre," *Semeia* 36 (1986): 86-87.

34. David Hill, "Prophecy and Prophets in the Revelation of St. John," *NTS* 18 (1971–72): 405. Frederick David Mazzaferri, *The Genre of the Book of Revelation* (Berlin: Walter de Gruyter, 1989), 374-78.

35. Jacques Ellul, *Apocalypse: The Book of Revelation*, trans. George W. Schreiner (New York: Seabury Press, 1977), 30.

36. A. M. Farrer, *A Rebirth of Images* (Westminster: Dacre Press, 1949), 305.

37. Ibid., 305-6.

38. Wikenhauser, *Offenbarung*, 6-8, 13-14, 27.

39. Dupuis, *Origine de tous les cultes*, 3:187-323. For the link with the Passover, see ibid., 3:321. See also Dupuis, *Origin of All Religious Worship*, 20-22, 63-66, 71-78, 255, 409-26.

40. See 215, on Pryse and Steiner.

41. P. Touilleux, *L'Apocalypse et les cultes de Domitien et de Cybèle* (Paris: Libraire Orientaliste Paul Guenther, 1935), 184.

42. Ethelbert Stauffer, *Christ and the Caesars*, trans. K. and R. Gregor Smith (Philadelphia: Westminster Press, 1955), 166-91.

43. Farrer, *Rebirth*, 94-95, sees a pattern of six quarters in the book: (1) from the Feast of Dedication (1–3); (2) Passover to Pentecost (4–7); (3) including the Jewish New Year (8–11); (4) from the Feast of Tabernacles (12–14); (5) from Dedication (15—18); (6) Passover to Pentecost (19–22).

44. Ibid., 177-84.

45. D. T. Niles, *As Seeing the Invisible* (London: SCM Press, 1962), 106-15, also argues that the Apocalypse is designed on the basis of the Jewish liturgical year, beginning and ending with the Feast of Dedication. Within each feast he detects the influence of a weekly cycle, extending from Sunday to Sunday.

46. Massey H. Shepherd, *The Paschal Liturgy and the Apocalypse* (Richmond: John Knox Press, 1960), 77-97, sees five liturgical divisions in the Apocalypse: (1) Scrutinies (1–3)—that is, the examination of candidates for baptism; (2) Vigil (4–6), a preparation for the Paschal; (3) Initiation (7)—that is, baptism, as indicated by the washing, sealing, and white clothes; (4) Synaxis (8–19), including scripture readings, psalms, a sermon, and prayers; (5) Eucharist (19–22).

47. Pierre Prigent, *Apocalypse et Liturgie* (Neuchatel: Éditions Delachaux et Niestlé, 1964), 39-79.

48. M. D. Goulder, "The Apocalypse as an Annual Cycle of Prophecies," *NTS* 27.3 (April 1981): 342-67.

49. David L. Barr, "The Apocalypse of John as Oral Enactment," *Interpretation* 40.3 (1986): 243-56; "The Apocalypse as a Symbolic Transformation of the World: A Literary Analysis," *Interpretation*, 38.1 (1984): 45.

50. J. Lambrecht, "A Structuration of Rev. 4,1-22,5," in *L'Apocalypse johannique et l'Apocalyptique dans le Nouveau Testament*, ed. J. Lambrecht (Gembloux: Éditions J. Duculot; Leuven: University Press, 1980), 77-104, divides the book into three parts: chapters (1) 4–5, (2) 6–7; (3) 8:1–22:5, with 1–3 as a prologue and 22:6-21 as an epilogue. Hartenstein, *Der wiederkommende Herr*, 26-28, divides it into four parts, an introduction, two main divisions, and a conclusion. Jacques Ellul, *Apocalypse* 36-64, argues that the parts are chapters (1) 1–4; (2) 5–7; (3) 8:1–14:5; (4) 14:6–19:8; (5) 19:9–22:21. Yarbro Collins, *Combat Myth*, 13-19, divides it into eight parts: (1) prologue; (2) seven messages; (3) seven seals; (4) seven trumpets; (5) seven unnumbered divisions; (6) seven bowls; (7) seven unnumbered visions; (8) epilogue. According to Schüssler Fiorenza, *Revelation: Justice and Judgment*, 159-80, the parts are (1) the inaugural vision and the seven letters (1:9–3:22), (2) the scroll (4:1–9:21; 11:15-19; 15:1, 5:16–21; 17:1–19:10); (3) the small scroll (10:1–15:4), (4) visions of judgment and salvation (19:11–22:9). The chiastic plan of the work is (A) 1:1-8; (B) 1:9–3:22; (C) 4:1–9:21 and 11:15-19; (D) 10:1–15:4; (C') 15:1, 5–19:10; (B') 19:11–22:9; (A') 22:10-21. A striking feature of

Schüssler Fiorenza's analysis is her theory of intercalation, according to which the author narrates two units that belong together and interposes a different unit between them. For example, he inserts a heavenly liturgy (Rev. 8:3-5) between the first appearance of the trumpet angels (Rev. 8:2) and the beginning of the trumpet visions (Rev. 8:6). In a new and complex approach to the question, David Hellholm, "Problem of Apocalyptic Genre," 44-46, examines the different levels of communication in the Apocalypse and the way in which sequences of text are embedded in each other.

51. Kraft, *Offenbarung*, 14-15.

52. Carl Gustav Jung, *Answer to Job*, trans. R. F. C. Hull (London: Routledge & Kegan Paul, 1954), 121.

53. Ibid., 129-32.

54. Ibid., 142, 154.

55. Yarbro Collins, *Crisis*, 156.

56. Yarbro Collins offers an alternative explanation, saying that the Apocalypse transfers the aggression to God, who will carry out judgment on sinners. Ibid., 156-57.

57. Ibid., 152-53. David L. Barr, "The Apocalypse as a Symbolic Transformation," 49-50, however, understands "catharsis" not primarily in terms of emotional relief but in terms of giving people a new understanding of the world, in which they see themselves as "*actors* in charge of their own destiny."

58. Cohn, *Pursuit*, 281-86.

59. Michael Barkun, *Disaster and the Millennium* (New Haven, Conn.: Yale University Press, 1974), 89-90.

60. Hanson, *Dawn*, 432-44.

61. Yarbro Collins, "Persecution and Vengeance in the Book of Revelation," in Hellholm, ed., *Apocalypticism*, 746; *Crisis*, 132-34.

62. Schüssler Fiorenza, *Revelation: Justice and Judgment*, 24.

63. Leonard L. Thompson, *The Book of Revelation, Apocalypse and Empire* (New York: Oxford University Press, 1990), 191-97.

64. John G. Gager, *Kingdom and Community: The Social World of Early Christianity* (Englewood Cliffs, N.J.: Prentice-Hall, 1975), 49-57.

65. See, for example, Douglas Robinson, *American Apocalypses: The Image of the End of the World in American Literature* (Baltimore: The Johns Hopkins University Press, 1985).

66. See 109-10, 182-29.

67. Charles, *Revelation*, 1:cxv, 63.

68. Augustine *Civ. Dei*. 21.17.

69. Origen *De Princip*. 1.6.3; 3.6.5.

70. Mathias Rissi, *Was ist und was geschehen soll danach. Die Zeit-und Geschichtsauffassung der Offenbarung des Johannes* (Zürich: Zwingli Verlag, 1965), 122-24.

71. Thomas Hobbes, *Leviathan* 3.38 (London: J. Dent & Sons; New York: E. P. Dutton & Co., 1947), pp. 246-47.

72. Caird, *Revelation*, 260.

73. M. Eugene Boring, *Revelation*, Interpretation Commentaries (Louisville: Westminster Press/John Knox, 1989), 226-31.

74. André Feuillet, *The Apocalypse*, trans. Thomas E. Crane (Staten Island, N.Y.: Alba House, 1964), 80-82.

75. Eugenio Corsini, *The Apocalypse: The Perennial Revelation of Jesus Christ*, trans. Francis J. Moloney (Wilmington, Del.: Michael Glazier, 1983).

76. Allo, *L'Apocalypse*, 307, 328; Prigent, *Apocalypse de Jean*, 301; Leon Morris, *Revelation*, 2nd ed. (Leicester: Inter-Varsity Press; Grand Rapids: Eerdmans, 1987), 230-32; Ernest Lee Stoffel, *The Dragon Bound: The Revelation Speaks to Our Time* (Atlanta: John Knox Press, 1981), 93-95; M. Robert Mulholland, Jr., *Revelation: Holy Living in an Unholy World* (Grand Rapids: Francis Asbury Press of Zondervan Publishing House, 1990), 304-11.

77. B. B. Warfield, *Works* 10 vols. (New York: Oxford University Press, 1929; reprint, Grand Rapids: Baker Book House, 1981), 643-64.

78. Zahn, *Offenbarung*, 593-97; Oscar Cullmann, *The Christology of the New Testament*, trans. Shirley C. Guthrie and Charles A. M. Hall (Philadelphia: Westminster Press, 1963), 226; Caird, *Revelation*, 254; George Elton Ladd, *Jesus and the Kingdom* (New York: Harper & Row, 1964), 333. Sickenberger, *Johannesapokalypse*, 182-83; Alfred Wikenhauser, *Offenbarung des Johannes* (Regensburg: Verlag Friedrich Pustet, 1949), 129-30. Cullmann's views are developed by Mathias Rissi, who differs from him by arguing that Paul also thought of a millennium in 1 Corinthians 15:23-26:

79. George E. Ladd, *Crucial Questions About the Kingdom of God* (Grand Rapids: Eerdmans, 1952), 141-50.

80. Hans Lilje, *The Last Book of the Bible: The Meaning of the Revelation of St. John* (Philadelphia: Muhlenberg Press, 1955), 253.

81. Caird, *Revelation*, 12, 32.

82. Boring, *Revelation*, 204-6.

83. William Milligan, *The Book of Revelation*, Expositors Bible (New York: A. & C. Armstrong, 1895), 335-48.

84. Abraham Kuyper, *The Revelation of St. John*, trans. John Hendrik de Vries (Grand Rapids: Eerdmans, 1964), 277.

85. Ellul, *Apocalypse*, 208.

86. George Eldon Ladd, *A Theology of the New Testament* (Grand Rapids: Eerdmans, 1974), 631.

87. Zahn, *Offenbarung*, 608-25.

88. Milligan, *Revelation*, 264.

89. Caird, *Revelation*, 254, 298-301. According to Traugott Holtz, *Die Christologie der Apokalypse des Johannes*, TU 85, 2nd ed. (Berlin: Akademie-Verlag, 1971), the Apocalypse affirms that evil has already been overcome and the New Jerusalem is already present, but at the same time there is an element of the "not yet" in the present existence.

90. Richard L. Jeske and David L. Barr, "The Study of the Apocalypse Today," *RelSRev* 14.4 (Oct., 1988): 337-44.

10. CHURCH, STATES, AND NATIONS

1. Donald W. Dayton, "Millennial Views and Social Reform in Nineteenth Century America," in M. Darrol Bryant and Donald W. Dayton, eds., *The Coming Kingdom; Essays in American Millennialism and Eschatology* (Barrytown, N.Y.: International Religious Foundation, 1983), 132-33.

2. H.-M. Féret, *L'Apocalypse de Saint Jean: vision chrétienne de l'histoire* (Paris: Corrêa, 1943), 308-10, 318-21, divided church history into three parts: (1) Roman persecution and the church's triumph; (2) the time of the ten kings, beginning sometime between 300 and 600, a period of strife between the gospel and the political powers; (3) the millennium, which will begin in the future, when Christ and his saints will reign invisibly.

3. Hartenstein, *Der wiederkommende Herr*, 85, 174.

4. See Ernst Sackur, *Sibyllinische Texte und Forschungen* (Halle: Niemeyer, 1898), 185-86; McGinn, *Visions*, 49-50; Reeves, *Prophecy*, 301.

5. Reeves, *Prophecy*, 334-46.

6. Cohn, *Pursuit*, 119-26.

7. Adso, *De Ortu* CCM 45:25-26; Martin of Leon, *Expositio Libri Apocalypsis* PL 209:359-60.

8. Reeves, *Prophecy*, 320-23, 416-17; J. Bignami-Odier, *Études sur Jean de Roquetaillade* (Paris: Vrin, 1952), 53-109, 113-29, 40-8; McGinn, *Visions*, 230-33. Later de Roquetaillade modified his views and predicted that in the last period a French king would reign in Jerusalem.

9. Reeves, *Prophecy*, 328-31, 354-58, 374-86, 388.

10. McGinn, *Visions*, 222; Reeves, *Prophecy*, 317.

11. Christopher Columbus, *The Libro de las profecías of Christopher Columbus*, trans. and commentary by Delno C. West and August Kling (Gainesville: University of Florida Press, 1991), 33-35, 104-05, 110-11.

12. Reeves, *Prophecy*, 366-72.

13. Donald Weinstein, *Savonarola and Florence: Prophecy and Patriotism in the Renaissance* (Princeton, N.J.: Princeton University Press, 1970), 69, 143-45, 182, 285.

14. Ibid., 27-66, 216.

15. Foxe, *Actes*, 86.

16. John Foxe, *Eicasmi seu meditationes in sacram Apocalypsim* (London: Impensis Geor. Byshop, 1587), 12. See Firth, *Apocalypse*, 108.

17. Bernard Capp, "The Political Dimension of Apocalyptic Thought," in C. A. Patrides and J. Wittreich, eds., *The Apocalypse in English Renaissance Thought and Literature*, (Ithaca, N.Y.: Cornell University Press, 1984), 183.

18. Andrew Marvell "The First Anniversary of the Government under O. C." 126-30.

19. See B. R. Capp, "The Fifth Monarchists and Popular Millenarianism," in J. F. McGregor and B. Reay, eds., *Radical Religion in the English Revolution* (Oxford: Oxford University Press, 1984), 183.

20. John Dryden, *Britannia Rediviva, a Poem on the Birth of the Prince*, 52-53.

21. Frederic Thruston, *England Safe and Triumphant*, 2 vols. (Coventry: F. C. and J. Rivington, 1812), 2:315.

22. Ibid., 1:33; 2:349.

23. Ibid., 2:358.

24. Ibid., 2:383.

25. George Croly, *The Apocalypse of St. John*, 3rd ed. (London: J. G. & F. Rivington, 1838), vii.

26. Henry Drummond, *A Defence of the Students of Prophecy* (London: James Nisbet, 1828), 115; *The Fate of Christendom*, 3rd ed. (London: Thomas Ainsworth, 1854), 3-7, 32.

27. Cecelia Tichi, *New World, New Earth: Environmental Reform in American Literature from the Puritans Through Whitman* (New Haven, Conn.: Yale University Press, 1979), 18, 51, 63, 263.

28. John Mellen, *A Sermon Preached at the West Parish in Lancaster* (Boston: Printed and sold by B. Mecom, 1760), 16, quoted in James W. Davidson, *The Logic of Millennial Thought: Eighteenth-century New England* (New Haven: Yale University Press, 1977), 209. Samuel Langdon, *Joy and Gratitude to God for the Long Life of a Great King, and the Conquest of Quebec* (Portsmouth, N.H.: Printed and sold by Daniel Fowle, 1760), 42-43, quoted in Nathan Hatch, *The Sacred Cause of Liberty: Republican Thought and the Millennium in Revolutionary New England* (New Haven, Conn.: Yale University Press, 1977), 42.

29. Hatch, *Sacred Cause*, 55. See Samuel West, *A Sermon Preached Before the Honorable Council* (Boston: Printed by John Gill, 1776).

30. David Austin, *The Downfall of Mystical Babylon: Or a Key to the Providence of God, in the Political Operations of 1793–94*, in Joseph Bellamy, *The Millennium*, ed. David Austin (Elizabethtown, N.J.: Printed by Shepard Kollock, 1794), 392-93, 409-10.

31. Timothy Dwight, *A Discourse on Some Events of the Last Century* (New Haven, Conn.: Printed by Ezra Read, 1801) 55, cited in Ernest Lee Tuveson, *Redeemer Nation: The Idea of America's Millennial Role* (Chicago and London: The University of Chicago Press, 1968), 112. See also Davidson, *Logic*, 287-97.

32. Edward Hine, *Forty-seven Identifications of the British Nation with the Lost Ten Tribes of Israel: Founded upon Five Hundred Scripture Proofs* (London: W. H. Guest, etc., 1874), 1-35.

33. Ibid., 40-41, 49-50.

34. Ibid., 118.

35. Ibid., 252-54, 278-79.

36. C. A. L. Totten, *The Hope of History: The Millennium* (New Haven, Conn.: The Our Race Publishing Company, 1892), 22, 78-87, 127, 130, 160-62.

37. W. H. Poole, *Anglo-Israel or the Saxon Race Proved to Be the Lost Tribes of Israel* (Toronto: William Briggs, 1889), 240-41.

38. Herbert W. Armstrong, *The United States and Britain in Prophecy* (Pasadena, Calif.: Worldwide Church of God, 1980), 151-84.

39. Hengstenberg, *Revelation*, 2:291-92.

40. Vondung, *Apokalypse*, 156-57.

41. Arlie J. Hoover, *The Gospel of Nationalism: German Patriotic Preaching from Napoleon to Versailles* (Stuttgart: Franz Steiner, 1986), 38.

42. Adolf Deissmann, *Inneres Aufgebot. Deutsche Worte im Weltkrieg* (Berlin: A. Scherl, 1915), reprinted in Gerhard Besier, *Die protestantischen Kirchen Europas im Ersten Weltkrieg. Ein Quellen- und Arbeitsbuch* (Göttingen: Vandenhoeck & Ruprecht, 1984), 125-27.

43. Adolf Deissmann, "Der Krieg und die Religion," *Deutsche Reden in schwerer Zeit* (Berlin: Die Zentralstelle für Volkswohlfahrt und der Verein für volkstümliche Kurse von Berliner Hochschullehrern, 1915), reprinted in Besier, *Die protestantischen Kirchen*, 120-21.

44. Adolf Deissmann, *Deutsche Schwertsegen* (Stuttgart and Berlin: Deutsche Verlags-Anstalt, 1915), 57-65.

45. Friedrich Gogarten, "Volk und Schöpfung," in *Protestantenblatt* 48 (1915): 55. See Vondung, *Apokalypse*, 191.

46. Joseph Goebbels, *The Early Goebbels Diaries 1925–1926*, ed. Helmut Heiber, trans. Oliver Watson (New York: Frederick A. Praeger, 1963), 92.

47. "In the next thousand years there will be no more revolution in Germany." Hitler's proclamation at the Nuremberg Rally, September 5, 1934. Max Deimarus, *Hitler, Reden und Proklamationen 1932–1945*, 2 parts in 4 vols. (Munich: Süddeutscher Verlag, 1965), 1.1:448.

48. Bryan R. Wilson, *Magic and the Millennium: A Sociological Study of Religious Movements of Protest Among Tribal and Third-world Peoples* (London: Heinemann, 1973), 50.

49. Bengt G. N. Sundkler, *Bantu Prophets in South Africa*, 2nd ed. (London: Oxford University Press, 1961), 291-92.

50. Vittorio Lanternari, *The Religions of the Oppressed: A Study of Modern Messianic Cults* (New York: New American Library, 1965), 41, 43.

51. Wilson, *Magic*, 64-9; Lanternari, *Religions*, 160-62; Karlene Faith, "One Love-One Heart-One Destiny: A Report on the Ras Tafarian Movement in Jamaica," in G. W. Trompf, ed., *Cargo Cults and Millenarian Movements: Transoceanic Comparisons of New Religious Movements*, Religion and Society 29 (Berlin and New York: Mouton de Gruyter, 1990), 297-99.

52. Priestley, *Works*, 14:486-88.

53. Bicheno, *Signs of the Times*, iv, 46-53, 312-14. Not everyone regarded the French Revolution as an act of divine deliverance. Samuel Horsley (1733–1806) described "the Atheistical democracy of France" as the little horn of the fourth beast of Daniel and expressed a sympathy for the pope that was uncharacteristic for an Anglican of that period. There was, he said, "nothing in the sufferings of the aged Pope, which can be the cause of exultation and joy, in the heart of any Christian" (Samuel Horsley, *Critical Disquisitions on the Eighteenth Chapter of Isaiah* [London: Printed by J. Nichols for F. Robson, 1799; Philadelphia: reprinted by J. Humphreys, 1800], 21, 94, 98-100; W. H. Oliver, *Prophets and Millennialists* (Auckland: University Press, 1978), 51-54.).

54. Cited in Arlie J. Hoover, *God, Germany, and Britain in the Great War* (New York: Praeger, 1989), 24-25.

55. James Plowden-Wardlaw, *The Test of War: War Addresses Given at Cambridge* (London: Scott, 1916), 77. Cited in Hoover, *God, etc.*, 29.

56. Hoover, *God, etc.*, 122.

57. Beckwith, *Apocalypse*, 308.

58. Charles, *Revelation*, 2:87; 1:xv.

59. Lynn Harold Hough, *The Clean Sword* (New York: Abingdon Press, 1918), 128-29. See Ray H. Abrams, *Preachers Present Arms* (Scottdale, Pa.: Herald Press, 1969), 65.

60. Abrams, *Preachers*, 104-5.

61. German artist Otto Pankok supported this theory. See Ulrike Camilla Gärtner, "Die wenig beachteten Lieblingskinder. Apokalypsefolgen im 20. Jahrhundert," in Richard W. Gassen and Bernhard Holezek, eds. *Apokalypse: ein Prinzip Hoffnung? Ernst Block zum 100. Geburtstag* (Heidelberg: Edition Braus, 1985), 193. See also Barclay, *Revelation*, 2:100. For Mussolini as Antichrist, see Paul Boyer, *When Time Shall Be No More: Prophecy Belief in Modern American Culture* (Cambridge, Mass.: Harvard University Press, 1992), 108-9, 218, 275.

62. Nathaniel Micklem, *May God Defend the Right!* (London: Hodder & Stoughton, 1939), 119-20.

63. Rowley, *Relevance*, 157-59.

64. Féret, *L'Apocalypse*, 294.

65. The Apocalypse played a part in Russian controversy. In the sixteenth-century dispute between the cities of Pskov and Moscow, the supporters of Pskov identified Moscow with the sixth head of the beast. But Philotheus, a champion of Moscow, who described the city as "the third Rome," explained it as the wilderness where the woman of Revelation 12 took refuge. During the seventeenth-century controversy about reform in the Russian Church, the Patriarch Nikon founded a monastery called the New Jerusalem, which his opponents, the Old Believers, described as Antichrist's kingdom. People expected Antichrist to arrive in 1666, a date they reached with the aid of the apocalyptic number 666, and opponents of church reform identified Nikon and Tsar Alexis with the beast. This kind of speculation continued in Russia, especially in connection with the tsars. The language and ideas of the Apocalypse were the coinage of religious and political controversy. James H. Billington, *The Icon and the Axe: An Interpretative History of Russian Culture* (New York: Vintage Books, 1970), 58-59, 142-44, 180, 201. See also Frederick C. Conybeare, *Russian Dissenters* (New York: Russell & Russell, 1962), 90, 94-101.

11. THE TRANSFORMATION OF SOCIETY

1. Samuel Hopkins, *A Treatise on the Millennium* (Boston, 1793), 45.

2. Ibid., 51, 56, 57.

3. Ibid., 59, 60-65, 75-78.

4. Ibid., 70-71.

5. Ibid., 71-73.

6. Ibid., 75.

7. Ibid., 116.

8. Joseph Emerson, *Lectures on the Millennium* (Boston, 1818), 276.

9. Samuel Taylor Coleridge, *The Collected Works of Samuel Taylor Coleridge*, vol. 2 (London: Routledge & Kegan Paul, 1970), 65-66.

10. Ibid., 2:66.

11. Charles Kingsley, *National Sermons* (London: Macmillan, 1880), 3.

12. Ibid., 28, 108-33.

13. *Songs of Praise: Enlarged Edition* (London: Oxford University Press, Humphrey Milford, 1931), No. 285.

14. Arthur S. Peake, *The Revelation of John* (London: Joseph Johnson, Primitive Methodist Publishing House, 1919), 376.

15. Charles, *Revelation,* 1:xv.

16. Beckwith, *Apocalypse,* 309.

17. Kingsley, *National Sermons,* 5.

18. Tichi, *New World,* 63.

19. Barlow's dreams are stated in two poems, the "Vision of Columbus" (1787) and "The Columbiad" (1806). See Tichi, *New World,* 114-50, and Tuveson, *Redeemer Nation,* 66.

20. Timothy Dwight, *The Conquest of Canaan: A Poem, in Eleven Books* (Hartford: Printed by Elisha Babcock, 1785), 10.535-612, 254-56. Reprint in *The Major Poems of Timothy Dwight,* intro. William J. McTaggart and William K. Bottorff (Gainesville, Fla.: Scholars' Facsimiles & Reprints, 1969). See also Tuveson, *Redeemer Nation,* 106-8.

21. Philip Freneau, *The Poems of Philip Freneau,* ed. Fred Lewis Pattee, 3 vols. (Princeton, N.J.: The University Library, 1907), 3:16.

22. Tuveson, *Redeemer Nation,* 81; *Millennial Harbinger,* 1, 1, January 4, 1830, 1.

23. Tuveson, *Redeemer Nation,* 123.

24. Washington Gladden, "Migrations and Their Lessons," *Publications of the Ohio Archaeological and Historical Society,* 3 (1891), cited in Tuveson, *Redeemer Nation,* 129.

25. Warren Lewis, "What to Do After the Messiah Has Come Again and Gone: Shaker 'Premillennial' Eschatology and Its Spiritual Aftereffects," in Bryant and Dayton, eds., *The Coming Kingdom,* 88-89.

26. Ricardo Foulkes, *El Apocalipsis de San Juan* (Buenos Aires-Grand Rapids: Nueva Creación and Eerdmans, 1989), 150.

27. Ibid., 77-78.

28. Dagoberto Ramírez Fernández, "La idolatría del poder. La Iglesia confesante en la situación de Apocalipsis 13," *Revista de Interpretación Bíblica Latinoamericana* 4 (1989): 109-28.

29. Dagoberto Ramírez Fernández, "El juicio de Dios a las transnacionales," *Revista de Interpretación Bíblica Latinoamericana* 5-6 (1990): 55-74.

30. Allan A. Boesak, *Comfort and Protest: Reflections on the Apocalypse of John of Patmos* (Philadelphia: Westminster Press, 1987), 14.

31. Ibid., 38.

32. Ibid., 105. Boesak admits that eventually the church renounced this position.

33. Ibid., 116.

34. Ibid., 72.

35. Ibid., 102-3, 120-21.

36. Ibid., 127-28.

37. Ibid., 135, 129.

38. Daniel Berrigan, *Beside the Sea of Glass: The Song of the Lamb* (New York: Seabury Press, 1978), 96.

39. Ibid., 103-7.

40. William Stringfellow, *An Ethic for Christians and Other Aliens in a Strange Land* (Waco, Tex.: Word Books, 1973), 25-37, 67-114.

41. Ibid., 56, 59-60, 155-56.

42. David Chilton, *Paradise Restored: A Biblical Theology of Dominion* (Tyler, Tex.: Reconstruction Press, 1985), 149-22; *The Days of Vengeance: An Exposition of the Book of Revelation* (Fort Worth, Tex.: Dominion Press, 1986), 1-6, 582-83, and passim. Chilton thinks that the fall of Babylon stands for the fall of Jerusalem in 70.

43. Robert Owen, *A Supplementary Appendix to the First Volume of the Life of Robert Owen. Containing a Series of Reports, Addresses, Memorials, and Other Documents Referred to in that Volume. 1808-1820* (London, 1858), 133; cited in Oliver, *Prophets*, 187.

44. Robert Owen, *The Life of Robert Owen, Written by Himself. With Selections from His Writings and Correspondence* (London, 1858), 1:36. Cited in Oliver, *Prophets*, 191.

45. Blair, *New Harmony Story*, 13-36.

46. Ibid., 197-216.

47. Karl Marx and Friedrich Engels, "Manifesto of the Communist Party," in Karl Marx and Friedrich Engels, *Basic Writings on Politics and Philosophy*, ed. Lewis S. Feuer (Garden City, N.Y.: Anchor Books, Doubleday & Co., 1959), 35-39.

48. Friedrich Engels, "On the History of Early Christianity," in Marx and Engels, *Basic Writings*, 168-78, 184-85. Engels was uncertain about the identity of its author but thought he might have been the apostle John.

12. THE CULTURAL HERITAGE

1. See Frederick van der Meer, *Apocalypse: Visions from the Book of Revelation in Western Art* (London: Thames and Hudson, 1978), 52. For similar examples in the Eastern churches see N. Thierry, "L'Apocalypse de Jean et l'iconographie byzantine," in R. Petraglio et al., *L'Apocalypse de Jean: Traditions exégétiques et iconographiques* (Geneva: Libraire Droz, 1979), 322-24.

2. Meer, *Apocalypse*, 237-51.

3. Thierry, "L'Apocalypse," 324.

4. Meer, *Apocalypse*, 189-91.

5. Susan Pfleger, "Die Apokalypse in der Gegenreformation," in *Apokalypse*, eds. Gassen and Holeczek, 112-14.

6. Meer, *Apocalypse*, 136-37, 144-46.

7. Ibid., 44.

8. Helmut von Erffa and Allen Staley, *The Paintings of Benjamin West* (New Haven, Conn.: Yale University Press, 1986), 391.

9. Meer, *Apocalypse*, 148.

10. Ibid., 176-87, 314-31.

11. Ibid., 258-71.

12. Ibid., 22-23; M. V. Alpatov, *Early Russian Icon Painting* (Moscow: Iskusstvo, 1978), Plates 159-62.

13. Meer, *Apocalypse,* 40, 93-107.

14. Ibid., 108-27.

15. Ibid., 129-31, 172-73; Florens Deuchler, Jeffrey M. Hoffeld, and Helmut Nickel, *The Cloisters Apocalypse* (New York: The Metropolitan Museum of Art, 1972); A. G. and W. O. Hassall, *The Douce Apocalypse* (New York: Thomas Yosseloff, 1961).

16. Meer, *Apocalypse,* 152-70.

17. Ibid., 202-35.

18. Ibid., 285, 289, 294, 300.

19. Raymond Lister, *The Paintings of William Blake* (Cambridge: Cambridge University Press, 1986), Plate 17.

20. Gassen and Holeczek, eds., *Apokalypse,* 131, 133.

21. Ibid., 189-90.

22. E. J. de Jager, ed., *Contemporary African Art in South Africa* (Cape Town: C. Struik, 1973), plate 40.

23. Gassen and Holeczek, eds., *Apokalypse,* 244-46.

24. For example, Vladimir Baranoff-Rossiné, Julius Diez, Paul Weber (ibid., 248-49, 254-55, 266-67).

25. See 58.

26. See Florence Sandler, "The Faerie Queene: An Elizabethan Apocalypse," in Patrides and Wittreich, *Apocalypse,* 148-74.

27. Milton, *Paradise Lost* 6.

28. Ibid., 12.549-51. Milton's sonnet on the massacre of the Waldensians also echoes the Apocalypse.

29. See 167.

30. William Blake, *Complete Writings,* ed. Geoffrey Keynes (Oxford: Oxford University Press, 1969), 533 (*Milton,* 2.41, 5). See also ibid., 636, 708, 741 (*Jerusalem,* 1. Plate 15, 15-16; 3. Plate 70, 15; 4. Plate 93, 20-25).

31. Ibid., 506 (*Milton,* 1.22, 40-62). But Swedenborg receives adverse criticism in Blake's "Annotations to Swedenborg's 'The Wisdom of Angels Concerning Divine Providence' " (Ibid., 131-33).

32. Ibid., 532 (*Milton,* 2.40, 20-22).

33. Much of Blake's imagery is ambiguous, and when he aspires to build Jerusalem "In England's green and pleasant Land," he is probably dreaming of a life of both inward and outward liberty (ibid., 481, *Milton,* Preface, 9, 13-16).

34. Ibid., 652 (*Jerusalem, to the Jews,* 85-88).

35. Vicente Blasco Ibañez, *The Four Horsemen of the Apocalypse,* trans. Charlotte Brewster Jordan (New York: E. P. Dutton and Company, 1918), 179.

36. Ibid., 420.

37. Katherine Anne Porter, *Pale Horse, Pale Rider* (New York: Harcourt, Brace and Company, 1939), 264.

38. John Mason Brown, *The Ordeal of a Playwright, Robert E. Sherwood and the Challenge of War* (New York: Harper & Row, 1970), 41.

39. Ibid., 288-89.

40. Ibid., 292.

41. Mary Wilson Carpenter and George P. Landow, "Ambiguous Revelations: The Apocalypse and Victorian Literature," in Patrides and Wittreich, eds. *The Apocalypse in English and Renaissance Thought,* 301-4.

42. Yeats, *Vision* 279-80.

43. Kermode, *Sense of an Ending*, 88.

44. Joseph Wittreich, "The Apocalypse in *King Lear,*" in Patrides and Wittreich, *Apocalypse*, 184-85.

45. Robert Payne. "Introduction," *The Apocalypse of Our Time and Other Writings by Vasily Rozanov* (New York: Praeger Publishers, 1977), 10-17; see also 226, 236-40.

46. C. S. Lewis, *The Last Battle: a Story for Children* (Harmondsworth: Penguin Books, 1972), 135-43, 162-62.

47. Paul Claudel, *Oeuvres complètes* (Paris: Éditions Gallimard, 1965), 25:446. This allusion is to his *Paul Claudel interroge l'Apocalypse*, written during the war but published in 1952. It was not his only work on this theme. The posthumously published *Au milieu des vitraux de l'Apocalypse* (*Oeuvres*, 26) was finished in 1932 (*Oeuvres*, 26:315-36). His *Introduction à l'Apocalypse* (*Oeuvres*, 21) was a lecture given in 1946.

48. Claudel, *Oeuvres*, 25:196-98, 168-72.

49. Ibid., 25:422-28.

50. Ibid., 25:110, 182.

51. Ibid., 21:95; 25:82-83; 26:137.

52. Ibid., 25:148-49, 128.

53. D. H. Lawrence, *Apocalypse*, with an Introduction by Richard Aldington (Harmondsworth: Penguin Books, 1960), 14.

54. Ibid., 87-88.

55. Ibid., 17-18.

56. For the influence of theosophy, see ibid., 60-69.

13. THE INNER LIFE AND WORSHIP

1. Andreas, *Apokalypse,* 51, 124.

2. St. John of the Cross, *The Complete Works*, trans. and ed. E. Allison Peers, 3 vols. in 1 (London: Burns and Oates, 1964), 1:101-2.

3. Ibid., 2:311.

4. Ibid., 2:261.

5. John Ruusbroec, *The Spiritual Espousals and Other Works*, intro. and trans. James A. Wiseman (New York: Paulist Press, 1985), 160.

6. Ibid., 170.

7. George Fox, *Gospel Truth Demonstrated* (Philadelphia: Marcus T. Gould, 1831), 1:178, 180, 182, 190.

8. Isaac Penington, *Works* (Sherwoods, N.Y.: David Heston, 1861), 1:318-19.

9. Ibid., 1:334.

10. Alex. R. MacEwen, *Antoinette Bourignon, Quietist* (London: Hodder & Stoughton, 1910), 92. Antoinette Bourignon, *Oeuvres*, 16 (Amsterdam: Jean Rieuvert & Pierre Arent, 1681): 18-80, 124. See also 18.1 (1679): 102. Pierre Serrurier (or Serrarius) (1600–69) shared this concern for both inward and outward change. He combined the expectation of a future millennium with an emphasis on the possibility of a present change in the inner life of individuals (Ernestine G. E. van der Wall, trans. Cartine van Heesewijk, "Petrus Serrarius [1600-1669] et le millénarisme mystique," in *Etudier*, 155-68).

11. See Nils Thune, *The Behmenists and the Philadelphians* (Uppsala: Almquist & Wiksells, 1948).

12. Jane Lead, *The Signs of the Time, Forerunning the Kingdom of Christ, and Evidencing When It Is Come* (London, 1699), 6.

13. Ibid., 29.

14. Jane Lead, *The Revelation of Revelations* (London: Printed by A. Sowle, & J. Lead, 1683), 25.

15. Emanuel Swedenborg, *The True Christian Religion*, 3 vols. (Boston: Houghton, Mifflin and Company, 1907) 3:989 (sec. 779).

16. Ibid., 3:982-84 (secs. 772-75).

17. Emanuel Swedenborg, *The Apocalypse Revealed*, 3 vols. (Boston: Houghton Mifflin and Co. 1907), 2:575-93 (secs. 532-44).

18. Ibid., 2:623, 645, 655 (secs. 567, 594, 606).

19. Ibid., 1:238-42 (secs. 241-44).

20. Ibid., 1:295-317 (secs. 298-323).

21. Ibid., 2:457-65 (secs. 449-55).

22. Ibid., 2:529 (sec. 493).

23. Ibid., 2:774 (sec. 707).

24. Helen Keller, *My Religion* (New York: Swedenborg Foundation, 1927).

25. Helena Petrovna Blavatsky, *The Secret Doctrine*, vols. 1 and 2 (Los Angeles: The Theosophy Company, 1947), 2:103, 229, 355-56, 383-84, 482-85, 497, 748. The original edition was published in 1888.

26. James M. Pryse, *The Apocalypse Unsealed* (London: John M. Watkins; New York: J. M. Pryse, 1910), 1.

27. Ibid., 9.

28. The acts are (1) the seal visions, the conquest of the seven centers of the nervous system; (2) the trumpet visions, the conquest of the seven centers of the brain; (3) Revelation 12 and 13, the elimination from the mind of all impure thoughts; (4) Revelation 14, the conquest of the seven cardiac centers; (5) the bowl visions, the conquest of the generative centers and the birth of the spiritual body; (6) Revelation 17–19, the extinction of the phantasmal demon in the individual; (7) the last judgment, the summing up of completed cycle of lives that have taken place by means of reincarnation. Pryse thinks, as Plato did, that a thousand years elapse between each of a person's incarnations. The seven-headed beast is the desire for a sentient existence, and it causes the soul to be reincarnated. Ibid., 33-35, 48-50, 62, 66-67, 70-73.

29. Rudolf Steiner, *The Apocalypse of St. John*, rev. M. Cotterell (London: Anthroposophical Publishing Company, 1958), 34, 38.

30. Steiner, *Christianity as Mystical Fact*, 3rd ed. (New York: G. P. Putnam's Sons, 1914), 183-88.

31. Jeanne-Marie Bouvier de la Motte Guyon, *Autobiography of Madame Guyon*, trans. T. T. Allen, 2 vols. (London: Kegan Paul, Trench, Truebner & Co., 1897), 1:153.

32. Ibid., 2:31.

33. Ibid., 2:263-64.

34. Jeanne-Marie Guyon, *La sainte Bible ou le Vieux et le Nouveau Testament, avec des explications et réflexions qui regardent la vie intérieure*, 20 vols. (1790), 20:86-87, 99-100, 140, 156, 189, 200, 258.

35. Christina G. Rossetti, *The Face of the Deep: A Devotional Commentary on the Apocalypse* (London: Society for Promoting Christian Knowledge, 1892), 331.

36. Ibid., 406.

37. Ibid., 459.

38. Andreas, *Apokalypse*, 44; Primasius *In Apocalypsin* 1.3 (CCL 92:44-45); Bede *Expositio*, PL 93:142.

39. Bridget of Sweden, *Revelationes Caelestes* (Monachii: Sumptibus Joannis Wagneri & Joannis Hermanni à Gelder, Typis Sebastiani Rauch, 1680), 4.39 (p. 261).

40. John Wesley, *Explanatory Notes upon the New Testament*, 932.

41. Claudel, *Oeuvres*, 26:11-12.

42. Guyon, *Autobiography*, 2:90.

43. Rossetti, *Face of the Deep*, 174.

44. Ibid, 176.

45. Ibid., 201.

46. Ibid., 381-82.

47. Ibid., 384.

48. See C. Heitz, "Retentissement de l'Apocalypse dans l'art de l'époque carolingienne," in Petraglio, etc., *L'Apocalypse*, 219-21.

49. *The Liturgies of S. Mark, S. James, S. Clement, S. Chrysostom, and The Church of Malabar*, trans. J. M. Neale (London: J. T. Hayes, 1859; reprint, New York: AMS, 1969), 21. Since the reference to the cherubim was probably not in the earliest forms of the liturgy, it is unlikely that the Apocalypse derived it from an early liturgy. The probability increases that the Apocalypse influenced the liturgy. See Geoffrey J. Cuming, *The Liturgy of St Mark*, Orientalia Christiana Analecta, 234 (Rome: Pontificium Institutum Studiorum Orientalium, 1990): 69-74, 120.

50. Neale, *Liturgies*, 49. The liturgies of St. Chrysostom and the Malabar Church of India, like the Apocalypse, combine the tens of thousands of angels with the six-winged seraphim. Ibid., 114, 145.

51. "White-robed" rather than "noble" is the meaning of the Latin *candidatus*.

52. "Beate Martyr, prospera," Prudentius *Perit* 5.9-12 (*Opera* CCL 126:294), trans. Athelstan Riley, *English Hymnal* (London: Oxford University Press, Humphrey Milford, and A. R. Mowbray, 1906), 155 (No. 185).

53. John Mason Neale, *Hymns of the Eastern Church* (London: J. T. Hayes, 1862), 52, 65.

54. "Urbs beata Hierusalem" (Guido Maria Dreves, *Ein Jahrtausend Lateinischer Hymnendichtung*, revised by Clemens Blume, 2 vols. [Leipzig: O. R. Reisland, 1909], 2:385-86; *Analecta Hymnica*, 55 vols. [Leipzig: Fues's Verlag (O. R. Reisland), 1886–1922] 51:110), trans. John Mason Neale, *Mediaeval Hymns and Sequences*, 2nd ed. (London: Joseph Martin, 1863), 18-19.

55. Dreves, *Jahrtausend*, 1:130; *Anal. Hymn.* 50:285; trans. Robert Campbell, *Hymns Ancient and Modern* (London: William Clowes and Sons, 1861?), No. 106.

56. Neale, *Mediaeval Hymns*, 81-82.

57. Neale, *Hymnal Noted*, pt. 1 (London: Novello, Eve, & Co., et al., 1851), 203-4 (No. 104), from "Jerusalem luminosa," F. J. Mone, *Lateinische Hymnen des Mittelalters*, 3 vols. (Freiburg im Breisgau: Herder, 1853–55), 1:433-34 (No. 209).

58. Catherine Winkworth, *Lyra Germanica*, 2nd ser. (New York: Anson D. F. Randolph, 1858), 291.

59. Frances Elizabeth Cox, trans., *Hymns from the German* (London: Society for Promoting Christian Knowledge, 1890), 46 (No. 23).

60. W. Prid, *The Glasse of vaine-glorie* (Printed at London by John Windet, Baynard's Castle, 1585).

61. W. T. Brooke, in John Julian, *Dictionary of Hymnology*, 2 vols. (New York: Dover Publications, 1957), 1:580-83.

62. Francis T. Palgrave, *Amenophis and Other Poems Sacred and Secular* (London: Macmillan and Co., 1892), 95.

63. Walter Russell Bowie, *The United Methodist Hymnal* (Nashville: The United Methodist Publishing House, 1989), 726.

64. See 179.

65. Percy Dearmer and Archibald Jacob, *Songs of Praise Discussed* (London: Oxford University Press, 1933), 239-41. See also 203.

66. John Mason, *Spiritual Songs, or Songs of Praise to Almighty God upon Several Occasions*, and Thomas Shepherd, *Penitential Cries* (London: D. Sedgwick, 1859), 1.

67. Isaac Watts, *The Psalms and Hymns of the Late Dr. Isaac Watts*, ed. Robert Goodacre, 2 vols. in 1 (London: Printed for Francis Westley, 1821), 2:56.

68. From "Give me the wings of faith to rise," in Watts, *Psalms and Hymns*, 2:282.

69. John and Charles Wesley, *Poetical Works*, 4:51.

70. Paul Gerhardt, *Dichtungen und Schriften*, ed. Eberhard von Cranach-Sichart (Munich: Verlag Paul Müller, 1957), 381-84.

71. *The Story of the Jubilee Singers: With Their Songs*, 3rd ed. (London: Hodder and Stoughton, 1876), 168. The spiritual is entitled "Ride on, King Jesus." According to John Lovell, Jr., *Black Song: The Forge and the Flame. The Story of How the Afro-American Spiritual Was Hammered Out* (New York: Macmillan, 1972), 253, the second line is "No man can hinder him."

72. *Jubilee Singers*, 137.

73. Dreves, *Jahrtausend*, 1:357; *Anal. Hymn.* 50:584.

74. Wesley and Wesley, *Poetical works*, 3:64.

75. (New York: Biglow and Main, 1872), no. 106.

76. Ibid., 149 (no. 210).

77. In John 16:33, Jesus says that he has overcome the world. According to 1 John 5:4-5, faithful believers overcome the world, and in the Apocalypse there are numerous references to those who overcome (Rev. 2:7, 11, 17, 26; 3:5, 12, 21, etc.).

78. *Coget omnes ante thronum* ("It [the trumpet] will gather all before the throne"). *Liber scriptus proferetur* ("The written book will be brought forth"). Dreves, *Jahrtausend*, 1:329-30.

79. *Jubilee Singers*, 141.

80. The sun clothes her, according to Conrad of Hamburg, and she treads underfoot the changeable moon and the unstable world. Dreves, *Jahrtausend*, 1:422; *Anal. Hymn.*, 3:21.

81. Markus Jenny, *Luther/Zwingli/Calvin in ihren Liedern* (Zürich: Theologischer Verlag, 1983), 142-45.

82. Dreves, *Jahrtausend*, 317; *Anal. Hymn.*, 9:161.

83. Watts, *Psalms and Hymns*, 2:53 (*Hymns*, Bk. 1, No. 58).

84. Johann Ludwig Conrad Allendorf, trans. Catherine Winkworth, *Lyra Germanica*, 1st ser. (New York: Delisser & Procter, 1859), 251.

85. An anthem by John Blow (1649–1708) sets to music the verse "I beheld, and lo, a great multitude, which no man could number" (Rev. 7:9). Charles Villiers Stanford (1852–1924) selected a group of verses from the vision of Revelation 7, beginning with "I saw another angel ascending from the east" (Rev. 7:2-3, 9-12).

86. See, for example, Thomas Weelkes (c.1575–1623), Thomas Tomkins (1572–1656), and John Goss (1800–80). All of the above compositions are listed together with many other settings of passages from the Apocalypse in James Laster, comp., *Catalogue of Choral Music Arranged in Biblical Order* (Metuchen, N.J., and London: Scarecrow Press, 1983), 330-54.

87. Charles Sanford Terry, *Joh. Seb. Bach: Cantata Texts Sacred and Secular* (London: The Holland Press, 1964), 454-60. Two other cantatas, "Man singet mit Freuden vom Sieg" ("They Sing with Joy of the Victory") and "Herr Gott, dich loben alle wir" ("Lord God, We All Praise Thee"), mentioned by Terry, refer to the defeat of Satan.

88. "Worthy is the Lamb that was slain to receive power, and riches, and wisdom, and strength, and honour, and glory, and blessing" (Rev. 5:12 AV); "And hath redeemed us to God by his blood" (based on Rev. 5:9 AV); "Blessing, and honour, and glory, and power, be unto him that sitteth upon the throne, and unto the Lamb for ever and ever" (Rev. 5:13 AV). The last of these verses provided the words for an anthem by William Boyce (c.1710–79).

SELECT BIBLIOGRAPHY

The following list of patristic writers alludes to the series in which they are to be found. Further details are given in the endnotes.

Abbo, PL 139; Adso Dervensis, CCM 45; Alcuin, PL 100; Ambrosius Autpertus, CCM 28; Anselm of Havelberg, PL 188; Arethas, PG 106; Augustine, Loeb; CCM 28; Barnabas, SC 172; Bede, PL 93; Berengaud, PL 17; Bruno of Segni, PL 165; Caesarius of Arles, PL 35 (Augustine); Commodianus, CCL 128; Cyril of Jerusalem, PG 33; Dionysius bar Salibi, CSCO 60; Epiphanius, PG 42; Eusebius, PG 20, 22; Gennadius, PL 58; Haimo, PL 117; Hippolytus, PG 10; GCS 1.2, PG 10; Irenaeus, SC 34, 152, 153, PG 7A, 7B; Jerome, CCL 8; Justin, PG 5; Lactantius, CSEL 19; Martin of Leon, PL 209; Methodius, SC 95; Origen, PG 13; Primasius, CCL 92; Quintus Julius Hilarianus, PL 13; Quodvultdeus, CCL 60; Richard of St. Victor, PL 196; Rupert of Deutz, PL 167, 169; Sulpicius Severus, CSEL 1; Tertullian, CCL 1, 2; Theophylact, PG 123; Victorinus, CSEL 49. Andreas, Apringius, Beatus, and Oecumenius are listed below.

* * *

Abauzit, Firmin. *Oeuvres diverses,* 1. London, 1770.
'Abdu'l-Baha. *Some Unanswered Questions.* Translated by Laura Clifford Barnett. 4th ed. Wilmette, IL: Bahá'i Publishing Trust, 1954.
Alcazar, Luis de. *Vestigatio Arcani Sensus in Apocalypsi.* Antwerpiae: Apud Ioannem Keerbergium, 1614.

Alexander Minorita. *Expositio in Apocalypsim*. Edited by Alois Wachtel. Monumenta Germaniae Historica. Quellen zur Geistesgeschichte des Mittelalters, 1. Weimar: Hermann Böhlaus Nachfolger, 1955.

Allo, E-B. *Saint Jean, L'Apocalypse*. 4th ed. Paris: Libraire LeCoffre, J. Gabalda et Cie, 1933.

Alsted, Johann Heinrich. *Diatribe de Mille Annis Apocalypticis . . .* 2nd ed. Frankfurt: Sumptibus Conradi Eifridi, 1630. ET., William Burton, *The Beloved City* (London, 1643). In Beate Griesing et al., *J. H. Alsted, Herborns calvinistische Theologie und Wissenschaft*. Aspekte der englischen Geistes-und Kulturgeschichte, 14. Frankfurt am Main: Verlag Peter Lang, 1988.

Andreas. *Der Apokalypse-Kommentar des Andreas von Kaisareia*. Part 1 of J. Schmid, *Studien zur Geschichte des griechischen Apokalypse-textes*. Münchener theologische Studien. Munich: Karl Zink Verlag, 1955-56.

Apringius de Béja. *Son commentaire de l'Apocalypse*. Edited by Marius Férotin. Paris: Bibliothèque patriologique, 1900.

Auberlen, Carl Gustav. *The Prophecies of Daniel and the Revelations of St. John*. Translated by Adolph Slater. Edinburgh: T. & T. Clark, 1856.

Bale, John. *The Image of bothe churches*. 1543?

Barclay, William. *The Revelation of John*. 2nd ed. 2 vols. Philadelphia: Westminster Press, 1976.

Barkun, Michael. *Disaster and the Millennium*. New Haven: Yale University Press, 1974.

Baur, Ferdinand Christian. *The Church History of the First Three Centuries*. 3rd ed. Translated by Allan Menzies. London: Williams and Norgate, 1878.

Beasley-Murray, G. R. *The Book of Revelation*. New Century Bible Commentary. Rev. ed. Grand Rapids: Eerdmans; London: Marshall, Morgan, & Scott, 1978.

Beatus. *In Apocalipsin Libri Duodecim*. Edited by Henry A. Sanders. Papers and Monographs of the American Academy in Rome, 7. Rome: American Academy in Rome, 1930.

Beckwith, Isbon T. *The Apocalypse of John: Studies in Introduction*. New York: Macmillan Co., 1919.

Bengel, Johann Albrecht. *Erklärte Offenbarung Johannis oder vielmehr Jesu Christi*. 2nd ed. Stuttgart, 1773.

———. *Gnomon Novi Testamenti*. London: David Nutt, and Williams and Norgate, 1855.

Berrigan, Daniel. *Beside the Sea of Glass: the Song of the Lamb*. New York: Seabury Press, 1978.

Bicheno, James. *The Signs of the Times, A New Edition*. London: Printed by J. Adlard, sold by Johnson et al., 1808.

Blake, William. *Complete Writings*. Edited by Geoffrey Keynes. Oxford: Oxford University Press, 1969.

Bleek, Friedrich. *Lectures on the Apocalypse*. Edited by Th. Hossbach and Samuel Davidson. London and Edinburgh: Williams and Norgate, 1875.

Blevins, James L. *Revelation as Drama*. Nashville: Broadman Press, 1984.

Böcher, Otto. *Die Johannesapokalypse.* Erträge der Forschung 41. Darmstadt: Wissenschaftliche Buchgesellschaft, 1975.

Boesak, Allan. *Comfort and Protest: Reflections on the Apocalypse of John of Patmos.* Philadelphia: Westminister Press, 1987.

Boring, M. Eugene. *Revelation.* Interpretation Commentaries. Louisville: Westminster/John Knox Press, 1989.

Bossuet, Jacques Bénigne. *Oeuvres complètes.* 11 vols. Lyon: Libraire Ecclésiastique de Briday, 1877.

Bousset, Wilhelm. *Die Offenbarung Johannis.* 2nd ed. Göttingen: Vandenhoeck & Ruprecht, 1906.

Bowman, J. W. *The Drama of the Book of Revelation.* Philadelphia: Westminster Press, 1955.

Brightman, Thomas. *Apocalypsis Apocalypseos. A Revelation of the Revelation.* Amsterdam, 1615.

Burkitt, F. C. *The Rules of Tyconius,* in *Texts and Studies* 3.1. Cambridge: University Press, 1894.

Burnet, Thomas. *The Sacred Theory of the Earth.* London: Centaur Press, 1965.

Caird, G. B. *A Commentary on the Revelation of St. John the Divine.* New York: Harper & Row, 1966.

Charles, R. H. *A Critical and Exegetical Commentary on the Revelation of St. John.* 2 vols. Edinburgh: T. & T. Clark, 1920.

—————. *Studies in the Apocalypse.* 2nd ed. Edinburgh: T. & T. Clark, 1915.

Chilton, David. *Paradise Restored. A Biblical Theology of Dominion.* Tyler, Tex: Reconstruction Press, 1985.

Claudel, Paul. *Oeuvres complètes.* 26 vols. Paris: Éditions Gallimard, 1955-65.

Cohn, Norman. *The Pursuit of the Millennium.* London: Granada, 1970.

Collins, Adela Yarbro. *The Combat Myth in the Book of Revelation.* HDR, 9. Missoula, Mont.: Scholars Press, 1976.

—————. *Crisis and Catharsis: the Power of the Apocalypse.* Philadelphia: Westminster Press, 1984.

—————. ed. *Early Christian Apocalypticism: Genre and Social Setting.* Semeia, 36. Decatur, Ga. Scholars Press, 1986.

Collins, J. J. "Apocalypse: The Morphology of a Genre." *Semeia* 14 (1979).

Corrodi, Heinrich. *Kritische Geschichte des Chiliasmus.* 3 vols. Frankfurt and Leipzig, 1781–83.

Corsini, Eugenio. *The Apocalypse.* Translated by Francis J. Moloney. Wilmington, Del.: Michael Glazier, 1983.

Cullmann, Oscar. *The Johannine Circle.* Philadelphia: Westminster Press, 1976.

Darby, J. N. *Collected Writings.* Edited by William Kelly. Kingston on Thames: Stow Hill Bible and Tract Depot, 1962-.

Döllinger, J. J. Ignaz von. *Beiträge zur Sektengeschichte des Mittelalters.* 2 vols. Munich: Beck, 1890. Reprint. New York: Burt Franklin, 1960.

Dupuis, Charles-François. *The Origin of All Religious Worship.* New Orleans, 1872. Reprint. New York: Garland Publishing, 1984.

Dupuis, Charles-François. *Origine de tous les cultes, ou religion universelle.* 3 vols. Paris: H. Agasse, l'an 3 (1795).

Düsterdieck, Friedrich. *Critical and Exegetical Handbook to the Revelation of John.* Translated by Henry E. Jacobs. New York: Funk & Wagnalls, 1887.

Edwards, Jonathan. *Apocalyptic Writings.* Edited by Stephen J. Stein, *The Works of Jonathan Edwards.* New Haven and London: Yale University Press, 1977.

Eichhorn, Johann Gottfried. *Commentarius in Apocalypsin.* Gottingae: Typis Jo. Christ. Dieterich, 1791.

———. *Einleitung in das Neue Testament.* 2 vols. Leipzig: Weidmannische Buchhandlung, 1810.

Ellul, Jacques. *Apocalypse: the Book of Revelation.* Translated by George W. Schreiner. New York: Seabury Press, 1977.

Erasmus, Desiderius. *Opera Omnia,* 6. Lugduni Batavorum: Petri Vabder, 1705. Reprint. Hildesheim: Georg Olms, 1961.

Ewald, Georg Heinrich August. *Commentarius in Apocalypsin Johannis.* Lipsiae: Sumtibus Librariae Hahnianae, 1828.

Farrer, A. M. *The Revelation of St. John the Divine.* Oxford: Clarendon Press, 1964.

———. *A Rebirth of Images.* Westminster: Dacre Press, 1949.

Féret, H.-M. *L'Apocalypse de Saint Jean: Vision chrétienne de l'histoire.* Paris: Corrêa, 1943.

Firth, Katharine R. *The Apocalyptic Tradition in Reformation Britain 1530-1645.* Oxford: Oxford University Press, 1979.

Ford, J. Massyngberde. *Revelation.* Anchor Bible. Garden City, New York: Doubleday, 1975.

Foulkes, Ricardo. *El Apocalypsis de San Juan.* Buenos Aires-Grand Rapids: Nueva Creación and Eerdmans, 1989.

Foxe, John. *Actes and Monuments of Matters Most Speciall and Memorable.* 1583.

———. *Eicasmi seu meditationes in sacram Apocalypsim.* Londini: Impensis Geor. Byshop, 1587.

Froom, LeRoy Edward. *The Prophetic Faith of Our Fathers.* 4 vols. Washington, D.C.: Review and Herald, 1948-50.

Frye, Northrop. *The Great Code. The Bible and Literature.* New York: Harcourt Brace Jovanovitch, 1983.

Gager, John G. *Kingdom and Community: The Social World of Early Christianity.* Englewood Cliffs, New Jersey: Prentice-Hall, 1975.

Garrett, Clarke. *Respectable Folly: Millenarians and the French Revolution in France and England.* Baltimore: Johns Hopkins University Press, 1975.

Gassen, Richard W., and Bernhard Holezek, eds. *Apokalypse: ein Prinzip Hoffnung?* Heidelberg: Edition Braus, 1985.

The Geneva Bible. The Annotated New Testament 1602 Edition. Edited by Gerald T. Sheppard. Pilgrim Classic Commentaries. New York: Pilgrim Press, 1989.

Grotius, Hugo. *Opera Theologica.* 3 vols. in 4. Amsteldaemi: Heredes Joannis Blaev, 1679. Reprint. Friedrich Frommann, 1972.

Gunkel, H. *Schöpfung und Chaos in Urzeit und Endzeit.* Göttingen: Vandenhoeck & Ruprecht, 1895.

Guyon, Jeanne-Marie Bouvier de la Motte. *Autobiography of Madame Guyon.* Translated by T. T. Allen. 2 vols. London: Kegan Paul, Trench, Truebner & Co., 1897.

————. *La sainte Bible ou le Vieux et le Nouveau Testament, avec des explications & réflexions qui regardent la vie intérieure.* 20 vols. 1790.

Hammond, Henry. *A Paraphrase and Annotations upon all the Books of the New Testament.* 4 vols. Oxford: University Press, 1845.

Hanson, Paul. *The Dawn of Apocalyptic.* Philadelphia: Fortress Press, 1979.

Harrison, J. F. C. *The Second Coming. Popular Millenarianism, 1780-1850.* New Brunswick, N.J.: Rutgers University Press, 1979.

Hartenstein, Karl Wilhelm. *Der wiederkommende Herr: eine Auslegung der Offenbarung des Johannes für die Gemeinde,* Stuttgart: Evangelische Verlag, 1953.

Hatch, Nathan. *The Sacred Cause of Liberty: Republican Thought and the Millennium in Revolutionary New England.* New Haven: Yale University Press, 1977.

Hemer, Colin J. *The Letters to the Seven Churches of Asia in their Local Setting.* Journal for the Study of the New Testament Supplement Series 11. Sheffield: JSOT Press, Department of Biblical Studies, University of Sheffield, 1986.

Hengstenberg, Ernst Wilhelm. *The Revelation of St John.* Translated by Patrick Fairbairn. 2 vols. Edinburgh: T. & T. Clark, 1851.

Herder, Johann Gottfried von. *Sämmtliche Werke.* Edited by Berhard Suphan. 33 vols. Berlin: Weidmannsche Buchhandlung, 1877-1913.

Hill, Christopher. *Antichrist in Seventeenth-Century England.* London: Oxford University Press, 1971.

————. *The World Turned Upside Down.* Harmondsworth: Penguin Books, 1975.

Hofmann, J. Chr. K. *Weissagung und Erfüllung im alten und im neuen Testament.* 2 vols. Nördlingen: C. H. Beck, 1841, 1844.

Hopkins, Samuel. *A Treatise on the Millennium.* Boston, 1793.

James I of England (James VI of Scotland). *A Paraphrase Upon the Revelation of the Apostle S. Iohn.* In *The Workes of the Most High and Mighty Prince, Iames.* London: Printed by Robert Barker and Iohn Bill, 1616.

Joachim of Fiore. *Expositio in Apocalypsim.* Venice, 1527. Reprint. Frankfurt am Main: Minerva, 1964.

————. *Liber Concordiae novi ac veteris Testamenti.* Venice, 1519. Reprint. Frankfurt am Main: Minerva, 1964.

John of the Cross, St. *Complete Works.* Translated and edited by E. Allison Peers. 3 vols. in 1. London: Burns and Oates, 1964.

Jung, Carl Gustav. *Answer to Job.* Translated by R. F. C. Hull. London: Routledge & Kegan Paul, 1954.

Jurieu, Pierre. *The Accomplishment of the Scripture Prophecies.* London, 1687.

Kamlah, Walter. *Apokalypse und Geschichtstheologie. Die mittelalterliche Auslegung der Apokalypse vor Joachim von Fiore.* Berlin: Verlag Dr. Emil Ebering, 1935.

Kermode, Frank E. *The Sense of an Ending. Studies in the Theory of Fiction.* New York: Oxford University Press, 1967.

Koch, Klaus. *The Rediscovery of Apocalyptic.* London: S. C. M. Press, 1972.

Kraft, Heinrich. *Die Offenbarung des Johannes.* Tübingen: J. C. B. Mohr (Paul Siebeck), 1974.

Kretschmar, Georg. *Die Offenbarung des Johannes: Die Geschichte ihrer Auslegung im 1. Jahrtausend.* Stuttgart: Calwer Verlag, 1985.

Kuyper, Abraham. *The Revelation of St. John.* Translated by John Hendrik de Vries. Grand Rapids: William B. Eerdmans, 1964.

Ladd, George E. *Crucial Questions about the Kingdom of God.* Grand Rapids: Eerdmans, 1952.

———. *A Theology of the New Testament.* Grand Rapids: Eerdmans, 1974.

Lanternari, Vittorio. *The Religions of the Oppressed: a Study of Modern Messianic Cults.* New York: New American Library, 1965.

Laster, James, comp. *Catalogue of Choral Music Arranged in Biblical Order.* Metuchen, N.J., and London: Scarecrow Press, 1983.

Lawrence, D. H. *Apocalypse.* Intr. Richard Aldington. Harmondsworth: Penguin Books, 1960.

Lead, Jane. *The Revelation of Revelations.* London: Printed by A. Sowle, & J. Lead, 1683.

———. *The Signs of the Time.* London, 1699.

Leff, Gordon. *Heresy in the Later Middle Ages.* 2 vols. Manchester: Manchester University Press, 1967.

Lilje, Hans. *The Last Book of the Bible.* Philadelphia: Muhlenberg Press, 1955.

Lindsey, Hal. *There's a New World Coming: "A Prophetic Odyssey."* New York: Bantam Books, 1973.

———. *The Late Great Planet Earth.* New York: Bantam Books, 1973.

Lohmeyer, Ernst. *Die Offenbarung des Johannes.* Tübingen: J. C. B. Mohr (Paul Siebeck), 1953.

Lovell, John Jr. *Black Song: the Forge and the Flame.* New York: Macmillan Company, 1972.

Lowman, Moses. *A Paraphrase and Notes on the Revelation of St. John.* 2nd ed. London: John Noon, 1745.

Lubac, Henri de. *Exégèse médiévale: Les quatre sens de l'Écriture.* 2 vols. in 4. Paris: Aubier, 1959-61.

Lücke, Friedrich. *Versuch einer vollständigen Einleitung in die Offenbarung des Johannes.* 2nd ed. Bonn: Eduard Weber, 1852.

Luther, Martin. *Works* 35. Philadelphia: Muhlenberg Press, 1960.

Maier, Gerhard. *Die Johannesoffenbarung und die Kirche.* Wissenschaftliche Untersuchungen zum Neuen Testament, 25. Tübingen: J. C. B. Mohr (Paul Siebeck), 1981.

Maitland, S. R. *An Enquiry into the Grounds on which the Prophetic Period of Daniel and St. John has been supposed to consist of 1260 years.* 2nd ed. London: Rivington, 1837.

Marx, Karl, and Friedrich Engels. *Basic Writings on Politics and Philosophy.* Edited by Lewis S. Feuer. Garden City, New York: Anchor Books, Doubleday & Co., 1959.

Matthews, Ronald. *English Messiahs: Studies in English Messianic Pretenders, 1656-1927.* London: Methuen & Co., 1936.

Maurice, Frederick Denison. *Lectures on the Apocalypse.* Cambridge and London: Macmillan and Co., 1861.

Mazzaferri, Frederick David. *The Genre of the Book of Revelation from a Source-critical Perspective.* Berlin: Walter de Gruyter, 1989.

McGinn, Bernard. *Visions of the End: Apocalyptic Traditions in the Middle Ages.* New York: Columbia University Press, 1979.

————. *The Calabrian Abbot: Joachim of Fiore in the History of Western Thought.* New York: Macmillan Publishing Company, 1985.

Mede, Joseph. *The Works of the Pious and Profoundly Learned Joseph Mede, B.D.* 2 vols. London: Printed by James Flesher, for Richard Royston, 1664.

Michaelis, Johann David. *Introduction to the New Testament.* Translated by Herbert Marsh. 2nd ed. 4 vols. in 6. London: F. and C. Rivington, 1802.

Minear, Paul S. *I Saw a New Earth: An Introduction to the Visions of the Apocalypse.* Washington/Cleveland: Corpus Books, 1967.

More, Henry. *Opera Omnia 1. Opera Theologica.* London: Impensis Gualteri Kettilby, 1674. Reprint, ed. Serge Hutin. Hildesheim: Georg Olms Verlagsbuchhandlung, 1960.

Morgan, Thomas. *The Moral Philosopher.* 3 vols. London, 1738-40. Reprint, edited by Günter Gawlick. Stuttgart-Bad Cannstatt: Friedrich Frommann, 1969.

Morosow, Nikolaus. *Die Offenbarung Johannis: Eine astronomisch-historische Untersuchung.* Stuttgart: W. Spemann, 1912.

Morris, Leon. *Revelation.* 2nd. ed. Leicester: Inter-Varsity Press; Grand Rapids: William B. Eerdmans, 1987.

Mounce, R. H. *The Book of Revelation.* Grand Rapids: William B. Eerdmans, 1977.

Mulholland, M. Robert Jr. *Revelation: Holy Living in an Unholy World.* Grand Rapids: Francis Asbury Press, Zondervan, 1990.

Napier (Napeir), John. *A Plaine Discovery, of the Whole Revelation of S. Iohn.* Edinburgh: Printed by Andrew Hart, 1611.

Newman, John Henry. *Essays Critical and Historical.* 4th ed. 2 vols. London: Basil Montagu Pickering, 1877.

Newton, Isaac. *Observations upon the Prophecies of Daniel and the Apocalypse of St. John in Two Parts.* London: Printed by J. Darby and T. Browne, Sold by J. Roberts et al., 1733.

Niles, D. T. *As Seeing the Invisible.* London: S. C. M. Press, 1962.

Oecumenius. *The Complete Commentary of Oecumenius on the Apocalypse.* Edited by H. C. Hoskier. Ann Arbor: University of Michigan, 1928.

Oliver, W. H. *Prophets and Millennialists: the Uses of Millennial Hope in England from the 1790s to the 1840s.* Auckland: University Press, 1978.

Oman, John. *Book of Revelation.* Cambridge: University Press, 1923.

Owen, Robert. *The Life of Robert Owen, Written by Himself.* London: E. Wilson, 1858.

———. *A Supplementary Appendix to the First Volume of the Life of Robert Owen.* London: E. Wilson, 1858.

Palmer, Frederic. *The Drama of the Apocalypse.* New York: The Macmillan Company, 1903.

Pareus, David. *A Commentary upon the Divine Revelation of the Apostle and Evangelist John.* Translated by Elias Arnold. Amsterdam: C. P., 1644.

Patrides, C. A., and J. Wittreich, eds. *The Apocalypse in English Renaissance Thought and Literature.* Ithaca, N.Y.: Cornell University Press, 1984.

Peake, Arthur S. *The Revelation of John.* London: Joseph Johnson, Primitive Methodist Publishing House, 1919.

Penton, M. James. *Apocalypse Delayed: The Story of Jehovah's Witnesses.* Toronto: University of Toronto Press, 1985 .

Petraglio, R., et al. *L'Apocalypse de Jean: Traditions exégétiques et iconographiques.* Geneva: Libraire Droz, 1979.

Priestley, Joseph. *Theological and Miscellaneous Works.* 25 vols. in 26. London: Printed by G. Smallfield, 1817-32.

Prigent, Pierre. *Apocalypse et Liturgie.* Neuchatel: Éditions Delachaux et Niestlé, 1964.

———. *L'Apocalypse de Saint Jean.* 2nd. ed. Geneva: Labor et Fides, 1988.

Prophet, Elizabeth Clare. *The Great White Brotherhood.* Los Angeles: Summit University Press, 1978.

———, recorded by. *Saint Germain on Prophecy.* Livingston, Montana: Summit University Press, 1986.

Pryse, James M. *The Apocalypse Unsealed.* London: John M. Watkins; & New York: John M. Pryse, 1910.

Ramírez Fernández, Dagoberto. "La idolatría del poder. La Iglesia confesante en la situación de Apocalípsis 13." *Revista de Interpretación Bíblica Latinoamericana* 4 (1989): 109-28.

———. "El juicio de Dios a las transnacionales." *Revista de Interpretación Bíblica Latinoamericana* 5-6 (1990): 55-74.

Ramsay, William M. *The Letters to the Seven Churches of Asia.* New York: A. C. Armstrong & Son, 1905.

Reeves, Marjorie. *Prophecy in the Later Middle Ages: A Study in Joachimism.* Oxford: Clarendon Press, 1969.

Reiter, Richard R., et al. *The Rapture: Pre-, Mid-, or Post-Tribulational.* Grand Rapids: Zondervan, 1984.

Renan, Ernest. *Antichrist.* Translated and edited by Joseph Henry Allen. Boston: Roberts Brothers, 1897.

Ribera, Francisco. *In sacram Beati Ioannis Apostoli & Evangelistae Apocalypsin Commentarij.* Lugduni: Ex Officina, 1593.

Rissi, Mathias. *Was ist und was geschehen soll danach.* Zürich: Zwingli Verlag, 1965.

Robinson, Douglas. *American Apocalypses.* Baltimore: The Johns Hopkins University Press, 1985.

Robinson, J. A. T. *Redating the New Testament*. Philadelphia: Westminster Press, 1976.

Rossetti, Christina G. *The Face of the Deep: A Devotional Commentary on the Apocalypse*. London: S.P.C.K., 1892.

Rowley, H. H. *The Relevance of Apocalyptic*. 2nd ed. London: Lutterworth Press, 1947.

Rozanov, Vasily. *The Apocalypse of Our Time and Other Writings by Vasily Rozanov*. New York: Praeger Publishers, 1977.

Ruusbroec, John. *The Spiritual Espousals and Other Works*. Introduction and translated by James A. Wiseman. New York: Paulist Press, 1985.

Schüssler Fiorenza, Elisabeth. *Revelation: Justice and Judgment*. Philadelphia: Fortress Press, 1985.

Scofield, C. I., ed. *The Holy Bible . . . with a New System of Connected Topical References:* Oxford: Humphrey Milford, 1917.

Scott, Thomas. *The Holy Bible . . . with Explanatory Notes*. 3 vols. New York: Collins & Hannay, 1832.

Semler, Johann Salomo. *Abhandlung von freier Untersuchung des Canon*. 4 vols. Halle: Henmerde, 1771-75.

Servetus, Michael. *Christianismi Restitutio*. Vienna, 1553. Reprint. Frankfurt am Main: Minerva, 1966.

Seventh-day Adventists Believe . . . : A Biblical Exposition of 27 Fundamental Doctrines. Washington, D.C.: Ministerial Association, General Conference of Seventh-day Adventists, 1988.

Shepherd, Massey H. *The Paschal Liturgy and the Apocalypse*. Richmond: John Knox Press, 1960.

Sickenberger, Joseph. *Erklärung des Johannesapokalypse*. 2nd ed. Bonn: Peter Hanstein, 1942.

Spener, Philip Jacob. *Pia Desideria*. Translated and edited by Theodore G. Tappert. Philadelphia: Fortress Press, 1964, 76-78.

Spitta, Friedrich. *Die Offenbarung des Johannes*. Halle: Waisenhaus, 1889.

St. John, Henry, Viscount Bolingbroke. *The Philosophical Works*. 5 vols. London, 1754-1777. Reprint. New York & London: Garland Publishing, 1977.

Stauffer, E. *Christ and the Caesars: Historical Sketches*. Translated by K. and R. Gregor Smith. Philadelphia: Westminster Press, 1955.

Steiner, Rudolf. *Christianity as Mystical Fact . . . of Antiquity*. 3rd ed. Edited by H. Collinson. New York: G. P. Putnam's Sons, 1914.

———. *The Apocalypse of St. John*. Edited by M. Cotterell. London: Anthroposophical Publishing Company, 1958.

Stierlin, Henri. *Le livre de feu: L'Apocalype et l'art mozarabe*. Geneva: La bibliothèque des arts, Paris, 1978.

The Story of the Jubilee Singers: With Their Songs. 3rd ed. London: Hodder and Stoughton, 1876.

Stringfellow, William. *An Ethic for Christians and Other Aliens in a Strange Land*. Waco, Texas: Word Books, 1973.

Stuart, Moses. *A Commentary on the Apocalypse.* 2 vols. New York: Van Nostrand and Terrett, 1851.

Swedenborg, Emanuel. *The Apocalypse Revealed.* 3 vols. Boston: Houghton Mifflin and Co., 1907.

———. *The True Christian Religion.* 3 vols. Boston: Houghton, Mifflin and Company, 1907.

Sweet, J. P. M. *Revelation.* Pelican Commentaries. Philadelphia: Westminster Press, 1979.

Swete, Henry Barclay. *The Apocalypse of St. John.* 3rd ed. London: Macmillan, 1909. Reprint. Grand Rapids, Michigan: Wm. B. Eerdmans, 1951.

Talia, Shawqi N. *Bûlus al-Bûsi's Arabic Commentary on the Apocalypse of St. John. An English Translation and Commentary.* Ph.D. dissertation, The Catholic University of America. Ann Arbor: University Microfilms International, 1987.

Testimony of Christ's Second Appearing. 4th ed. Albany: The United Society Called Shakers, 1856.

Thompson, Leonard L. *The Book of Revelation: Apocalypse and Empire.* New York: Oxford University Press, 1990.

Thruston, Frederic. *England Safe and Triumphant.* 2 vols. Coventry: F. C. and J. Rivington, 1812.

Tichi, Cecelia. *New World, New Earth.* New Haven: Yale University Press, 1979.

Tindal, Matthew. *Christianity as Old as the Creation.* London, 1730; Reprint, ed. Günter Gawlick. Stuttgart-Bad Cannstatt: Friedrich Frommann, 1967.

Toon, Peter, ed. *Puritans, the Millennium and the Future of Israel: Puritan Eschatology 1600 to 1660.* Cambridge: James Clarke & Co., 1970.

Totten, C. A. L. *The Hope of History: The Millennium.* New Haven: Conn.: Our Race Publishing Company, 1882.

Touilleux, P. *L'Apocalypse et les cultes de Domitien et de Cybèle.* Paris: Libraire Orientaliste Paul Guenther, 1935.

Tuveson, Ernest Lee. *Redeemer Nation: The Idea of America's Millennial Role.* Chicago and London: The University of Chicago Press, 1968.

Ubertino da Casali. *Arbor Vitae Crucifixae Jesus.* Venetiis: Andrea de Bonettis, 1485. Reprint. Turin: Bottega d'Erasmo, 1965.

van der Meer, Frederick. *Apocalypse: Visions from the Book of Revelation in Western Art.* London: Thames and Hudson, 1978.

Vischer, Eberhard. *Die Offenbarung Johannis, eine jüdische Apokalypse in christliche Bearbeitung.* TU 2.3 (1886).

Vitringa, Campegius. *Anakrisis Apocalypseos.* Franeker: Franciscus Halma, 1705.

Vogel, Paul Joachim Sigismund. *Sacra Paschalia . . . Commentationis de Apocalypsi Ioannis Pars Tertia.* Erlangen: Kunstmann, 1813.

Voltaire, F. M. de. *Oeuvres complètes.* 52 vols. Paris: Garnier Frères, 1877-85.

Völter, Daniel. *Die Entstehung der Apokalypse.* Freiburg im Bresgau: J. C. B. Mohr (Paul Siebeck), 1882.

———. *Die Offenbarung Johannis neu untersucht und erklärt.* Strassburg: J. H. Ed. Hertz, 1904.

Vondung, Klaus. *Die Apokalypse in Deutschland*. Munich: Deutscher Taschenbuch Verlag, 1988.

Wakefield, Walter L., and Austin P. Evans, eds. and trans. *Heresies of the High Middle Ages*. New York and London: Columbia University Press, 1969.

Walvoord, John F. *The Revelation of Jesus Christ*. London: Marshall, Morgan & Scott, 1966.

Walvoord, John F., and John E. Walvoord. *Armageddon: Oil and the Middle East Crisis*. Grand Rapids: Zondervan, 1974.

Weinstein, Donald. *Savonarola and Florence*. Princeton, New Jersey: Princeton University Press, 1970.

Weizsäcker, Carl Heinrich von. *Das apostoliche Zeitalter der christlichen Kirche*. Freiburg i. Br., 1886.

Wesley, John. *Explanatory Notes upon the New Testament*. London: Epworth Press, 1950.

Wette, W. M. L. de. *Kurzgefasstes exegetisches Handbuch zum Neuen Testament*. 3 vols. Leipzig: Weidmann'sche Buchhandlung, 1847-48.

Wettstein, Joannes Jacobus. *Novum Testamentum Graecum*. 2 vols. Amsterdam: Officina Dommeriana, 1752.

Whisenant, Edgar C. *On Borrowed Time: The Bible Dates of the 70th Week of Daniel, Armageddon, the Millennium*. Nashville: World Bible Society, 1988.

Whiston, William. *A New Theory of the Earth*, 5th ed. London: Printed for John Whiston, 1737.

Whitby, Daniel. "A Treatise of the True Millennium." In *Paraphrase and Notes on the New Testament*. 2 vols. London: Printed for Awnsham & John Churchill, 1703.

Wikenhauser, Alfred. *Offenbarung des Johannes*. Regensburg: Verlag Friedrich Pustet, 1949.

Wilson, Bryan R. *Magic and the Millennium*. London: Heinemann, 1973.

Wordsworth, Christopher. *Lectures on the Apocalypse*. Philadelphia: Herman Hooker, 1852.

Zahn, Theodor. *Die Offenbarung des Johannes*. Leipzig & Erlangen: Deichert, 1924-26. Reprint. Wuppertal: Brockhaus, 1986.

Züllig, Jakob. *Die Offenbarung Johannis*. 2 vols. Stuttgart: E. Schweizerbarts Verhandlung, 1834, 1840.

Extensive bibliographies of works on the Apocalypse are to be found in: C. A. Patrides and J. Wittreich, eds. *The Apocalypse in English Renaissance Thought and Literature;* L. E. Froom, *The Prophetic Faith of Our Fathers;* Gehard Maier, *Die Johannesoffenbarung und die Kirche.* A bibliography of books written since 1700 is given in Otto Böcher, *Die Johannesapokalypse.*

SCRIPTURE INDEX

OLD TESTAMENT

NEW TESTAMENT

APOCRYPHA AND PSEUDEPIGRAPHA